MOUNTAINS
OF THE PYRENEES

KEV REYNOLDS

Cirque de Gavarnie, 'Grande Cascade' (left).

MOUNTAINS OF THE PYRENEES

KEV. REYNOLDS

Illustrations by the author except where otherwise noted.

ACKNOWLEDGMENT

My thanks are due to many authors from the past whose works I have freely drawn upon to supply information for this book. Edward Pyatt, retiring editor of the *Alpine Journal,* gave permission to use material from the Journal, and I am grateful to him. At the Alpine Club library which houses the recorded history of our sport, Mrs Pat Johnson is thanked for her ready help in burrowing among the archives on my behalf.

From France I am indebted to Jean and Pierre Ravier of Bordeaux, and to Robert Ollivier of Pau, for their advice and encouragement, and for allowing me to use some of their photographs.

Pete Smith suffered the leanings of friendship, reproduced some difficult prints, and also gave me access to his own fine photographic collection, whilst Brian Evans at Cicerone Press put the whole thing together. I thank them both. And to those partners on a rope - Keith, Mike, Hugh, Pete and Alan - my thanks for sharing so many good Pyrenean days, and for making the mountains and valleys so memorable.

Finally, for her forbearance in sharing our home with my dreams, a vast clutter of notes and thousands of photographs, my wife is to be congratulated; and for typing the manuscript against considerable odds, I thank her publicly. To her I dedicate this book with my love.

Contents

Preface

When first I went to the Pyrenees to climb I was struck immediately by three things; by the beauty of the mountains and their moating valleys, by the sheer exuberance of the flowers, and by an over-whelming sense of solitude. After the Alps and the hills of Britain it was an unusual experience to have some of the grandest scenery, and the most delightful of peaks, to oneself. There was a rare enchantment in sharing a stream with isard a few paces from the tent, in scrambling day after day without seeing sign of human life, in the plants discovered among remote and untouched crags and the butterflies on a sun-warmed ridge. It seemed only natural then to return, and natural, too, to learn as much about these mountains and their history as I possibly could. But although there were plenty of books dealing with the range as a whole, very little could be found that concentrated on mountaineering other than in very general terms. For whilst the Alps have been charted and recorded in every detail the Pyrenees, so far as climbing history is concerned, have been virtually ignored on this side of the Channel. To unearth this history has involved a long and protracted - but enjoyable - research.

Many of the sport's pundits, it soon became clear, have casually dismissed the range as of little importance to the climber. One scorned their summits as being easily attainable by anyone with workable lungs and sturdy legs, and another commented; '... there is practically no climbing these days in the Pyrenees'. This comment, be it noted, was published at a time when members of the GPHM were creating routes of a difficulty matched only by the more advanced activists in the Alps! This book, then, is an attempt to redress the balance, to create a picture of these mountains in the light of their exploration and development; a survey of the range through the activities of its pioneers, and to introduce some of these pioneers - many of whom were colourful characters - whose names may be unfamiliar to British enthusiasts. In addition, appendices have been designed to offer some items of practical information which might aid the climber and walker in planning to explore the Pyrenees for himself.

*

Since that distant first visit I have returned to climb and wander both peak and valley more than a dozen times, and over the years there has been a definite increase in activity there. Solitude may still be found, but the popular areas have become more popular, and at a time when Europe's finest ranges are being buffeted by the pressures of tourism, I am very conscious of the dangers in drawing attention to the riches of these challenging, yet vulnerable mountains, but it is evident that the climbing and hill-walking fraternity has already 'discovered' the Pyrenees. It is to be hoped that by making the reader aware of the range's history of remote isolation and perfection, this book will serve to remind him of his duty to ensure that future generations of enthusiasts may experience the enchanted massifs in a similar manner. Only by such awareness can mountaineering's future be assured. Only by such willingness can the Pyrenees survive.

*

In a range that borders two major countries, with differing languages and several separate dialects, it is natural to find the names of the mountains, their valleys and their individual features, vary considerably from one side of the frontier to the other. Thus it is with the Pyrenees.

It is difficult and unnecessary to be pedantic with such names, therefore I have taken the obvious solution of giving the title of each mountain and valley as adopted by the current map published by the body responsible for each specific region. For example, French mountains as per IGN maps, and Editorial Alpina names for Spanish mountains, but even here difficulties arise, for different editions often use different spellings, and sometimes overlapping sheets adopt alternative names!

Heights, too, can vary by a few metres; but all this seems to me to be of only secondary importance. Nomenclature and altitude measurements have their place, but the mountains remain the same whatever their title or spot height. Maps create dreams. Mountains provide the arena for making them come true.

*

No-one can indulge in recording history, be it of nations or of mountains, without drawing upon the works of others, and this I have done throughout. I have taken the liberty of quoting, extensively in places, briefly in others, from the writings of the actual pioneers. I offer no apology for this, for it is my belief that the words of the man who creates history retain a certain vivacity that the onlooker, from the distance of a century or more, can scarcely hope to reproduce. Some of these pioneers were erudite, their words ringing today with a poetic clarity. Some were less so, perhaps concerned more for the statement of unadorned fact than for the delivery of a literary style, but each statement has a value, whether taken down as rough notes during the adventure or written afterwards in the comfort of a valley hotel or spartan hut.

Of course, I never had the pleasure of meeting Ramond or Russell, Packe or Brulle, and so to write of them demands first an enquiry of those who did. In some instances it was not difficult to trace references which would lead to information, for mountaineering literature is as rich and varied as the men who built it; yet there remain blind spots. On occasion clues would lead to vague snippets of insight, while others remain elusive, enigmatic, simply faceless men who came by chance to the Pyrenees, climbed a peak for the first time, and went away again. Who were they, these men whose names survive, yet little else? What were the limits of their involvement? Did they climb elsewhere? Alas, we shall never know. Their experiences may here be crudely encapsulated within the compass of a brief paragraph, but where personal accounts survive to tell of those experiences I have readily borrowed from them, the better to understand the men behind their actions.

It would be futile to speculate on the achievements of the pioneers and weigh them against the undertakings of today's masters of *Pyrénéisme*. Each generation is a product of its age. Some of the names from the past, undoubtedly, are remembered simply because circumstances allowed them to make the first ascent of a peak that had not been previously attempted. Their names live on by chance when others, possibly with a greater devotion to their mountains, are forgotten purely because they neither wrote of their experiences nor had the fortune to be active at a time when virgin summits were there for the taking. Such is the nature of the sport. Such is the nature of recorded history. It is to be hoped, therefore, that the reader will view both the mountains and the pioneers who first climbed them in the context of their age, rather than ours.

*

Finally, piecing together the patchwork of this book has been a pleasurable experience, not only from the viewpoint of resurrecting the masters of yesteryear, but also because it has of necessity meant reliving so many of the scenes from past climbs of my own. These, however, were simply modest repetitions of routes worked out long ago by other, more talented, climbers than I, but to my mind this is of no account, for my own outlook follows closely to that summarised many years ago by Godley: 'I appear then as a member of that class of not altogether respectable persons who ascend hills merely for pleasure. They have no particular principles ... if they cannot have a peak they will take a pass, if they cannot have a pass they will be content with a glacier. They are smatterers and general readers in an age of specialism; they are wedded to no dogmatic formulae'. No mountains could be more suited to this attitude than the mountains of the Pyrenees.

*

PART ONE

Introduction to the Pyrenees

'The Alps astound, the Pyrenees attract and soften us. They have a supreme and indefinable poetry ... Their waters are pure as crystal, their forests are like waving robes of green or black velvet ... Their lakes ... sleeping and lost in the snows whence they came, are there to sparkle on the forehead of the Pyrenees ... The mountains have an Oriental grace and langour, and their colours ... are richer and more burning than in the Alps ... It is to the Pyrenees that the smiles of the artist and the heart of the poet will always turn'.

(Henry Russell)

Seen from the north the Pyrenees rise as a sudden, dramatic wall out of the vibrant green plains of Gascony; an abrupt, imposing line of peaks that stretches apparently unbroken from the Atlantic to the Mediterranean. To the south, on the other hand, the mountains fall away in a confusion of successive ridges - or sierras - to a maze of low and shadeless hills that merge into the badlands of the Ebro basin.

It is a range of great contrasts. The hills of the Basque country in the west are cloaked with dense forests of oak and pine, well-watered by virtue of the heavy, moisture-laden winds that come sweeping from the Bay of Biscay. At the eastern end Catalonia is a blistering region of sun-baked hillsides, barren plateaux and valleys dressed with orchards and vineyards; but between these two extremes, in the High Pyrenees, there lies an alpine landscape of immense variety and charm. There are sharp, jagged peaks riven by crumbling gullies; slender snowfields and shallow, napkin glaciers; granite massifs and ochre canyons of weathered limestone. Mountains there are, soft and downlike, washed with a subtle light that plays on their spreading flanks, and yet heights, too, of a stark austerity, whose panoramas reveal mysterious visions of lesser summits and surrounding regions of wilderness apparently held in a lifeless shadow. There are impressive amphitheatres - or cirques - and numerous tiny, glistening tarns; luxurious virgin forests and valleys containing a diverse and unique flora; the peculiar silence of a country slumbering as under a spell, and the never-ceasing boom of broad cascades. There are naked, soaring aiguilles, cloud-girt and remote, and streams that plunge into motionless hollows and disappear.

The Pyrenees stretch for almost four hundred kilometres - in two chains of approximately equal length - between ocean and sea, narrow to the north of the watershed with short, deep valleys to add to the impression of height, and contrastingly broad and aggravated by parallel massifs to the south. They rise from the waters of the Atlantic just south of the sharp bend of the Bay of Biscay,

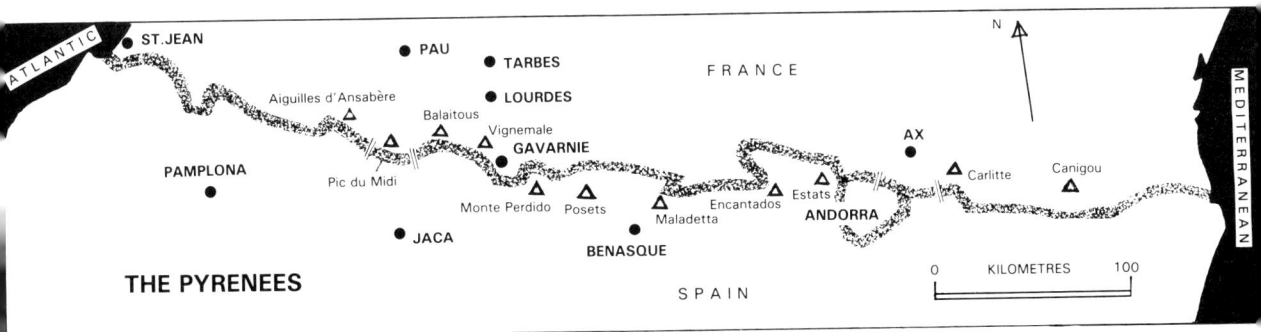

THE PYRENEES

to run in a castellated line a little south of east to fade in the peaks of Saboredo, a group attached to that of the Encantados. This western chain contains all the major summits and valleys and is about 200 kilometres in total length. The other, eastern, chain overlaps by some twelve kilometres to the north and sweeps similarly south-eastwards, rising and falling in linking massifs, to end in the Mediterranean at Cape Cerbere. Where the two chains overlap runs the pleasant green sward of the Vall d'Aran, and the gap is bridged by the grassy saddle of the Port de la Bonaigua. With a few notable exceptions the watershed is traced by the political frontier crest, along which are generally positioned the more interesting peaks. There are, however, important and isolated massifs to either side of the watershed, with the highest summits - Aneto, Posets and Perdido - all stationed above Spanish valleys.

As a natural division between nations the range could scarcely be bettered. 'Europe ends at the Pyrenees' is a well-established cliché born of a geographical half-truth. The mountain barrier separates not only nations and cultures, but also climate and vegetation. To the north spreads the main body of Western Europe with its mosaic of variegated, yet uniting communities, while beyond the range to the south stretches the anachronism that is the Iberian Peninsular, whose vast expanse seems to be dusted with the hot, dry breath of Africa.

*

Of all the great mountain regions of Western Europe, the Pyrenees are second only to the Alps. Lower and less extensive though they may be, geologically speaking they are of a similar vintage to the Alps, being formed during the relentless upheavals of Tertiary times, between 50 - 100 million years ago. Driven by enormous pressures from the south - pressures whose effects were further aggravated by the restrictions imposed by the stubbornly rigid Central Plateau to the north, and by the huge block of the Spanish Meseta to the south - the pliable sedimentary rocks that had previously been acting as the bed of a warm sea, were thrown to the surface where they became folded against - and contorted by - the harder crystalline core which forms the serrated backbone of the range.

Through the proximity of the neighbouring Atlantic with its moist air-streams, the western portion of the range - composed primarily of limestones - has suffered violent erosion, with former ridges rounded by weathering, and deep valleys cut by regular torrents. By contrast, the erosion of Catalonian heights is due to Mediterranean dryness and heat, and the flaring white limestone presents a very different picture, equally severe in its weathering, but naked and drought-ridden by nature. However, the contrast between the extremities of the range is not more marked than that between north and south. On the French side glaciers carved deep valleys, and the precipitation that regularly dashes these northern slopes ensures that the valleys are fertile, that forests and meadows receive encouragement to prosper. On the southern slopes away from frontier heights there is an air of solemn thirst, where man has worked against the needs of nature, and instead of protecting the vegetation that once clothed the sierras, he has joined forces with natural erosion and hastened the march that leads irrevocably from waste to exploitation, and from exploitation to ultimate ruin. The vision that greets the south-bound traveller now is often more of barren acres of arid, semi-desert, and mountains crumbling under the enervating power of the sun.

*

Although the range lay far to the south of the main zone of Quaternary glaciation, the tiny glaciers of the present day are yet remnants of the extensive ice-sheet which once existed here and, during the Würmian period, actually bore a front of almost three hundred kilometres. The widespread snowfields and glaciers of this impressive front pushed northwards as far as 55 kilometres from their source, and attained a maximum depth in the valley of the Gave de Pau of 900 metres. Glaciers also spread southwards, but to a much lesser degree. They sculpted the land, moulded and scoured and enriched the valleys, and left behind a luxurious testament to their industry. In the central part of the range the evidence of ancient periods of glaciation is everywhere to be seen. Peaks have been carved and fretted into distinct pyramid shapes, sharp arêtes and cirque basins are common, and primitive moraines are clearly visible in a number of valleys. Truncated spurs and hanging valleys confirm with added proof the moulding effects of the subconscious flow of ice. In the high mountains, too, there remain some 1,070 glacial lakes, deposited without favour by the retreating rivers of archaic frost.

Ossoue Glacier, Vignemale.

Compared with those of the Alps, today's icefields are of an insignificant size; minute draperies of the 'cirque' variety, slung in the hollows of high peaks. Their aggregate area is probably less than 40 square kilometres, yet their presence adds character and a sense of grandeur which is quite unrelated to mere quantity. A hundred years or so ago the story was rather different. Illustrations from old books, and the stories of the pioneers, show that many of these glaciers were as impressive as those of Switzerland; aiguilles of ice towering 50 metres high where plants now blossom, icefields pouring over now-naked rocks, crevasses of hollow blue where only moraines reflect the heat of summer today. Of those that remain, the largest individual is the Ossoue Glacier which flows down the eastern flanks of the Vignemale. It is the only one in the whole range to conform with the generally accepted idea of an alpine glacier, with an upper catchment area, moraine banks, a number of fearsome crevasses and a lower icefall; but this too has shrunken considerably from its former glory. On the North Face of Monte Perdido, not far from the Vignemale, but on the Spanish side of the frontier, hangs perhaps the most impressive glacier whose double terrace of séracs is of a most threatening, but at the same time attractive, nature. Most of the range's glaciers, however, form mere caps to the peaks; others are contained in sheltered, north-facing cirques. In the Maladetta massif lies a collection of small snowfields and shawls of ice out of which rises the high granite ridge with its many summits topping 3,000 metres. In the Balaitous, Gavarnie, Posets and Estats areas icefields of varying quantities and degrees of grandeur are to be found, with lesser *néves* protected in the hollows of other massifs.

The recession of Pyrenean glaciers is due to a combination of the range's southerly lattitude and to the influence of Mediterranean air-streams. Although winter snowfall is surprisingly high, with a depth which exceeds that of many regions of the Alps, the thaw comes with a dramatic rapidity early in summer, turning winter-clad hillsides into full summer dressing in only a few short weeks, with the thunder of avalanche and gurgle of melting pastures accompanying the fragrance of transitory spring. Once disrobed of winter, the mountains wear the livery of permanent snow as high as 2,800 metres.

11

The western limits of the Cirque de Troumouse.

If the glaciers of the Pyrenees are of an insignificant size, the many lakes, in both area and volume, likewise compare unfavourably with those of the Alps. There is no single sheet of water to match the lakes of Lucerne, or of Geneva, and the largest natural lake of the range - the Lac de Lanoux on the western perimeter of the Carlitte massif - is little more than three kilometres long. These lakes, or tarns, are to be found in abundance throughout the High Pyrenees, clustered often under the final ridges of tortuous peaks, and some way above the benevolence of vegetated valleys. Grouped as they frequently are in wild country presents a pleasing spectacle to the climber, for in these sometimes savage regions they add colour and a fresh dimension. Characteristic of these is the well known group found to the west of the Pic du Midi d'Ossau, both above the Bious valley - the Lacs d'Ayous - where the popular Refuge d'Ayous is situated, and another sprinkling trapped directly below the mountain itself. Slung in tormented hollows, or spread neatly on hillside shelves, the waters dapple reflections of peak and pasture and in so doing apply a sense of tranquility to the landscape.

Sparkling pools adorn corners of other massifs; around the otherwise solemn Balaitous, the Pic des Posets and the southern heights of the Maladetta; among the haunted valleys of the Gourgs Blancs, in the Encantados and the Estats, and the granitic jumble of the Carlitte. Wherever they are discovered their presence induces an air of timeless serenity, a peace unchanged through the passage of geological epochs, contrasting the sometimes sullen mountain heights with a distinctive calm and beauty that otherwise might be wanting.

Even more than the countless tarns and the glacial remnants, it is the existence of dramatic cirques which lends a character of individuality to the mountains of the Pyrenees. Gouged by the sculpting forces of ancestral ice, valley-heads here and there end abruptly in steep, smooth-sided walls or horse-shoe grouped mountains, thereby offering grand opportunities for climbing and ridge-walking in the most perfect of settings; by far the best known of all these cirques, and the most instantly impressive, is that of Gavarnie. In spring its huge walls are laced with feathery cascades, the snow and ice which plasters the limestone terraces creating an impression of even greater height and severity, and offering an almost irresistible challenge to the rock climber.

In a range as varied as that of the Pyrenees there are a great many cirques of contrasting size; those of Estaubé and Troumouse immediately to the east of Gavarnie enclose whole valleys, cirques with green pastures cradled in their basins. That which blocks the Pineta valley so deeply below the glaciated slopes of Monte Perdido creates an impression - albeit a false one - of impregnability. Much farther to the east the whole contorted region of the Encantados is a wilderness containing an assortment of minor cirques that trap unsettling, echoing corries, while back in the west, where the Basque hills give way to the first of the High Pyrenees, gentle grasslands - lush pastoral valleys - lead to sudden, upthrusting spires that form amphitheatres again of a very different nature.

*

In common with most other mountainous regions of Europe, the Pyrenees are under threat. The pressures of industrial expansion have put fresh demands upon the resources mountains have to offer. Once-tranquil lakes have been dammed and valleys flooded to enable hydro-electric stations to produce power for distant towns and villages. Engineers force roads where no roads intruded before, where once only the burdened mule floundered. Tunnels are blasted through the mountains as an alternative to sending fresh highways winding over passes, to speed communication. Tourism is understandably magnetised by peak and valley as ski centres are created in order to tap the same source of wealth that made Austria and Switzerland successful in economic terms. Areas of virgin wilderness are rapidly diminishing to meet man's voracious appetite for domination over his environment, and as Fernando Barrientos Fernandez commented: 'It would not be over-dramatic to say that the coming years will be extremely critical, due to the impacts of urban motorised man, who has no responsible conservationist regard for nature'.

The creation of large areas as National Parks may be seen, possibly, as a working compromise to protect some of these threatened upland regions, though others will see the Parks as a threat in themselves. Mountaineering, in its many forms, has long been happily anarchistic, free of beurocratic management and policing, and few climbers or mountain walkers bent on experiencing the mountain wilderness of the pioneers, will approve wholeheartedly of a concentration of tourists in specially designated Parks. Yet climbers are tourists too, and the mountaineering fraternity should allow itself no superior attitude since their numbers are guilty also of despoiling with their waste the very wilderness environment they seek to maintain. The alternative threat of wholesale marketing on a commercial scale - as has happened in so many parts of the Alps - or, worse, a widespread destruction in the name of industrial progress, is hardly worth considering; so perhaps the National Parks already set up, and those still in the planning stages, may achieve a successful method of mountain protection. It is fortunate that a number of the finest peaks lie in such remote country that all but the most determined of mountain lovers will avoid their recesses, consequently denying a heavy concentration upon them and thereby enabling that spirit of adventure with its sense of exploration of a mysterious and little-known country, to be experienced by generations of climbers yet uninitiated.

On the northern slopes the National Park of the Western Pyrenees was set up in 1967, and is the largest of the three to be established in the range. The objects of its foundation were to preserve the character of an outstanding area; to protect the wild life within it; to discourage industrial and commercial activities, and to provide facilities for mountain ramblers - the latter it has done with the construction of several new refuges, and the waymarking of numerous trails. By 1976 the successes of the venture were officially recognised by the Council of Europe, who awarded it their 'Diploma', a distinction given to landscapes and reserves of outstanding interest.

*Isard - the Pyrenean chamois,
enjoying the protection of the
National Parks.
Illustration by Whymper,
from Buxton's 'Short Stalks'.*

The Park - known locally as the Parc National des Pyrénées (PNP) - follows the frontier crest for some 110 kilometres, from the high valley of Aspe in the west, to the valley of Aure in the east, and contains some of the more important peaks on the French side of the border. Notable among these are; Pic du Midi d'Ossau, Balaitous, Vignemale, Pic du Marboré, as well as the cirques of Gavarnie, Estaubé and Troumouse. Information centres have been located at the road-head of several popular valleys and new paths created in certain areas, but climbers' peaks have suffered little from the establishment of the Park, and regulations that are governed by common sense and with a priority of preservation, have little effect on the true lovers of the heights whose freedom of choice over routes and activity remains unimpaired.

On the Spanish side of the watershed, and situated to the south of the Cirque de Gavarnie, lies the National Park of Ordesa. It is the smallest, and the oldest, of the Parks - its status was granted in 1917 - but from the sheer grandeur of its vibrantly coloured walls it is in some respects the most outstanding. It includes all the upper reaches of the glorious Arazas river which drains the south-western slopes of Monte Perdido and then comes roaring through its wild canyon; and some quite spectacular limestone cliffs, with the toppling form of Tozal del Mallo taking pride of place. Recently its boundaries were extended to include the magnificent Anisclo valley, whose tremendous gorge is still little visited. This addition greatly enlarged the Park, and hopefully has quashed plans to flood the lower portion of the gorge for hydro-electric purposes.

Although Ordesa has enjoyed National Park status for more than sixty years, the sole concessions to tourism are a road of only 4 kilometres which ends in a rough car park; a hotel and a restaurant. Paths, there are, but beyond these the magnificent forests of beech, silver fir and pine are quite unspoiled, the rock walls challenging in the extreme, and the open pastures at the head of the valley, rich in wild flowers.

Spain's other National Park within the Pyrenean range lies some way to the east, where the western chain subsides above the Vall d'Aran. The Aigües-Tortes/San Mauricio National Park has an area in excess of 35,000 acres, an area of wild and tangled country wedged between the valleys of Noguera de Tort and the Noguera Pallaresa, a confusion of tiny lakes, sudden jagged peaklets and idyllic intimate cirques. There is the possibility that an extension will be made to this Park in the foreseeable future, with parts of the upper Aran valley being included within its limits;

a plan which may halt the march of 'progress' through these pleasant chequered pastures, but within the Park's present boundaries hydro development at several of the accessible tarns has had the effect of taming an otherwise virgin landscape, although the heartland remains as remote and seemingly uncharted as ever.

In the Encantados are to be found climbs of quality, yet the whole region abounds with fine opportunities for scrambling, walking, and the study of an impressive flora. Here, as in many parts of the main Pyrenean range, the modern climber may wander and scramble at will, enjoying for a transient period the experiences of solitude and unbounded vistas of little-known country; landscapes wrapped in a cocoon of timelessness that were enjoyed first by the pioneers of a century and more ago.

*

PART TWO

Pioneers

'In those distant times ... mountaineering was ... quite in its infancy, and climbing entailed all sorts of privations, hardships, and even risks, unknown to the present generation ... '

(Henry Russell)

The Early Days

There is ample evidence pointing to areas of confusion, and not a little contradiction, in the accounts of early geographers as to the location and, indeed, even the existence of the Pyrenees. According to Herodotus, the father of historians, they were not a range of mountains, but a European town; Aristotle believed Pyrene to be a mountain which contained the sources of both the Danube and Guadalquivir. Denys of Halicarnassus maintained that the range was situated in south-east Gaul, while Strabo located it running north to south and parallel with the Rhine; and the historian, Diodorus Siculus, likening the name for the Greek word for fire, relates the story of a forest blaze of such intensity that it caused streams of molten silver to flow down the hill-sides.

The valleys were settled many hundreds of years ago, and over the passage of centuries peasant farmers, shepherds and hunters learned to move freely at the head of their glens where summer pastures were grazed by livestock. Theirs was a simple, basic existence, unchanged until comparatively recent times. They had neither reason nor feelings of curiosity or compulsion to explore the stark walling peaks that marked the limits of their world, but smugglers there were, and itinerant merchants too, who negotiated high passes in order to continue trade with settlements on either side of the frontier; a frontier breached also in times of hostility, and routes became established over certain 'ports', some of which were surprisingly difficult and complicated of access.

Hannibal crossed the range in 218 B.C., Vandals and Visigoths followed. The Moors swept over them and were driven back again. Legends grew, and the ephemeral mists of the high peaks were reflected in the clouds of mythology sustained by the simplicity of successive generations of valley-dwellers.

Superstitions developed from this innocence, they bred in the dark corners of winter-locked villages, they matured and were aggravated by the moaning of the winds and the frowning precipices of looming crags. Swollen streams and the white hell of avalanche disturbed the minds of men who sought answers, not in logic, but in the fashionable obscurity of legend, and the mountains recorded this unease in their names; the *Enchanted Mountains*, the *Lost Mountain*, the *Peak of the Thirteen Winds* and the *Accursed Mountain*. Later, as the first tentative, halting steps were taken to discover the haunting recesses of the heights, their savage characteristics were likewise afforded names of a legendary nature; the *Hole of the Bull*, the *Abandoned Pass*, *Mohammed's Bridge* and the *Hole of the Tinkers*.

*

Throughout history isolated examples of mountain exploration occur in the records of Man's endeavour. In the Middle Ages a number of such records point to a period of enquiry, although these examples inspired no great surge of adventuring and would indicate little more than the curiosity of a few men. One such was Peter III of Aragon (1236-85), 'a man of splendidly stout heart .... a man of great courage'. He it was who made an attempt on the Pic du Canigou (2784m.) in 1276.

It was a time of almost universal superstition, even among the most enlightened minds of Europe who readily believed in the existence of demons, dragons or fairies dwelling among the inaccessible heights. As for the Canigou, it gives the impression of some isolation, quite the most impressive peak in this eastern corner of the Pyrenees and which, at the time, was considered by many to be the highest in the range. 'On that mountain no man has ever lived, nor has any son of man ever dared to ascend it, both on account of its excessive height, and by reason of the difficulty and toil of the journey'.

On this pioneering expedition, one of the first ever recorded in the Pyrenees, King Peter took with him two knights, a quantity of provisions, and '... the weapons that seemed appropriate'. Having tethered their horses in the woods which clothe the foot of the mountain, they began the ascent on foot.

> 'When they had ascended a considerable distance they began to hear very horrible and terrible thunder claps; in addition to this, flashes of lightning began to appear and storms of hail to fall: all which things so terrified them that they threw themselves upon the ground, and lay there, as it were, lifeless, in their fear and apprehension of the calamities which had overtaken them'.

Considering the degree to which superstition had so aligned itself with a general ignorance of the conditions likely to be encountered upon mountains, it is perhaps not really surprising that a sudden storm should so affect these early adventurers. Peter, however, was made of sterner stuff and he cajoled the knights to continue with him once the storm had abated, but again they balked with fear, and he had no alternative but to leave them behind with orders to wait until the following nightfall for his triumphant return.

> 'So Peter, with great labour made the ascent alone; and when he was on top of the mountain he found a lake there; and when he threw a stone into the lake, a horrible dragon of enormous size came out of it, and began to fly about in the air, and to darken the air with its breath.'

*

Almost three hundred years were to pass before another attempt on a Pyrenean peak was recorded. Superstitions were still rife, but successes had been achieved elsewhere - Antoine de Ville, for example, had climbed Mont Aiguille in 1492 - and a fresh acceptance of mountains other than places of abhorrence had been voiced by Conrad Gesner in 1541. It was a time, then, for an appraisal of Pyrenean heights, and the particular mountain chosen was the fine, dramatic-looking Pic du Midi d'Ossau; the man responsible for the initiative being Francois de Foix, the Count de Candale.

Francois de Foix, a celebrated mathemetician and Bishop of Aire, was born in 1502 and died at the grand age of 92, in 1594. During a visit to the spa of Eaux Bonnes - then known as Bains du Bearn - in the spring of 1552, he organised an expedition to climb the Pic du Midi with the principal purpose of determining its height. Among those who elected to accompany him were several '... gentlemen and other young persons' who openly mocked the suggestion that ample warm clothing should be taken to combat the cold which they were bound to experience. The warnings were to ring true, as the record shows. 'At four o'clock', the account explains, 'they got high enough to see clouds under their feet; ... the cold gripped the young people who were in so great a hurry, so that they could go no further'. The Count de Candale, on the other hand, called for his fur coat and continued with the climb.

Although the attempt to reach the summit failed - and it is not possible, from the second-hand account available, to ascertain the exact height gained - it was a notable effort for two particular reasons in an historical context. The first of these is to be found in the narrative of de Thou which contains probably the earliest reference to 'mountain sickness' when he tells how '... the cold and rarefied air which surrounded them caused sensations of giddiness which made them fall down in their weakness'. The second concerns de Foix's equipment, '... when the rock resisted their endeavours, they made use of grapnels, and climbing irons'. This, a very clear indication of an early dependance upon specialised apparatus to aid the ascent of mountain obstacles, pre-dates the artificial age of *Pyrénéisme* by more than three hundred and fifty years.

*

In 1672 Montvalier was climbed by a bishop who set up a cross on the summit in honour of Saint Valier, after whom the peak is named and who, according to legend, had already made the ascent in the 5th century.

At the end of the seventeenth century, Hubert Jaillot conducted his survey of the mountains and produced a map of dubious value. Marshall de Noailles followed with a study of the range for primarily military purposes, and it was during his travels that he made the novel discovery that sometimes the sun would be shining on the peaks while rain was falling in the valleys. During the first half of the eighteenth century an astronomer from Montpellier, Plantade, made several ascents of the isolated Pic du Midi de Bigorre in order to carry out scientific observations. As an old, but apparently contented man, he died upon its slopes, in 1741. Darcet and Monge were next, making barometrical experiments, followed by Baron de Dietrich, who published in 1784 the results of his mineralogical studies.

Then came the geographers, Reboul and Vidal, from the Academy of Toulouse. They measured a number of summits, and lived in a rough hut which they erected on the summit of the Pic du Midi de Bigorre. They were to have an influence on the early mountaineering history of the range, climbing together the first 3,000m. summit to be won there, the Turon de Néouvielle, in 1787 and, two years later, Reboul ascended Pic Quayrat in the Gourgs Blancs and eventually ascertained Aneto as the highest point in the Pyrenees. But in, or a little before, 1787, they encouraged an unknown shepherd from the Aspe valley to climb the Pic du Midi d'Ossau '...in order to construct a triangulation turret on the summit'. Bearing in mind the rather formidable appearance of this mountain, its first ascent signifies a landmark in the climbing history of the Pyrenees.

Until the appearance of Ramond de Carbonnieres though, the peaks and hidden valleys in the heart of the range were an unknown quantity to the pioneers of the newly-evolving sport of mountaineering.

*

Ramond de Carbonnieres

Not only was Ramond the first of the real pioneers of mountaineering exploration within the Pyrenean range, he was a worthy successor to de Saussure, combining scientific observation with an acknowledged delight in climbing which, through his lucid literary style, he managed to convey to a broader public. It was a period of slow awakening in Europe to a new understanding and appreciation of mountain scenery. The heralds of enlightenment - Gesner, von Haller and Rousseau - glow as candles in the dim corridors of fear and superstition, yet their eulogies were inspired principally by the 'middle view', as Ruskin's were to be similarly restricted a century and more later; but Ramond ventured to the regions of eternal snow and ice, found there a peculiar kind of beauty, and returned to the lowlands to illuminate the darkness of ignorance with an elegant and honest prose.

Baron Louis-Francois Ramond de Carbonnieres (1755-1827) came from Colmar in the pleasant green countryside of Alsace. As a student at the University of Strasbourg he was influenced by Goethe, also at Strasbourg, but some six years his senior. He harboured early literary ambitions, but it was not until he had visited Switzerland at the age of twenty-two that he at last threw off the shackles of youthful morbidity and found inspiration to mature his pen. Having achieved modest success with his translation and annotation of Archdeacon Coxe's '*Letters on the Civil and Political State of Switzerland*', he received an invitation to become Confidential Secretary to the Cardinal Rohan. It was to prove a demanding appointment, for the Revolution was rumbling, and many heads were to fall. As a consequence, he visited the Pyrenees in 1787, a factor which was to have a considerable influence on his life, and especially on the history of Pyrenean exploration.

Ramond de Carbonnieres (1755-1827)
First of the real mountaineering pioneers
in the Pyrenees.

On the summit of the Pic du Midi de Bigorre Ramond met Reboul and Vidal, and there, with a vast multitude of unknown, untrodden peaks displayed before him, made plans for his summer's activity. Subsequently he crossed many a high pass, traversed virgin valleys and scrambled at will where none save the isard and its hunter had been before him, and crowned his adventuring with a brave attempt on the Maladetta's lofty and mist-girt summit. Wherever he went his eyes were alert to the upland wastes, to the play of the clouds, the profusion of flowers and the geology of the heights, but more than this, his passion was for the sheer exhileration of travelling through a wild and uncharted landscape, a landscape which he drew so graphically with his descriptively romantic pen. Writing of his attempt upon the Maladetta, he described the tarn now known as the Lago de Paderna above the Renclusa:

'Already far above the valley which we had traversed, we had nothing about us but blackened rocks and ravines; the snows were suspended above our heads, and flowers and rivulets the most distant from our thoughts, when a little platform, entirely surrounded with the most menacing ruins, presented us the smiling spectacle of a little lake, whose borders were clad with the freshest turf, and tufts of pines of the smallest stature. This is the last retreat of vegetation, the most secret of her solitudes: the universe disappears at its very entrance; it seems to be the remains of a world which has been buried up beneath its ruins.'

Again, in a passage which describes a sudden storm trapping him above the snowline with a meagre rock his only shelter, he dreams of building a hut there in order to observe better the convulsions of this rarely-trod world. Had Rousseau been a mountaineer to experience this world, he too may have written in a similar vein:

'What a spectacle it would be, when the storms of autumn descended upon the place, as though it were their own peculiar domain; when the fleet izard and the mournful crow, sole dwellers in this wilderness, had fled before them from the heights; when the light and powdery snow, falling from slope to slope, and blown from rock to rock, had swamped the whole waste beneath its capricious billows; when the mountain peaks, wrapped in impenetrable mist, had disappeared from view! What battles then! What whirlwinds! ... And what a stillness when the skies no longer thundered, and winter, victorious at last, had no more battles to fight.'

Ramond was a politician, a gifted amateur botanist and geologist, and later, under the direct order of Napolean, Prefect at Puy de Dome. He climbed at a time when science was the single justification for adventure, but through his writings it becomes clear that scientific knowledge was but a portion of the reward for the hardships endured during his travels among mountains.

Passages from his books and journals suggest that his involvement in mountaineering, albeit somewhat pedestrian compared with the standards of today, was not so far removed from that of many alpinists of the present. He wrote without restraint of the emotions experienced whilst climbing, and long before the motives of climbers came under the general scrutiny of curious laymen, Ramond wrote as no single-minded scientist would write:

'Such persons as have not traversed mountains of the first order, will with difficulty form an idea of what repays the dangers which are undergone there. Still less will they be able to imagine that these fatigues are not without their pleasures, and these dangers not without their charms.'

He returned again to the Pyrenees in 1792 in order to escape the terrors of life in Paris where the Revolution - which he had prophesied, and even welcomed - had gained momentum, but even in the apparent sanctuary of Garvarnie's sheltering mountains, where he shared not only the coarse, hard bread of the peasants, but their sometimes harsh and simple life too, the long arm of the Revolution reached out and found him, and for several months he was interned in the festering and gruesome horror of gaol. Upon his release he turned once more to the mountain fastnesses which, more than ever before, must have represented pure freedom. There he scrambled time and again, whenever the opportunity presented itself, but nearly always with one eye open for an unusual plant, or a rock with a history to read. Among his excursions at this time was an abortive attempt on the Pic de Néouvielle, an attempt which failed through faulty route-finding and resulted in the party reaching a minor summit. Separated from the main peak by a steep snow-covered slope of scree, Ramond glissaded into the tracks of avalanches with his guide, leaning on their sticks. Several times more he visited the summit of the Pic du Midi de Bigorre, but apparently his favourite outing was to the insignificant Pené du Lieris in the valley of Adour, a mountain which presented ample opportunities for botanising, as well as a noted view.

His knowledge of the range grew, and as it did so his faith in the maps decreased until, in obvious frustration, he wrote in his journal: 'May Heaven preserve the Pyrenees from an earthquake big enough to make the map correct!'

In historical terms Ramond's mountaineering fame rests on the pioneering achievement of Monte Perdido's first ascent, in 1802. His was the inspiration, but the ascent was made by others on his behalf. He had seen the 'lost mountain' on numerous occasions from afar, but two attemps to climb it in the summer of 1797, by way of the lovely Estaubé glen and the Brèche de Tuquerouye, fell some way short of completion; but they were nonetheless gallant efforts which involved some

Monte Perdido from below the Brèche de Tuquerouye, the route pioneered by Ramond in 1797

Illustration: Franz Schrader

difficult and at times dangerous ice-work. Ramond went away, leaving the mountains and valleys of the Pyrenees until the chance came to renew his acquaintance with them in 1802. This time he thought of Perdido perhaps with subdued enthusiasm, for he decided to conserve his energies until success could be judged fairly certain. He therefore employed his old friend and guide Laurens to reconnoitre the route on his behalf. Together with another local man, Rondau, and a Spanish shepherd met on the way, they actually completed the ascent on 7th August. Three days later Ramond made his own ascent in the company of Laurens and his brother Palu.

It was the culmination of Ramond's mountain career; the days of freedom and of limitless horizons were ending, and the years which remained were never successfully to replace the joys he had found among the savage heights.

> 'What is civilisation,' he wrote, 'if it still leave in our hearts an imperishable regret for our old independence? What is society if man, who she has fashioned to her will, and attached to her by habit and necessity, cannot escape an instant from the crowd which constrains him without shedding a tear at the thought of necessity which plunges him back into it?'

*

1802 - 1858 A Golden Age

The first half of the nineteenth century saw a period of slow, but deliberate progress among the peaks of the High Pyrenees, when all the major summits were won. Although mountaineering was yet some way from becoming universally acceptable, the relatively small band of enthusiasts was growing, and so too was that determined brotherhood of men who were openly scrambling for the fun of the thing, refusing to hide behind a shield of respectability whose banner was scientific motivation. Some came with a short alpine experience behind them, inquisitive to the challenge of an unknown range. Others arrived in the foothills, vacationing at one of the popular watering places. They took excursions to Gavarnie and to the Port de Venasque, and found a dimension that was exciting, invigorating, and offering opportunities for adventures mysterious. Hunters and shepherds found a lucrative sideline in escorting these brave new adventurers to certain and safe vantage points; to the Bréche de Roland, the Piméné and Port de Venasque, but when it came to exploring untrodden heights from unfamiliar valleys, few guides worthy of the name could be found. Terrors remained, the peasant mind unwilling to rise to the demands of creating routes into the savage unknown. Yet that handful of aspiring *Pyrénéistes* with sufficient resolution to seek new ways could, and did, find the rare hunter or shepherd willing to be persuaded to forsake the comforts of the fragrant valley in exchange for those inhospitable regions where only the isard roamed. New routes were made, fresh summits rose as a challenge and one by one the lofty heights fell.

After the successful first ascent of the range's third highest mountain, Monte Perdido, - a considerable accomplishment which had demanded persistence, dedication and the overcoming of numerous ice-climbing and route-finding problems - the next noteworthy achievement came in 1817. Dr Frederic Parrot - the Russo-German professor at the University of Dorpat in Estonia, who is remembered for his first ascents of the Parrotspitze on Monte Rosa, and of Mount Ararat, in 1829 - set off on a walk across the Pyrenees, from the Atlantic to the Mediterranean. During the course of this lengthy ramble which took fifty-three days, Parrot succeeded where Ramond had failed thirty years before him, in making the first ascent of the Pico de la Maladetta (3308m.) with Pierre Barrau of Luchon as his guide. Other summits were likewise claimed by this little-known enthusiast as he made his way eastwards, among which were those of Gallinero and Basibe.

During the 1820s survey officers under the overall charge of Lieutenant-Colonel Coraboeuf began a campaign of detailed exploration in the highest and least accessible portions of the range in preparation for the *Carte de France*. Coroboeuf was a single-minded and dedicated master of his profession, and one who led a vigorous enterprise, conducting every phase with considerable emphasis on accuracy. In the course of his surveys a great many summits were reached, the carto-

The Port de Venasque with Aneto beyond.   *Lithograph by E.Paris*

graphers in most instances carrying delicate and cumbersome equipment. They were a hardy group of men; Coroboeuf and Testu concentrating on the eastern section, while Peytier and Hossard surveyed the west, and in order to complete their measurements they spent long periods in the remote heartland of the mountains, climbing here, surveying there, bivouacking wherever night caught them, in fair weather and in foul. In this manner the difficult Balaitous, in 1825 (Peytier and Hossard), and the Estats and its neighbouring Montcalm (by Coroboeuf and Testu) two years later, received their initial ascents.

*

James David Forbes, the Scots Professor of Natural Philosophy at Edinburgh who was to make such an impact on the early history of mountaineering in the Alps, was one of the better-known figures from the world of mountains to visit the Pyrenees during the early 1800s. Already he had been to the Alps, but the Pyrenees offered a fresh scene for his questioning mind, and in the summer of 1835 he came to the range to study its geology. His outings, however, were far from original and were limited to the well-known and much-trodden Brèche de Roland - 'The Brèche itself quite exceeded my expectations' - and to the Port de Venasque. Grand as the panorama most certainly is from the Port de Venasque, and as impressive as the Maladetta appears, his comments on the ice-fields of this huge massif reveal their former glory which is some way removed from the relatively insignificant drapery of today.

'... the mist cleared away so as to let me have a complete view of this giant mountain, with its prodigious glaciers, which seem to me to rival those of Mont Blanc, and to vie with the ice-fields of Grindelwald. The valley of Venasque is a fitting scene: bare rocks with only scattered pines, savage in the extreme.'

*

With the Pic du Midi d'Ossau, Perdido, Maladetta and the Balaitous all won, the two outstanding mountains remaining untouched, and of obvious provocation to ambitious mountaineers, were the Vignemale and Aneto. Both were protected by bands of ice and snow, defences which tended rather to intimidate the advances of the pioneers, but it was the Vignemale, with the largest glacier in the whole chain, which was first to capitulate.

It is understandable that the Vignemale should attract the attention of the early climbers. Since nearly every visitor to the Pyrenees made the pilgrimage to Gavarnie, many would have been inspired by the great white tongue of the Ossoue Glacier swelling in the upper reaches of its beckoning valley. From the Brèche de Roland it catches the eye, an expanse of snow and ice against a background of dull rock. It makes the half-circle of darkened ridge which cups the levels of snow at its head, appear even higher than it really is. It becomes a target of one's attention.

In 1837, two guides from Gedre, a village down-valley a short distance from Gavarnie, made the first ascent whilst prospecting a route for a client. It was a dramatic ascent, for Henry Cazaux and his brother-in-law, Bernard Guillembet, both managed to fall into the *Grande Crevasse* which at that time was the major obstacle on the Ossoue Glacier. Using a labyrinth of tortuous corridors in the ice they eventually escaped, climbed up to the vast snowfield at its head and scambled to the actual summit. So unnerved were they by their experience in the crevasse that, rather than reverse their route, they found an alternative way down, after a bivouac, by way of the Ara Valley, south of the frontier in Spain. The following year Cazaux led the first tourist ascent - via the Ara Valley - which was made by a certain Miss Anne Lister, from Halifax.

Miss Lister was a remarkable, indomitable lady; one of the pioneers of women's mountaineering. Having gained some experience of mountains through a walking tour of Switzerland, she first visited the Pyrenees in 1830 when she made a very early ascent of Monte Perdido - most probably the first ascent by a female. On her return in the summer of 1838 she met Cazaux on the summit of that fine viewpoint, but easy mountain, the Piméné, and made arrangements to tackle the Vignemale at the earliest opportunity. On August 7th the ascent was completed from the South. Characteristically, her journal entries are brief, indicating no-nonsense resolution.

'Off at 2¾. Sent back the horses at 4.55 ... Breakfast at 4.55 and set off at 5.20 on foot. At the first degree at 6.40. Climbed the chimney ... Put on crampons and off again at 8.18. On the snow without quitting it till 9.8 ... Took off crampons at 10.10 ... I lay down a little; put on my cloak and did not feel the air cold ... Off again 11¾, sick just before ... At the top at 1.'

A week later she learned the news that Cazaux had taken the Prince de la Moskowa, son of Napolean's Marshall Ney, to the summit a few days after her own ascent, but had misled the Prince into believing that his was the first successful tourist ascent. It appears that he explained Miss Lister's tracks in the snow by saying that she had been unwell on the glacier and had descended without completing the route. Angered by this, she refused to pay her guide until the affair was publicly cleared, even threatening legal action to speed a settlement. After some time a document was produced and duly signed by Cazaux. The Prince was informed of the deception, but this was evidently insufficient to discourage him from publishing his own account in a local newspaper shortly after.

'The Prince de la Moskowa and his brother Mons. Edgar Ney, accompanied by five guides made a successful ascent, on the 11th instant, to the summit of Vignemale, the second highest (sic) mountain of the Pyrenees ... which had hitherto been thought inaccessible.'

*

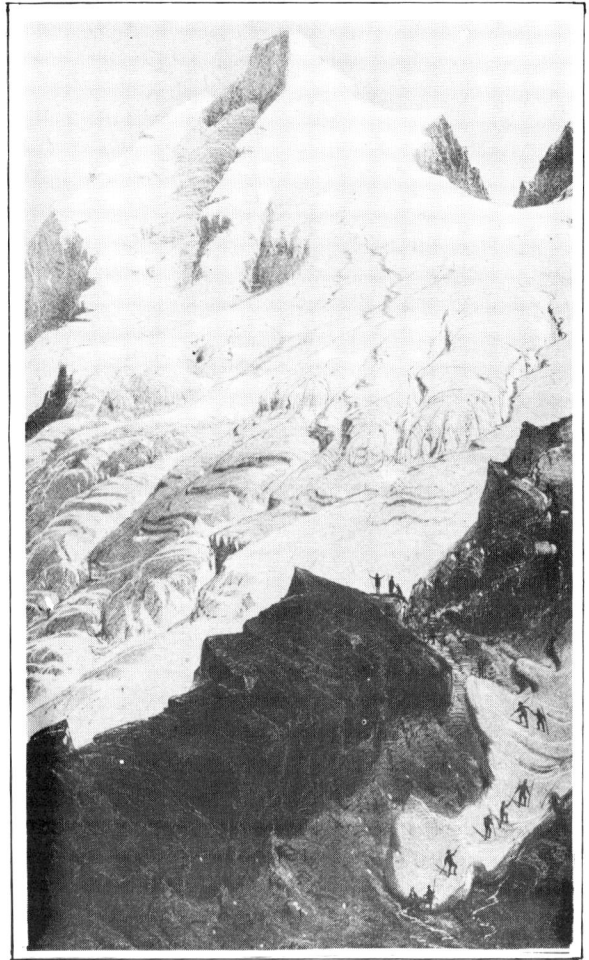

*The ascent of Aneto -
from the Cresta de los Portillones
- a 19th century impression.*

Lithograph by Victor Petit.

Five years after Cazaux and Guillembet climbed the Vignemale, the heights of the Maladetta were visited by an international party whose sights were set steady on Pico de Aneto, highest summit in the range, and its greatest prize remaining.

Count Albert de Franqueville, born in 1814, was a passionate botanist and hunter of isard, who was also haunted by the desire to be first on the summit of the Pyrenees. In Luchon he met a young Russian officer, Platon de Tchihatcheff, who shared his goal and was already organising an expedition bound for Aneto. Rather than be spurred in unwarranted competition for the prize, they pooled their resources for a joint expedition. Accompanying them were two isard hunters from Luchon, Bernard Ursule and Pierre Redonnet, who were familiar with the country approaching the Maladetta, and the guides Jean Argaret, also from Luchon, and Pierre Sanio from Luz.

Their route was a bewilderingly devious one, chosen in an effort to avoid what glaciers they could; but it met with success when, on 20th July 1842, they reached the highest point of the vast Maladetta massif, and the culminating peak of the range was theirs.

Few major peaks remained to be won. In 1847, more than fifty years after Ramond's aborted attempt, the Pic de Néouvielle was climbed by de Chausenque, a persistent *Pyrenéisté* who had earlier published *'Les Pyrénées ou Voyages Pédestres dans toutes les régions de ces montagnes depuis l'Océan jusqu á la Mediterranée'* in which he had commented that the Vignemale was inaccessible from France. Yet in his honour he was later to have one of the Vignemale peaks named after him.

In 1856 two important ascents were made. Pic Long (3192m.) is the highest of the Pyrenean peaks set entirely in France and it was first climbed by the Duc de Nemours, son of King Louis Philippe, with Marc Sesquet as his guide. Then Halkett, guided by Redonnet and Barrau, found a successful route to the top of the crumbling rocks which rise to the Pico des Posets, at 3375m. the second major Pyrenean peak and one which commands one of the broadest panoramas of the range.

Two years later the fine, double-headed Forcanada, standing above the sterile wastes of the Escaleta, was finally beaten into submission under the onslaught of the young and impetuous Alfred Tonnelle - again under the steady guidance of Redonnet, who by now had acquired something of a reputation for himself in Luchon.

By 1858 then, all the highest Pyrenean summits had been reached. The handful of enthusiasts who had found a virgin range had accepted the challenge and taken their prizes, leaving behind them only the more difficult peaks - or regions of unexplored wilderness - inviolate. There were other mountains to win, it is true, and fresh routes to be made on those already won. There were faces and gullies and tortuous ridges; but mountaineering was not yet ready for advances of this nature, although before the century had reached full maturity brave new developments would herald a new era.

One era was over, the first Golden Age had been half a century of sporadic activity. All major summits had been climbed because there had been so many tempting prizes available, but the heights of the Pyrenees had still to receive the scrutiny of a single-minded champion, a man prepared to devote time and energy to the cause of cataloguing the peaks and publicising their attractions to the swelling ranks of British climbers. Such a man was Charles Packe.

*

Packe and Russell

Although his name rarely appears in historical surveys of the mountaineering scene, Charles Packe (1826-96) was for many years one of the most influential of climbers. It was he who introduced John Ball, Hinchliff and William Longman - prominent names in the early days of the Alpine Club - to the mountains of North Wales and to the Lakeland fells. It was he who introduced the young Haskett-Smith - later to become the father of British rock climbing - to his first mountains with a walking and scrambling tour of the Pyrenees, in 1881. It was Packe, more than any other, who 'discovered' the full potential for mountaineering in the Pyrenees; who wrote long and informative articles, and produced the first climbers' guide book to the range; the man of whom it was said: 'Mr Packe is the king of the Pyrenees; he invented them'.

Packe's background was not altogether dissimilar to that of many of the Victorian pioneers. After Eton and Oxford he was called to the Bar in 1852, but he never practised seriously, preferring diversions of another order, and with the supreme confidence of one released by inheritance from the distractions of having to earn a living, he took readily to travel. Mountains, he found, were an inspiration, a source of never-fading fascination. They offered an ideal field for the indulgence of amateur studies and the finest of all opportunities for regular bodily exercise. The hunting fields of his native Leicestershire could not compete with the attractions of his mountains, and they became the centre of his interest. Throughout his life he undertook strenuous walking and climbing tours among them, concentrating mainly in the Pyrenees where he became the great British authority, but visiting also the Alps on numerous occasions.

The Alps already had an impressive band of protagonists working, climbing, writing about them, but so far as the outside world was concerned, the Pyrenees lay somewhere beyond the horizon or, at best informed, were the backcloth to some fashionable watering places. Packe was to alter all that with his passion and persistence, yet although he undoubtedly favoured those mountains above all others, he was not blind to the glories of other ranges, and he knew well the Sierra Nevada, the greater Alps and the homely hills of Britain.

His first visit to the Pyrenees was made in 1853. He returned four years later, and in 1859 began work on his systematic and detailed study of them. Travelling at first mostly alone, and taking guides only for the ascent of first-class peaks, he rapidly gained a considerable knowledge of the range, a knowledge unrivalled by any of his contemporaries. Both in appearance and, to a degree, in temperament, he was a little like Don Quixote; enigmatic, sincere yet transparent in his strong distaste for petty hypocrisies, prejudiced and warm-hearted. He was slight of build, yet he

Charles Packe (1826-96)
the Leicestershire landowner
who opened up the range
for climbers.

(Photo credit: Lt.Col. E.C.Packe)

possessed substantial powers of strength, and was capable of sustaining a high degree of physical exertion. During the many years of his explorations it was his habit to '... rise at daybreak after a night on the hard ground, take a cup of tea and a nibble of bread, and thereupon walk for five, six, or seven hours before breakfast; after that there was no more eating till we made our bivouac a little before sunset, and no rest, except perhaps an hour's siesta in the hottest part of the day'. With such energies, and an acknowledged devotion to detail, he absorbed all the range had to offer.

Charles Packe was an enthusiastic and competent botanist, and the Pyrenees gave him ample scope to exercise this interest. He also niggled at the geology of the range, enquiring into every facet of the mountains and their valleys, gaining invaluable knowledge which was to be the foundation for the production of his Guide. This *'Guide to the Pyrenees'* with a subtitle, *'Especially Intended for the use of Mountaineers',* was the product of four years of intensive exploration, and it was enlarged later as his experience unearthed yet more knowledge, until the compact volume - published by his friend, William Longman - contained more than a catalogue of peaks and the routes by which they might be climbed, but which was an observant and informative pocket companion.

Packe's experience was gained by way of climbs on every major summit, countless minor heights, the crossing of passes and glaciers, the forcing of untracked gorges and the descent into nameless valleys; but through all the years and all the magnificent days of pioneering, and in spite of his books and many articles, we know few of the summits whose first ascent he made. His character remains aloof from records of personal achievement, and it is only by courtesy of his friends and contemporaries that any such records exist. Pic Carlitte, the Picos de Valhiverna, Perdighero and Munia can likely be attributed to him. The Balaitous, unknown for forty years, was rediscovered by him in a tireless campaign inspired, to a certain extent, by the failure of John Ball, and it was not until he actually reached the summit that Packe found a cairn indicating that it had already been climbed. In the Posets he created new routes. In the Maladetta he crossed the Col de Salenques for the first time with William Matthews - one of the founding fathers of the Alpine Club - and made a long tour of discovery round that broad and chaotic massif. His exploration of the Ordesa Canyon in 1860 was virtually an act of discovery since, for nearly sixty years after Ramond's early glimpse of its wonders, it had completely neglected and forgotten.

The Maladetta came under close inspection when, in the early summer of 1865, Packe installed himself in the fragrant pastures of the Valhiverna with Captain Barnes, Firmin Barrau and Charles Gouchan - and his great cosseted dog, Ossoue - and spent two weeks of exploration there. By making a series of observations and measurements from the summits of countless peaks and ridges, he made what Russell considered to be '... his greatest service to the geography of the loftiest part of Aragon ... his admirable map of the Monts Maudits, of which the whole credit is due to him alone'. It was, without doubt, a magnificent achievement, but Packe was clearly in his element, for he had '... neither predecessors nor even books to guide him, and the wild and vast regions he so conscientiously explored and mapped .... covered no less than 1,000 square kilometres, where none but chamois hunters had trodden before him'.

Charles Packe, the Leicestershire landowner, the Barrister who climbed with a copy of *Horace* in his pocket, indulged - perhaps uncharacteristically - in the strangely eccentric habit of undertaking long excursions in the sole company of his two Pyrenean mountain dogs, even going to the lengths of negotiating crevassed glaciers roped between them in surely misplaced confidence. Like Coolidge in the Alps, Packe took one or more of his dogs to the top of a number of high peaks. They accompanied him on countless travels, and shared with him the frosty night bivouac and the glories of the spangled dawn.

*

Henry Russell (1834-1909)
Romantic eccentric, 'Grand Old Man
of the Vignemale'
Photo: M.Beys.

Packe's name is naturally linked with that of Henry Russell. 'Mon ami Packe' is a phrase which recurs time and again in the latter's writings, yet the two were of greatly differing temperaments. Packe was the studious, scientific 'plodder', systematic and single-minded. Russell was an unashamed romantic, an impulsive, jovial lover of the mountains, ready to be wooed by the moonlit snows without being side-tracked into seeking answers to unnecessary questions. Russell admitted their differences: '... we were the very best of friends, though we had not the same pursuits or tastes. Whilst I indulged in accentric, solitary ascents of untrodden and snowy peaks ...

Packe did more useful things. He mapped those peaks, he measured and named them, botanised in their valleys, and read their history in their rocks and fossils'. Whilst Packe ascended the peaks by their more logical, straightforward, routes, Russell scrambled - and descended - the unknown way. Packe was made in the traditional mould - 'he was the Tyndall of the Pyrenees' - Russell was the embodiment of the 'sporting mountaineer'. Though both were devoted to the Pyrenees, and both content to experience long periods of solitude in their mountaineering, Russell sought isolation in an almost mystical fashion. His whole attitude towards the mountains was summarised in a passage from his classic *'Souvenirs d'un Montagnard'*.

'I respect and envy those for whom the mountain is other than a goddess. I am jealous of those to whom geodesy and the structure of peaks mean more than the voice of the torrent, the purple of a precipice or the fire of the snows at sunset. But each to his own taste. Mine was to move and to feel.

Count Henry Patrick Marie Russell-Killough (1834-1909) was born at Toulouse, practically within sight of the Pyrenees, of an Irish father and French mother. It is said that he made his first mountain excursion at the age of six, when he walked from Cauterets to the Lac de Gaube from whose shores he gained his initial view of the Vignemale, the mountain with which his name will forever be associated.

His early longings were for the sea, but his journey round the Cape to Lima - where he made a brief acquaintance with the Andes of Peru - was something of a disaster. The wanderlust saw him travelling the world for several years; to Canada, to the United States and to Cuba; across Europe to the frozen wastes of the Gobi -where, he later claimed, he and his companions were forced to *eat* their brandy with the temperature at 90° below freezing - to China and Japan and India, to Australia and New Zealand - where he was lost, alone and without food for three days in the Southern Alps - before heading up to the foothills of the Himalaya.

Returning from his travels he found that the Pyrenees had lost nothing in the years of his absence, and the mountains were no less for his courtship with other, distant, heights. The swelling ridges and fragrant valleys of his home were to demand his full attention, and Russell was more than willing to give it. In 1861 he made the first of his many ascents of the Vignemale, under the guidance of Laurent Passet, uncle of Célestin, who was to become a regular companion and his favourite guide in the productive years ahead. From this date until shortly before his death, Henry Russell was to climb every Pyrenean mountain of note, often by new routes, often alone, experiencing the remote heights and the seclusion of cloud-wrapped summits in his own inimitable fashion. With an undiluted enthusiasm he strode across the range, exploring hidden corries and hanging valleys, wandering in a daze of adulation of the highland world. He climbed simply for the joy of being where none - or, at worst, very few - had been before. In his writings we learn nothing about these mountains save their colour at dawn and the caprices of the wind; they paint rainbow patterns of one man's impassioned excesses and his relationship with the naked arétes and the deep, blossomed valleys.

Russell and Packe met by the Lac Bleu near Baréges in the summer of 1863. In spite of their obvious differences they were at once united by a common love of their mountains, and a friendship grew that was to last until Packe's death. Two years after their first meeting they became instrumental in forming the *Société Ramond* - a specifically Pyrenean association, and a forerunner of the C.A.F. - and in 1874, when the C.A.F. emerged, Russell was a founder member. The Alpine Club in London, too, opened its doors to him, and it seems almost a contradiction to find that this great lover of solitude was at the same time an open, friendly, 'clubable' man, charming and entertaining, with a droll humour and some talent as a performer on the cello. Yet as he grew older, so his passion for seclusion in the mountains intensified. On one of his earliest solo expeditions this delight in being alone almost cost him his life. He climbed Monte Perdido and was returning to Gavarnie by way of the Brèche de Roland, when he was caught by a furious snowstorm. Night fell and marooned him near that monstrous gash in the Cirque de Gavarnie's high western wall where he was forced to spend twelve hours of bitter darkness, lashed by storm, without the comfort of shelter. The mystic in him found expressions of glory and splendour in the storm's savagery, and it is quite probable that in such instances his romantic zeal was as valuable to the act of survival as any natural mountaineering instinct or physical resource. When night was spent the storm abated, but the descent to Gavarnie was aggravated by white-out conditions that led him to the very brink of the precipices, and he was saved from disaster at the last moment only by the sound of the cascade, which is un-detected from the true route. At last in Gavarnie he was met by a party setting out to search for his remains.

On another occasion he made a solo ascent of Aneto in conditions that rapidly deteriorated, yet his poetical nature emerged with typical sentiments; 'Terrible weather; hungry; snow; fog; no compass; solitude!' The exclamation of 'solitude!' emphasises a certain wry satisfaction, and one can almost picture his tall, military frame bent under the force of the wind, but with a smile of deep contentment lighting his snow-crusted face.

Russell was a pioneer of winter climbing, and he made an attempt on the snow-bound Pic du Midi d'Ossau early in the 1860s, succeeded on the Pic de Ger in March 1863 and, in February 1869, recorded probably the first winter ascent of the Vignemale with Henri and Hippolyte Passet.

> 'It was, I admit, extremely fatiguing, as we walked in soft snow for sixteen hours, but dangers there were none, although this peak is almost 11,000 feet. Avalanches do not fall in winter. The eastern glacier, so fearfully crevassed in July, had quite disappeared under snow hills, undulating all over it like some monstrous waves on an ocean of milk or cream. Both heat and light became intense. The peak itself, which rises from the glacier like an island upon the sea, was free from snow, save a few specks here and there, which melted in the sun, and fell on the hot slopes with all sorts of murmers and whispers'.

He was also delighted to discover that the temperature was considerably higher upon the summit than that experienced down in the valleys. 'As for beauty and majesty,' he concludes, 'nothing ever surpassed or equalled them in the finest days of July'.

Russell's new climbs in the Pyrenees were far more numerous than those of any of his predecessors. While he began his career as a *'Gavarniste'* he soon found that the range had more to offer than those well-known peaks at the head of Gavarnie's surrounding valleys. He trod summits as far apart as Anie and Carlitte, filling the gaps between with his passion and flare for climbing, for scrambling undocumented ways. Although he discouraged unnecessary rashness in others, and openly spoke against the tendency by some to turn his mountains into one vast, open-air gymnasium, he was himself responsible for some fine rock climbs early in his career. Disclaiming any particular skills, he sought routes that offered challenge. 'Danger,' he wrote, 'is ... one of the charms of mountains, and in many cases their greatest attraction. It has a mesmeric effect. An easy peak is left alone, and deserves to be so'. However, when his favourite guide, Célestin Passet, together with Henri Brulle and others of his circle, brought a fresh emphasis to the mountaineering style of *Pyrénéisme*, deliberately seeking difficulties of a new order - and overcoming them - Russell could not help but find himself out of tune, and his own mountaineering changed direction. He became insular in his approach, almost incapable of keeping pace with changing attitudes that marked an evolution of mountaineering thought. He became old-fashioned.

Always an enthusiastic advocate of the bivouac, he rarely used a tent and scorned the huts which the C.A.F. began to erect in his mountains. His great desire for intimacy with the heights meant that literally hundreds of nights were spent in his lambskin sleeping bag; above the snowline and in the higher valleys, and even upon the summits themselves; on the Vignemale, on Monte Perdido and Aneto - remarking at sunrise on the snow turning blood-red where the first rays struck, while the hollows clutched shadows of deep blue. These were the delights, the simple delights that drew him again and again to the mountains, and which were expressed in the rich imagery of his writings.

For two decades - the 1860s and 1870s - Henry Russell's tireless explorations resulted in an ever-growing list of new routes. Towards the end of the seventies, in a fit of uncharacteristic melancholy, he confessed to Packe that there was little left to explore, and it was shortly after this that he entered a new phase of attachment to the range. He knew the individual peaks through personal experience. He knew their ridges and faces and deep-shadowed gullies, their glaciers and their hanging valleys, but one peak above all others lured him regularly to its flanks - the Vignemale. It retained his especial affection and devotion, drawing from him curious acts of eccentricity and fervour unequalled in the long history of mountaineering. That he actually loved the Vignemale cannot be disputed. He loved the turmoil of its glacier, the elegance of its domination over the immediate landscape, the way it beckoned from afar; and he loved its solitude. At least thirty-three times he wandered to its summit and sought out the hidden sanctuaries of its frosted ridges, 'watching the sunset fade or in grave meditation stalking slowly to and fro across the moonlit snows'.

By 1880 he was beginning to concentrate all his attention on this fine mountain. He wrote:

'It took me twenty years to discover that the exploration of the virgin, savage, and lofty regions of the Pyrenees was almost as hard as that of Greenland or the Sahara; but I discovered it at last, and, tired out with suffering so much, I decided either to beat a retreat, or to find some way of making long stays at the height of 10,000 feet or more on the summit of the Pyrenees without compelling myself to keep there a perpetual Lent.'

Retreat, of course, was never seriously considered; Russell was too deeply commited for that, but the answer to the nagging problem of finding a habitable spot on the Vignemale was not an easy one to overcome. It was to demand several years of dogged resolution, and frustrating disappointments, to resolve.

Better than any man, Henry Russell knew that the Vignemale, in its natural state, was quite uninhabitable. Perhaps to one with a lesser attachment an answer would be to construct a refuge from which to base these 'long stays', but to Russell any suggestion of building on sacred ground was abhorent; there was no possibility of a man-made structure conforming with the highest standards of aesthetic acceptance. A cave, on the other hand, would be a part of the mountain. It would offer shelter without intruding upon the mountain's individual architecture, but since there were no caves on the Vignemale, he embarked upon a survey designed to uncover any clue that might offer a solution to the problem. It resulted in the strangest of his growing eccentricities.

On August 16th, 1880, Henry Russell allowed himself to be placed in a shallow grave excavated on the very summit of the Vignemale, and there he spent the night in solitude. One man, his mountain, and the bitter chill of the 'cold lunar beams'. Reminiscing, he wrote: 'It was impossible to catch cold, for one was always cold - indeed, I was blue and frozen'.

Deciding finally to create his own caves, Russell subsequently spent two summers directing the labours of the peasants from Gedre whom he had enlisted for the work. For two summers they paced the path along the Ossoue valley, struggling with cumbersome loads of explosives, wood and food, picking their way cautiously among the crevasses of the glacier beside which the first of the grottoes was sited. Sometimes they floundered in the mist and falling snow, at others they cowered beneath a huge canvas as a storm erupted its fury about their heads. During the first attempt, in 1881, they were forced to retreat; 'pale, wild and livid'. Snow swirled about them, covering everything. 'We had the air of dead men rising again'.

The following July they were blessed with three weeks of calm weather, and on August 1st, Henry Russell took possession, sharing the honour with Francis Swan - after whom the couloir seaming the twin Astazou peaks is named. Other nights followed. Russell took up residence for several days at a time, and like so many valley-bound householders, he began to entertain visitors. The Abbé Pommes celebrated Mass in the grotto while a congregation of thirty knelt on the ice of the glacier outside.

Three years later he extended his estate by opening another grotto; and the following year, yet another. With the steady possession of the Vignemale, he became even more extravagent; entertaining dinner parties at which he wore evening dress. A banquet was arranged, and a large tent erected before the grottoes in which to house the guests. At its entrance columns were carved in the ice, Persian carpets unrolled, and the company feasted as well as at any valley hotel.

In 1889, in recognition of his peculiar attachment and devotion to the mountain, the *Syndicat* of

*'Grotte Bellevue'
one of Russell's
Vignemale caves.*

the valley of Baréges leased the four summits of the Vignemale to him - without right to forbid access - for a ninety-nine year term, at the not-exorbitant sum of one franc per year. In obvious delight he wrote: 'It is certainly the highest estate in Europe and, despite its sterility, I would not exchange it for the finest in France'.

As though to endorse the outside recognition of his tenancy, Russell created a seventh, and final, grotto only a few metres below the actual summit. *'Le Paradis'* faced south and was dry. Its entrance, though low, was sufficient to allow access and to secure the occupant from the wind; it was carpeted with straw and even had its own water supply by virtue of a steady trickle through a crack in the rock. It was here that the Grand Old Man of the Vignemale celebrated in his sixtieth year, what he referred to as the 'silver wedding' of his first ascent, and ten years later made his final pilgrimage to the mountain, paying homage for a period of seventeen days at *Le Paradis*, and spending hours of isolated meditation there, gazing with sentimental understanding and nostalgia from the ragged rocks of the summit.

*

Brulle and the Heroic Age

The influence of Packe and Russell was both considerable and lasting. John Ball, clearly inspired by Packe's example, made two visits to the range, in 1861 and '62, during which he made an unsuccessful attempt on the Balaitous, as already noted, but otherwise made no impression camparable to his work in the Alps. A little later W.D. Freshfield - one of the greatest of Victorian mountaineer-explorers - also came to the Pyrenees with his guide, Francois Devouassoud, but although they made a number of ascents, including those of Monte Perdido, Vignemale and Pic de Perdighero, they created no outstanding new routes.

Franz Schrader, who combined *Pyrénéisme* with science, began his work of mapping the range in 1874. Others made their own singular contributions to the exploration and subsequent knowledge of the mountains. Men like Lequetre and Wallon, Gourdon, Trutat, the Count de Saint-Saud and Emile Belloc, but almost without exception their mountaineering was traditional in concept, consisting of repeating known routes on the major peaks, or opening new peaks by their more obvious approaches. They climbed, as did the majority of these pioneers, with the minimum of

*Pioneers - early adventurers
in the heart of the range*

equipment. Alpenstocks were almost universally employed with, in some instances, a very small 'pocket axe' which was used to cut steps in steep slopes of hard ice. Ropes were seldom taken, and when they were standards of management were so appallingly low that it may well be true to say that it would have been safer to climb without a rope than to use one without understanding the correct procedure for its use. These were still early days, and techniques advance best on the mistakes of the founders.

Then Henri Brulle (1854-1936) came onto the scene, discovered the full scope of the talents of the Gavarnie guide, Célestin Passet, and heralded a new era of mountaineering adventure on peaks long recognised by the earlier pioneers.

Brulle was to enjoy one of the longest careers of any climber in the broad history of mountaineering, remaining active until only a few days before his death, which came as a direct result of an epic attempt on Mont Blanc at the age of 82. It was also an extremely productive career that included visits to many different ranges besides those of the Pyrenees and the Alps. He climbed throughout Europe, from Mount Etna to Skye, and from Corsica to the Lake District - where he did Napes Needle and Steep Ghyll with Aleister Crowley - and for a number of years concentrated his activities on climbs from Chamonix. In 1883 he became the first man to climb the Meije in a single day, but it is in the Pyrenees that his great industry assures him a place of honour.

*Henri Brulle (1854 -1936)
Father-figure of the Heroic Age.*

Henri Brulle came from Libourne, near Bordeaux, and at the age of twenty began his climbing activity with an ascent of the Vignemale with the Count de Saint-Saud, but his enormous appetite for mountaineering of a more strenuous and exploratory nature was not fully whetted until four years later, when he met Jean Bazillac and Célestin Passet. The trio made a formidable team; Bazillac was already a climber of experience, and Passet, trained by Russell, was to become the finest guide produced in the Pyrenees until recent years. Taking the Alps and the Pyrenees in alternate years they climbed as a team, and they developed together as a team, making at least fifty new or little-known ascents in the Pyrenees alone. The Heroic Age is a testament to their expertise and daring, but the route which effectively marks the inauguration of the brave new era - the Clot de la Hount Couloir on the Vignemale, of August 1879 - was made by Brulle and Bazillac without Passet, who was unavailable, his place being taken by the guides, Sarrettes and Bordenave.

It was in the Alps that Henri Brulle became familiar with routes of a demanding nature and of greater length than could be found in the mountains of his first love, and the lessons learned in the Alps were readily adopted for *Pyrénéisme*. From the Alps he gained an appreciation of snow and ice routes, and on lengthy rock climbs around Mont Blanc he found an additional challenge that inspired the development of fresh standards on peaks that previously had been overlooked. The potential for creating hard routes in the Pyrenees became recognised as an exciting reality.

> 'The Alps having given me a taste for difficulty ... I was led to 'operate' in the Pyrenees in the style of the new school. Why, after all, should they not tempt a true mountaineer? Their jagged crests, their craggy cliffs abound in problems of rock climbing ... and if it be true that their glaciers are few and far between, there are yet quite enough of them to supply us now and then with sport of an undeniably orthodox character.'

Brulle's first winter ascent was of Monte Perdido, in 1885, followed by two exhausting attempts on the Balaitous, but it was from Gavarnie, where he became for a while a 'centrist', that his most important outings began, with numerous routes being traced on the walls of the cirque. On the Casque, on the *'doigt'* of the False Brèche, and the North Face of the Taillon, as well as the Petit Pic Rouge de Pailla - likewise from the north - Brulle's eye for an interesting line led to a whole string of elegant ascents. However, this elegance deserted him on the last-named when he was unable to complete the ascent in the style to which he was accustomed, for his shoulders were too broad to enable him to worm through a narrow gap where the upper couloir was blocked by a great boulder. There, his companions on the rope, Passet and René d'Astorg, had to render assistance from above by hauling him from the outside, '... like a vile impedimentum'.

His greatest achievement, and the finest climb in the whole range of the Pyrenees during that eventful century, was the ascent of the Couloir de Gaube.

The Couloir de Gaube seams the northern aspect of the Vignemale; a great gash which separates the wedge of the Piton Carré from the huge block of the Pique Longue. A savage, yet tantalising corner; '... It is in itself so fierce-looking and vertiginous that it had been haunting my dreams'. On 7th August 1889, Brulle, with his enterprising team of Bazillac and de Monts, with Célestin Passet and Francois Bernard Salles as guides, attacked the couloir with immense vigour and not a little audacity. Nothing comparable had ever been considered outside of the Alps, and it is extremely doubtful whether another competent man could have been found in the Pyrenees capable of following in their wake. Even to approach the foot of the couloir across the turmoil of the glacier was an achievement, but once the actual climb had begun they made steady progress until the crux was reached - a large block, glazed with ice, which was found to be immovably wedged across the narrow gully of ascent. After two hours of exhausting effort Passet overcame the obstacle, and the Couloir de Gaube was won. Russell was furious, his mountain was being defiled by gymnastic antics; but, gentlemen that he was, he nonetheless offered celebratory drinks in his grotto to the victorious team on their descent.

Two days later the same team, maintaining the momentum, made the ascent of the North Face of Monte Perdido, a route originally created the year before by Passet, leading Roger de Monts and

Jean Bazillac and, once again, Francois Salles.

Brulle was perhaps the most outstanding of the amateur climbers active in the Pyrenees during the latter half of the nineteenth century, with his enthusiasm for difficult routes carrying through until the First World War. He was every bit as conscientious and determined in the mountains as in his professional capacity of lawyer; generous in friendships and in his attitude towards the adventures of others, he carried a philosopy to his climbing that elevated the actual struggle above any eventual outcome. If he failed to reach his summit due to the brutality of a storm, for example, it was of little consequence so long as it offered 'a sporting effort'. There was something of the romantic in his make-up, as indeed there must be in all who turn repeatedly to the heights in search of adventure. In his long career he suffered many hardships and not a few dangers, all of which complemented the countless ascents which were undertaken in a straightforward manner.

Writing of a difficult solo traverse of the Vignemale under the wild battering of a storm ' ... which made this expedition the pleasantest of my souvenirs,' it is possible to detect and understand the driving force that sustained him for more than sixty years of climbing activity.

> 'Enveloped in the morning in a dense fog, annoyed in the steep couloirs of the Cerbillonas by vultures which swept over me like avalanches, just grazing me with their long wings, assailed during three hours by hailstones of such a size that they bruised and stunned me, deafened by thunder, and so electrified that I was hissing and crepitating, I notwithstanding reached the summit at half-past four in the evening, amidst incessant detonations. In descending I got lost in a labyrinth of crevasses...As a climax night came on as black as ink, and I had to grope and feel my way down the endless valley of Ossoue. It was at 11 o'clock at night when I reached Gavarnie, almost starved and quite exhausted, but having lived the crowning day of my life.'

*

Whilst Henri Brulle undoubtedly spear-headed the Heroic Age, he was ably supported by Count René d'Astorg, who shared his rope on several notable climbs; North-West Arete of Pic d'Astazou (1892), North Face of the Pic du Midi d'Ossau via La Fourche (1896), and the splendid Petite Encantat, in 1902. Count d'Astorg was also actively involved in developing the Maladetta massif, where he has a summit named in his honour - first climbed with Brulle, Passet and Salles, in 1901.

Another of Brulle's contemporaries was Roger de Monts, whose great passion was for snow and ice routes. There was, of course, greater scope then for this type of climbing than may be found today, due to the retreat of the glaciers, but de Monts sought, and made, fine routes on the walls of the Cirque de Gavarnie - many with Brulle - and persisted until the ice-hung cliffs on the north of Monte Perdido had been adorned with a challenging line. He also made a speciality of winter ascents, catching the mountains in good condition and glorying in their magnetically icy veneer. Through his determination he gave added experience to various guides; to Haurine and Junté of Luchon, Célestin Passet of Gavarnie and Victor Chapelle of Héas; climbing Aneto in March, Perdido in December, Picos de Valhiverna, Posets, Pic du Midi d'Ossau, and countless others.

*

The Professionals

The Pyrenees produced few professionals to match the calibre of their counterparts of the Alps, those enduring guides whose skill and stamina had enabled standards to rise at a pace greater than here and whose names are recorded in the history books alongside their illustrious employers. Indeed, in the Pyrenees there was only a small band of the élite who knew more than the mountains of their own valleys, and few enough of these who were prepared to venture farther afield to satisfy the curious whims of an adventurous amateur with time on his hands. Of the two main centres, Gavarnie and Luchon, only the first inspired that true spirit of enterprise among its guides which was directly to lead to an upsurge in activity and harder routes being accomplished by both the professional and his client.

In Luchon there were too many excursions available for exploitation. Too many pleasant outings that led into mountain country to give the modest visitor a taste of adventure without any of the hazards or hardships that necessarily accompanied 'real' mountaineering. There were always guides available to give full encouragement to this style of adventure; their tariffs were displayed at the principal hotels and watering establishments, but invariably the visitor found himself the hirer also of horses, one for himself, and one for the guide. Packe found it necessary to put forward the names of a few whom he could recommend '... who will not grumble at being asked to use their own legs and carry your rucksack'. Of those included in the first edition of his *Guide,* Packe named Pierre and Firmin Barrau, Jacques Sors and Jean and Pierre Redonnet, this last named by then (1862) considered '... somewhat too old, but thoroughly trustworthy'.

In those days the usual charge was 5 francs a day per guide for the ordinary excursions, but for an ascent of the Maladetta, 30 francs per guide was the standard rate. Other, unlisted climbs, were arranged beforehand, and Packe gave the following advice:

'For any mountain excursion where the guide is required to sleep *sub Jove,* 10 francs a day seems to be required as remuneration, exclusive of provisions. For a course extending over more than 4 days, I should consider 8 francs per day quite as much as ought to be given.'

In addition to offering advice on which guide to use and how much ought to be paid, Packe also warned against the attitude adopted by some of those professionals:

'Most of the ... guides have been spoilt by being allowed too much of their own way, and are very apt to assume the position of master rather than the servant; but with an Englishman, especially when they find he is not a novice among the mountains, they are soon brought into their proper place.'

Gavarnie, however, bred men of a different calibre, and it is not mere coincidence that ignited here the spark that fired the Heroic Age, for the guides of this brave new era made a willing adjustment to the fresh emphasis placed upon their profession. The more active climbers of the day, no longer content to repeat the hackneyed *voie normale,* found among the encircling cliffs of Gavarnie's cirque, and the neighbouring peaks too, full scope for a more demanding sport. The guides who had cut their teeth on the rock and ice of standard routes had grown attentive to variations that might possibly exist, and to quicker ways from one point to another. They grew inquisitive and adventurous.

Of those working their trade from Gavarnie's simple base the Passet cousins, Henri and Célestin, outshone all others with their great natural mountaineering instincts, their competence on both rock and ice and, above all, their willingness to create new and demanding courses for their clients.

They came from guiding families; Laurent and Hippolyte Passett were brothers who had helped open the Cirque de Gavarnie, in particular by discovering the Brèche Passet, climbing the Point de Chute de la Cascade, Col d'Astazou and the Col de la Cascade from the north. They had been 'sturdy, capable, trustworthy guides', but the second generation cousins soon outstripped the reputations of their fathers and became universally recognised as the finest guides to be found throughout the range.

Henri Passet (1845-1919) was a master of tact, ever cheerful with a 'round, good-natured, rather stolid, Basque face'. For a good many years he accompanied Packe, not only in the Pyrenees where he gained great knowledge of the range's variety and scope, but also in the Alps and the Sierra Nevada - where they bivouacked together on the summit of Mulhacen. His experience of the Pyrenees was quite considerable and matched by a deep understanding, and although his ability was somewhat overshadowed by that of his highly talented cousin, he remained enormously popular with all who secured his services. Quietly intelligent, with a prodigious memory that stored information on various assorted subjects - which he had gained from his often intellectual employers - he was '... on rock, ice, or in bivouac... all that could be desired as a guide and comrade'.

Henri's cousin, Célestin, was the guide supreme whose enormous appetite for the mountains, coupled with an almost instinctive mastery of difficult rock or ice work, and an eye for an

*Célestin Passet - guide supreme of
the Heroic Age (1845-1917)
Illustration by Whymper
from Buxton's 'Short Stalks'.*

interesting line, led to a great many successes during the Heroic Age. Lean and lithe, Célestin cut a dashing figure. He had been employed for some years as a guide to isard and ibex hunters, and this gave him a keen understanding of mountainous terrain over which he was a fast mover. With Russell first, then with Brulle, he turned to adventurous climbing and travelled throughout the Pyrenees enlarging his repertoire of challenging routes wherever he went. He too made a number of distinctive climbs in the Alps, including ascents of the Meije, Matterhorn, the Dru and Ecrins. When Whymper was making plans for his expedition to the Andes he invited both Célestin and Henri to accompany him as his guides, but they declined, according to Russell, 'for sentimental reasons', adding, 'Exile will never be popular in France'!

During the latter half of the nineteenth century, wherever bold and enterprising lines were being established on Pyrenean faces, or in ice-choked gullies, the name of Passet subsequently became inscribed in the history books.

Another legendary figure of the period, and a man who took part in many of the more dramatic events which endorsed the Pyrenees as a first-class mountaineering centre, was Francois Bernard Salles. Salles was, of course, with Brulle's rope - as second guide - in the historic Couloir de Gaube. He was also with Brulle on the North Face of the Pic du Midi d'Ossau, on the Pointe d'Astorg, North Face of Monte Perdido, and took a leading part in the first ascent of the Grande Encantat in 1901, with de Negrin, Romeu, Angusto and Ciffre. Whilst his list of ascents is impressive, it is not so much for his climbing that he is best remembered, as for his incredible strength.

Salles, who was born in Gavarnie in about 1851, was a veritable giant of a man with a great hooked nose and high, gaunt forehead. When Russell required a stove to be carried up to one of his grottoes on the Vignemale, it was Salles who volunteered to do the work. Haskett-Smith tells how this great bear of a man looked at the stove for a moment, then went off for firewood with which to fill it! 'What use is a stove without wood?' he grunted. He, it was, who carried the bronze Virgin up to the Tuquerouye when no-one else could even lift it. On yet another occasion it is said that he caught a mule as it fell on a cliff path under a heavy load, and alone hauled it to safety. In her most readable mountaineering memoir, *'Climbing Days'*, Dorothy Pilley presents a fine word-picture of Francois Salles, and shows that even at the age of 72, he retained considerable strength, and was still active among the mountains of his native Gavarnie.

*

Maintaining the Momentum

Carrying the Heroic Age into the early years of the new century, were several ageing pioneers and a number of fresh faces willing to maintain the momentum that had so gracefully and conscientiously been bred. One of the foremost of these was the Viscount Jean d'Ussel, whose regular guide, Germain Castagné, was Célestin Passet's son-in-law. Together they pioneered the glorious Arête de Gaube which forms the north-western shoulder of the Vignemale, and explored the long Crête des Tempetes on Aneto. d'Ussel was also one of that rare breed of climber who sought adventures among the peaks at the eastern end of the range; making an early attempt on the

Dent d'Orlu - one of the outliers of the Carlitte massif - an ascent of the Pica d'Estats by way of the Riufred wall, and another of the Petite Encantat. Turning to the centre of the range, he climbed Perdido from the north and developed the North Face of Crabioules which graces the frontier ridge above the Lys valley, then pioneered sections of the Costerillou ridge on the Balaitous and picked out an elegant route up the face of Batcrabere.

During the interim period which linked the closing stages of the Heroic Age with the exciting developments that emerged with the dawning of the new century, one name persistently recurs in the record book; that of Cadier.

*

The family Cadier was prominent in the village of Osse in the Aspe valley, and the five sons of the pastor - Charles, Edouard, George, Henri and Albert - shared a genuine love of their mountains, and a common spirit of adventure. They combined to make one of the most formidable teams of inventive rock climbers to concentrate their efforts in the Pyrenees. With refreshing *joie de vivre* they sprang into action throughout the main part of the range, from Aspe to Aneto, creating new and often quite audacious routes as they went.

Theirs was a very personal style which owed little to others. 'Five brothers with but one spirit', they had no need for guides. Strong and solidly built, they possessed as much natural expertise as could be found among the majority of professional guides, and with the characteristic stamp of the exploratory mountaineer, managed to counter any obstacles set in their way. Sleeping out wherever night found them, they explored all the major peaks and worked out numerous new ways to scale them. Tracing a delightful route along the ridges, they completed two novel expeditions; working from Aneto to Munia, and from Pic Long to the Balaitous, bivouacking along the way.

Aneto was climbed by the eastern point which is now referred to as the Cap des Cinq Frères - Espalda de Aneto - and George made a fine solo first ascent of the Couloir Nord on the Pic des Tempêtes. They sought fresh routes among the Encantados, on the Grand Bachimale, on Crabioules amd Marboré, but reserved their most novel innovations for the tortuous ridges of the Balaitous, where George and Edouard in particular were in splendid form, strenuously devouring the Tour de Costerillou, the major obstacle on the bristling Costerillou arête. On the Pic du Midi d'Ossau, Charles and Edouard attempted on three occasions to force a route by the north-east; a route which defied all until the 'thirties when another generation of *Pyrénéistes* returned to the fray.

The Brothers Cadier, in 1919
Left to right: Charles, Edouard, George, Henri, and Albert.
Photo Credit: 'Sud-Ouest'

The brothers Cadier built for themselves a reputation that extended far beyond their own mountains, while in the Pyrenees they inspired great respect for the fashion of their climbing. As a seal of the wide range of approval their activities achieved, even Russell, by now ill at ease with the gymnastic feats of *Pyrénéistes,* described them as 'model mountaineers'. In delightful style, their experiences are recorded in the classic, *'Au Pays des Isards',* and a second volume devoted to the Balaitous, *'Marmuré ou Balaitous'.*

*

Arlaud and the GDJ

In the years immediately following the 1914-18 war, the mountains were visited by a man whose personality and sense of vocation were to have a considerable impact on the direction of Pyrenean climbing, and in particular, on the climbers themselves. Jean Arlaud (1896-1938), a Savoyard by birth, came to live at Toulouse to study medicine in the shadow of the Pyrenees. A brilliant, natural climber with a flair for the unconventional approach, he very soon became a true master of *Pyrénéisme,* and inspired a whole generation of young men eager to breathe the freedom of high places after the rigours and privations of four years' war.

Arlaud began his career by repeating the routes of past masters, and in particular those of Henri Brulle, but then turned in true virtuoso fashion to the creation of dynamic new routes of his own. For a while he concentrated substantial energies to the development of hard climbing in the heart of the range, transferring attention for a short period away from Gavarnie and the Pic du Midi to the Maladetta and Posets.

In 1922 he was instrumental in the establishment of the *Groupe des Jeunes* (GDJ), organising camps for aspirant mountaineers. From these camps there sprang a bevy of fine, accomplished leaders; men like Charles Laffont, Gaston Fosset, Pierre Abadie, and many others. Arlaud, in the role of entrepeneur, became the promoter of numerous new and exciting routes, finding a delight in the conception of provocative lines that members of his group could then claim with the boldness and vigour of youth. Arlaud was not content to remain a valley-bound pundit, though, directing the strenuous outings of others from the luxury of a tarn-side camp; he inspired by example, pushed himself on climb after climb, and in so doing achieved the respect and admiration of his fellow-climbers.

Between 1922 and 1935, Jean Arlaud organised a number of these camps beside the lake of San Mauricio in the Encantados, but he continued to seek the challenge of other areas, too. In 1922, for example he explored the beautifully firm granite of the Salenques arête in the Maladetta massif with Charles Laffont; and in 1925, also with Laffont, he climbed the Capéran de Sesques near the Pic du Midi, then repeated in one day all the classic routes of the period on the Pic du Midi itself, this with Pierre Abadie. From the Encantados camp, in 1926, he developed the Aiguilles de Trevessany and the North Face of the Gran Pic de Peguera, then moved westwards to the Gourgs Blancs where he climbed the West Face of Pic Lézat.

The following year, Arlaud and Laffont attempted to make the second ascent of the Couloir de Gaube - almost forty years after Brulle's tremendous breakthrough, it had still not been repeated - but were defeated by 'an impassable obstacle' at the very head of this frowning gully. Their descent was, understandably, '... an agony'.

Disappointments were destined to be short-lived, however, for the flurry of activity which followed was rewarded by a number of triumphs. Successes came among the peaks of the Cirque de Troumouse and on the Grande Aiguille d'Ansabère, on the Crête du Diable in the Balaitous, and on the lower of the Aiguilles de Ratera in the Encantados.

The GDJ camp of 1930 was set beside the haunted Cregüeña tarn under the wild western precipices of the Maladetta. From here, Arlaud, Barrué and Escudier tackled the 'crest of the fifteen gendarmes' - the western aréte of Pico de Alba - a superb expedition, magnificently executed.

In 1936, Arlaud went to Hidden Peak as doctor to the first French Himalayan expedition - for which Henri Brulle contributed 10,000 francs - but became restless upon his return and suffered subsequent depression. On 24th July 1938 he was climbing in the Gourgs Blancs when he fell from a ridge, and was killed.

Arlaud had served the Pyrenees and their advocates well. Through his enormous enthusiasm for adventure he inspired a great many young climbers. He explored the whole range systematically, not only in summer, but in winter, too, developing ski mountaineering with vigour; making long, high level traverses which enabled his commitment to the mountains - and that of members of the GDJ - to be continued all year round. He promoted ski competitions, instigated winter ascents of ice-sheathed peaks, and generally influenced mountaineering thought in the Pyrenees for many decades. His place in the history of climbing exploration in the range is assured.

*

Into the Modern Age

In 1926 there were signs of a revolution. In the west of the High Pyrenees the impressive Grande Aiguille d'Ansabère stood aloof and arrogant against the advances of man. It had received its first ascent in 1923, but the price paid for this success had been an exorbitant one; the deaths of both its assailants. However, three years after this bitter pioneering effort, Marcel Cames and Henri Sartou invented a new mode of overcoming the persistent overhangs that protect the faces of this peak, and in so doing dashed the myth of inaccessibility. Their innovation was the employment of 'an enormous rod of iron' - the first act of defiance against the traditions of Pyrenean mountaineering. In a similar vein, and with comparably crude aid, Cames, Romano Casabonne and Jean Santé pegged the overhangs of the Pombie-Suzon couloir on the Pic du Midi d'Ossau, but just as the new techniques were being mastered by the *avant-garde,* pitons of more durable quality were being introduced. As they did, so the old fears and prejudices, old limits of possibility were tossed aside, and *Pyrénéisme* leapt forward with an exciting prospect.

The confidence inspired by this acceptance of artificial aid, whilst putting fresh emphasis on the athletic nature of the sport, was bound to broaden climbing horizons, but there were still major strides being taken of a more traditional concept on hard routes. On the Capéran de Sesques, which Arlaud had climbed for instance, attempts at pushing a route with pitons failed, and so Pierre Bourdieu climbed it free; and on the first ascent of the North-West Arête of Balaitous, in 1932, Henri Lamathe, Henri Le Breton and Jean Senmartin conscientiously probed until they had created a clean, free ascent.

There remained one major route that seemed an affront to the rising generations of hard-men; the Couloir de Gaube. For almost half a century it had resisted the ambitions of the climbing fraternity. It could be ignored no longer, for in spite of the obvious advances that had been made in the mountains of the Pyrenees since its first ascent, the acknowledgement of Brulle's master-stroke somehow held a tight rein on each phase of development. Then, in 1933, there came two ascents in quick succession. On 13th July Henri Barrio, Aussat and Loustaunau succeeded where others - including Arlaud and Laffont - had failed, and in so doing buried the jinx. Two days later, Cazalet, Lamathe, Ollivier and Senmartin followed through as though to underline the victory.

With an end to the diversion of the Couloir de Gaube prospects for the future of *Pyrénéisme* could be viewed in a clear light, and with the creation of the *Groupe Pyrénéiste de Haute Montagne* (GPHM) in 1933, a nucleus of advanced climbers spearheaded the direction which mountaineering would pursue. The GPHM was formed of that élite band who had proved themselves in the Couloir, and their numbers were to be swelled only as routes of major importance were won, and there were soon to be considerable routes worthy of acceptance as new techniques evolved.

*

At the forefront of the new wave of quality climbers were men such as Bellocq, Sarthou, Roger Mailly and Henri Barrio, - one of the founder-members of the GPHM. On 8th August 1933, less

Robert Ollivier,
founder-member of the G.P.H.M.
whose routes in the thirties.
kept him at the forefront
of activity.
Photo: R.Ollivier

than a month after he had scrambled up the Couloir de Gaube, Henri Barrio with R. Bellocq turned his attention to that huge blank wall which is the highest in the range, the North Face of the Vignemale. This vast, bleak, compelling face had never before been attacked with such determination, but with the aid of a rucksack full of pitons, a demanding, exposed line was created. The result of this pioneering ascent was to virtually discard an already badly dented psychological barrier, and climbing within the Pyrenees entered a modern phase which successive generations of dedicated men have served to reinstate.

In many respects artificial climbing here mirrored developments that were being made in the Dolomites and other primarily rock-climbing regions of the Eastern Alps, and preceeded the full impact that pitons were to have on routes in the High Alps; while the impact within that relatively small band of advanced climbers in the Pyrenees, was quite considerable. After the brave initiative shown by Barrio and Bellocq had been digested, a rash of extreme climbs was created on varied peaks situated throughout the range, and in particular on the many diverse walls of the Pic du Midi. These walls were found to be ideal for perfecting the new techniques, and a spate of classic routes followed.

Among the first of these was the West Face of the Petit Pic which had resisted a number of attempts until, on the 3rd July 1934, the experienced and talented trio of Cazalet, Mailly and Ollivier finally achieved success through the aid of a single piton placed with deliberate care. The North-West Face of the Petit Pic followed, this time with Mailly and Ollivier on their own, having already been beaten back once. Their route was an imaginative one, aided by the placement of a dozen pegs. That same year (1935) Cazalet and Mailly climbed the vicious little aiguille of the Capéran de Sesques by its very difficult North Face. Even today the 130 metres of this route make a respectable outing that demands something like five hours of effort, and its first ascent confirmed the supremacy of the GPHM élite. The following year, Roger Mailly and Robert Ollivier turned once more to the Petit Pic du Midi, this time studying the North-East Face, and the ascent which resulted from their survey was the line that had originally defied three assaults from the brothers Cadier some twenty years earlier.

*

The *Groupe Pyrénéiste de Haute Montagne* was highly ambitious in concept, and the manner by which its finest achievements were created displayed the dynamic qualities of its constituent members. Individually, and as a body, they encouraged a truly professional approach that was absolutely essential to the cause of rising standards.

A natural extension of all the great activity on summer-lit peaks was the development of winter climbing. Forty years earlier Roger de Monts had pioneered a number of winter ascents. Arlaud and the GDJ had established activity on the snow-laden peaks of the central Pyrenees and pointed the way for further exploration; and in 1928 Douglas Busk, accompanied by the American, Caleb Gates, had made the first winter ascent of the North Face of the Pic du Midi. It was not until the competitive members of the GPHM turned to the ice-coated faces of their mountains during the late 1930s, that really difficult winter routes became fully established. On the same day - 12th February 1939 - two major climbs were successfully carried out. Aussat and Cazanave stormed the Pic du Midi by way of the South Cirque, and at the same time - on the Balaitous, several kilometres to the east - Cazalet, Mailly and Henri Sarthou were making the magnificent first winter traverse of the Costerillou ridge.

War again called a severe limit to mountaineering activity, and it was some time before a full return could be made to the challenge of extreme climbing. There were fresh faces, too, for some of the pre-war hard-men had failed to return, some had lost the years of their prime; but in their place there emerged an entirely new generation eager to fill the boots of past masters. Camps of *Jeunesse et Montagne,* based on Gavarnie and Cauterets, encouraged the redevelopment of adventurous expeditions; the first of these being claimed by Simpson and Boyrie on the north-west buttress of Pointe de Chausenque, in 1945. A year later Marcel Jolly led his rope on a splendid aussault of the vast Pombie wall of the Pic du Midi, making a strenuous line up to the Pointe Jean Santé.

In 1948, two major climbs in the heart of the range marked the resumption of technically difficult activity. On the North-East Face of Crabioules, Couzy and Georges succeeded - after eleven hours of sustained effort - in pushing a demanding route of some 350 metres with the aid of a moderate selection of pitons; and a little farther east, on the pyramid-shaped Pic de Maupas, the North Face was climbed by Céréza in fine style.

Perhaps the finest, and certainly the most audacious, ascent of the 'forties, was that of Marcel Jolly and Bernard Clos who, on 28th February, 1949, attacked the 800 metres of the North Face of the Vignemale. Their magnificent first ascent in winter, completed without the expected bivouac, set a fresh standard; it fired the imagination of aspiring *Pyrénéistes* and sparked an enthusiasm which brought about a spate of similarly demanding routes. These routes included a hard line on Pointe de Chausenque, on the North Face of the Tour du Marboré, and Marboré by the Cascade route combining the Crête des Druides and Arête Passet, thereby creating the longest winter climb in the length and breadth of the Pyrenees.

Jolly and Clos were consistent in their winter activities, and by their example were responsible for the establishment of advanced climbing throughout the range, their routes invariably pushing standards ever higher. Among his many successes, Bernard Clos, from Bagneres de Bigorre, claimed the superbly executed first winter ascent of the North Face of the Taillon, sharing his rope with Sauton and Escalona; while Marcel Jolly made the first winter route on the North-West Arête of the Balaitous, and a number of new ascents on the Pic du Midi in the late 1940s and 50s. As a ski-touring enthusiast he took part in the first crossing of the *Haute Route Pyrénéene*, between the Somport and Luchon, and as president of the GPHM in 1952, he strengthened its ranks by drawing together members of Arlaud's *Groupe des Jeunes* and those of the *Luchon Haute Montagne*. The union thus formed served to bond the energies of all the finest, and most ambitious climbers then concentrating in the Pyrenees.

*

The Age of Extreme Climbing

The age of extreme climbing dawned in the early nineteen-fifties. Many fine routes, conceived ahead of their time, had been forged on the challenging faces and ridges of these peaks in the decades of yesteryear, but with the upsurge of interest in climbing that came as an aftermath of War, technically difficult ascents became more than isolated events. The men at the front exhibited cool professionalism, but they displayed, too, an attachment that was reminiscent of that shown by the activists of a century ago; an attachment involving an interest in all things Pyrenean - the history of the range, the ascent of a modest peak by its *voie normale,* the wealth and diversity of its flora, as well as the creation of an exacting line on the most demanding of overhanging walls.

It was in 1953 that the Ravier twins, Jean and Pierre, took part in two notable climbs which effectively heralded this new age. The first, involving Jean Ravier with A.Armengaud, was an airy, 500 metre line up the South-East Face of Pointe Jean Santé which towers above the screes near the Pombie hut. It was a brave and exacting venture, but two months later Jean was joined by his brother on a pioneering climb that pushed another 500 metres up the West Face of Pic Quayrat. The following year, as though to endorse these earlier successes, they stormed the coldly-sinister verglased North Face of Piton Carré - that triangular block which walls the Couloir de Gaube - with J.Teillard; an exposed and somewhat meandering line that first demanded an approach through the lower section of the Couloir itself. Then, on 12th and 13th August, with Guy Santamaria and the aid of about 50 pitons, they worked their way up the North-East Diedre of the Grande Aiguille d'Ansabère. It was a direct, sustained line, and one which demanded complete familiarity with, and mastery of, artificial techniques; and their achievement - coming twenty-one years after the teams of Barrio and Bellocq, and Cazalet, Ollivier and Sarthou of the GPHM had all failed - was a shining example of the modern touch. The Age of Extreme Climbing had truly arrived.

At every subsequent stage of advancement the brothers Ravier have been at the very forefront, maintained there by dedication and a superbly dynamic style. It would be true to say that they have completely dominated the post-war period, proving without dispute their position as the finest pair of climbers ever to concentrate their efforts upon these mountains. For more than twenty years they have ranged back and forth along the Pyrenees, on both sides of the frontier, seeking out an untried challenge through which to pursue their mutual passion for Pyrenean adventure. Their routes have consistently been bold, radical and adventurous, calling for agility and the endurance of an extremely high degree of expertise on the sometimes dubious rock of their mountains. Their talent, though not unique in world mountaineering, is rare enough to warrant the use of superlatives, but the record of their ascents - which reads like a catalogue of the most advanced climbing yet seen in the range, - speaks for itself. In the history of *Pyrénéisme* the chapter which is rightly theirs, is that of the Age of Extreme Climbing.

The Ravier Twins, Jean and Pierre. Together they raised the standards of Pyrénéisme with a long series of first-rate climbs.

Photo: Ravier

In September 1956 the Tour du Marboré, one of the peaklets of the Cirque de Gavarnie, yielded a classic route over a two-day period to Jean Ravier and Claude Dufourmantelle. It set yet another standard, spurring *Pyrénéisme* into a headlong search for ever-greater difficulties, leading to the exploration of novel routes on little-touched spires and long-forgotten faces. Valleys of a virgin purity were scoured for unknown pinnacles where the ambitions of a new breed might be satisfied, and the ensuing decades were elevated as years of great productivity.

That teetering, doomed, dolomitic tower which looms over the lush forests of Ordesa, the Tozal del Mallo, was a target for the aspirations of a rope consisting of Jean Ravier, Dufourmantelle, Blotti, Jaccoux and Kahn. After a memorable two-day struggle, and the additional aid of about sixty pegs, they succeeded in tracing the first enterprising line up its South Face. This was in early 1957; an outstanding year which saw the emergence of the Spanish pair, J-A Bescos and R. Montaner, who claimed the East Face of the Cylindre du Marboré, and then, in October, an arduous ascent was made of the East Face of the Grande Aiguille d'Ansabère by Patrice de Bellefon, Raymond Despiau, Claude Dufourmantelle and, yet again, Jean Ravier.

The Aiguilles d'Ansabère took the main focus of attention the following year, too, but perhaps the highlight of 1958 was the forcing of the overhangs that guard the North Face of the Petit Vignemale, by Couzy and Soubis. Then the Pic du Midi came once more into its own, revealing still more opportunities for new ascents. After the development of the North-West Face of Pointe d'Espagne, the superb traverse of the four main peaks of the Pic - initially laced together in 1944 - was negotiated under full winter conditions in 1960, by Bescos and Montaner. Also in 1960, Patrice de Bellefon, with Sylvain Sarthou, created one of the hardest routes in the Pyrenees by climbing the West-North-West Face of the Grand Pic du Midi - Pointe de France - from the austere and crumbling base of the Cirque de l'Embarradére. The indefatigable Ravier brothers responded with their South-East 'direct' on Pointe Jean Santé, and another fine route on the northern buttress of the Petit Pic.

Year in and year out the incredible momentum was maintained. As techniques developed, and the invention of new devices of artificial hardware became increasingly accepted, so the limits of inaccessibility became more and more remote. Climbers here, as elsewhere, were forced to examine the future direction of their sport with regard to its ethical structure and the aesthetic value of the rock upon which they practised. Modern *Pyrénéisme* had become balanced precariously between the desire, on the one hand, to advance in terms of route-achievements, and the necessity to preserve the natural features of these magnetically attractive mountains, on the other. Tradition, and the ethical code which stems from it, is - and has always been - the guiding condition that governs mountaineering progress, and the mountaineers themselves remain responsible for the self-discipline and discretion of their actions. In the Pyrenees, as in the Alps, climbers therefore sought diligently for routes offering an ever-greater degree of challenge whilst straining within the unwritten boundaries of this ethical code. Harder winter climbs, demanding reserves of stamina and the maintenance of a high standard of performance, grew in popularity on account of the increased element of uncertainty over the outcome. The repetition of extreme aid climbs, only using less aid than the originators, became another challenge worth pursuing, as did the ultimate in mountaineering challenge, solo climbing.

Among the more dramatic of winter ascents at this time was the splendid Grande Diedre on Pic des Spijoles forced through by Sol and Valleau. In the same winter - 1964 - Patrice de Bellefon and Raymond Despiau turned to the Pointe de France and scaled the northern buttress first climbed in July 1938 by Mailly and Ollivier, and the following year the Ravier twins climbed the very difficult 'Y' couloir on the Vignemale.

The highlight of all this activity which makes the 'sixties one of the most exciting decades of Pyrenean exploration and achievement, came in a two-day sortie covering the 17th and 18th July 1965. Jean and Pierre Ravier, with Paul Bouchet, created a route which was heralded as the hardest in the whole range. This exposed, complicated, semi-direct line on the North Face of the Embarradére Pillar - which stands wedged between the Grand and Petit Pics du Midi - was an out-standing example of modern enterprise; a climb often compared in difficulty with the Bonatti

Pillar on the Dru, and one which helped define the scope of the upper spheres of *Pyrénéisme*. It became the yardstick by which levels of progress could be measured.

*

In the past two decades *Pyrénéisme* has forged ahead, unselfconsciously keeping pace with developments that mark the surge in Alpine trends. The brothers Ravier, though undisputed masters, are not alone in the richness of their successes. Raymond Despiau, Tony and Sylvain Sarthou, the guide Patrice de Bellefon, Jean Ollivier and Hervé Butel and another Ravier, Jacques, have likewise taken a leading part in a number of remarkable new climbs, adding their names to the roll of honour. Others, like Dominique Julien, Michel Boulang and Rainier Munsch, represent a more recent generation of adventurous climbers studying the countless faces, couloirs and ragged crests for the next great problem.

It is significant that French climbers should have been at the forefront of all the major developments in these mountains. Theirs is a century-old tradition of innovation and determination. Conservatism long since made way in the face of inspiration, and that inspiration led to relentlessly rising standards, but in recent years there has been a growth in activity from Spanish climbers too; climbers of initiative who have begun to make their mark on that elevated group of extreme *Pyrénéistes,* determining to create a degree of balance.

José Manuel Anglada, from Barcelona, is one of the best-known climbers from south of the border to cut his teeth on the granite and limestone of the range. His routes include a brace of eminent lines on Tozal del Mallo, but he has been tempted farther afield, too, climbing extensively in the Dolomites, making the first Spanish ascent of the Eigerwand, expeditioning in the Andes, the Hindu Kush and to Annapurna. Other Spaniards to respond effectively to the lead given by their French neighbours include Emilio Civis, J-J Dias, Rabada and Navarro - who died in 1963 on the Eiger - Bescos and Guillamon; and their numbers are increasing annually. With the vast array of pinnacles and faces, remote and unsung peaks and roadside outcrops stretching in a maze of sunlit sierras away from the better-known heights that congregate along the international frontier, the opportunities for the development of evolving techniques is considerable. So much so that the future of *Pyrénéisme* appears to be assured.

*

Most of the pioneers of mountaineering - and none more so than those of the Pyrenees - developed a great and lasting passion for their mountains. They climbed almost as an outward expression of attachment for the peaks on which they scrambled and sought adventure; an attachment which came sometimes to surpass the basically physical exaltation of overcoming artificially conceived problems. They bred a tradition of emotional involvement that began with Ramond, was carried by Packe and Schrader and through the peculiar excesses of Russell. Henri Brulle turned his back on the Pyrenees only when the loss of family and friends in the Great War meant that the peaks which they had shared held too many poignant memories, but he had gone on to climb in the Alps and elsewhere in search of lost youth. Arlaud lost his life through his commitment to the mountains, but he had already bequeathed his involvement to others, and the hard men of the 'twenties and 'thirties, spurred on by competitive impulses, rarely allowed personal triumphs to blurr their attachment to the soaring peaks and cradled pastures themselves.

This devotion may be seen almost as a Pyrenean tradition. It is not unique, of course, for the history of mountaineering is punctuated with examples of men concentrating the greater part of their energies to specific regions; Coolidge in the Alps, Kugy in the Julians, Slingsby in Norway, but the Pyrenees, although close enough to the Alps to suffer the indignities of comparison, sheltered a school of climbing that survived - and thrived - almost *because* of the alternatives available. Protagonists ascribed perhaps an even deeper romance to their sport - and to their mountains - which required no regular testing in other ranges, while those who did expand their careers on better-known heights were often content to return to the peaks of their origins, and

Pyrénéisme became enriched by their experiences.

Although this deep-rooted attachment has been attributed to the pioneers and founders of *Pyrénéisme,* it has been readily adopted by many of the talented young men who have since found that the mountains of the Pyrenees offer a worthwhile testing ground. As each stage of development in climbing strains to reach, and overcome, greater scales of difficulty; as hard climbs lead to technical climbs, and technical climbs reach extremes, so the commitment - and attachment - grows more acute.

*

Rich are the prospects for new ascents among these mountains. The modern climber in action there follows in the footsteps of a number of remarkable - yet little-known - men. What the Pyrenean climber requires is enthusiasm coupled with persistence, trademarks that underline the successes of men like Henri Brulle, Jean Arlaud and the brothers Ravier. They will not find their routes imbued with a charisma inspired by notoriety, neither will the rewards for outstanding performances include that of reputation, since the Pyrenees are not mountains of this order. Their greatest innovations do not make headlines, but what the Pyrenees do offer is a sense of pioneering and the sharing of a fascinating history, the charm of idyllic settings as an arena for adventure, and an 'air of unquiet mystery'. More, a climber may not ask.

*

A Review of Pyrénéisme

1276   The legendary first ascent of the Pic du Canigou is made by Peter III of Aragon who discovers a dragon on the summit.

1552   In May the Count de Candale leads a party on an attempt to climb the Pic du Midi d'Ossau in order to calculate its height. The attempt fails at an unspecified altitude.

1672   Montvalier, to the north of the Vall d'Aran, is climbed by a bishop who places a cross on the summit.

1787   After more than two hundred years, an unknown shepherd from the Aspe Valley reaches the summit of the Pic du Midi, and there erects a cairn to aid the observations of Reboul and Vidal. These two geographers from the Academy of Toulouse make a detailed study of the main peaks from the summit of the Pic du Midi de Bigorre, and also climb the Turon de Néouvielle, the first of the 3,000 metre peaks to be climbed. In the same year Ramond de Carbonnieres undertakes his first journey of exploration in the Pyrenees, including a spirited attempt on the Maladetta.

1802   Monte Perdido, third highest mountain in the range, is ascended by Rondau, Laurens and a Spanish shepherd. Ramond repeats the ascent a few days later.

          With Monte Perdido climbed, the Golden Age begins.

1817   Frederic Parrot crosses the range from the Atlantic to the Mediterranean, and makes the first ascent of the Maladetta, and several other peaks, on the way.

1825-27   Survey officers at work on the *Carte de France* make a notable contribution to the exploration of the Pyrenees. They make first ascents of the Balaitous, Pic de Troumouse, the Pica d'Estats and its neighbouring Montcalm.

1837   Cazaux and Guillembet find a route to the summit of the Vignemale, but have to descend via the Spanish Ara Valley for fear of falling a second time into the *Grande Crevasse* in the Ossoue Glacier.

1842   The highest point in the Pyrenees, Pico d'Aneto, is defeated by an international party; de Franqueville, Tchihatcheff, Ursule, Redonnet, Argarot and Sanio.

1847   Pic de Néouvielle receives its first ascent from de Chausenque.

1853   Charles Packe visits the range for the first time, and begins a passion that is to last more than forty years.

1856   Pic Long, highest of the peaks entirely in France, is climbed by the Duc de Nemours, son of King Louis Phillippe, and the guide, Marc Sesquet.

Farther east, Halkett, Barrau and Redonnet claim the second highest major peak, Pico des Posets. With this ascent the Golden Age draws to a close as all the highest summits have now been won.

1858   The young poet, Alfred Tonnelle, conducts a whirlwind journey through the mountains and climbs the difficult Forcanada.

1861   Henry Russell's attachment to the Vignemale begins with his first ascent; an attachment that will manifest itself in the strangest acts of eccentricity in mountaineering history.

1889   The advent of the Heroic Age is signalled by the audacious ascent of the Couloir de Gaube by Henri Brulle's rope.

Célestin Passet establishes himself as the Pyrenean guide supreme by displaying the full scope of his talents in leading this climb.

1901   A brief encounter with the peaks east of Aneto sees the first route made on the fine Grande Encantat by de Négrin, Romeu, Angusto, Salles and Ciffre.

1902   Next it is the turn of the neighbouring Petite Encantat, a slightly harder climb than that of the higher peak. Here, Brulle, René d'Astorg and the guide Castagne make their mark. With the turn of the century the five brothers Cadier sweep into action throughout the range in impressive style, creating a number of classic routes.

1922   The rise of the *Groupe des Jeunes,* with Dr Jean Arlaud at its head, brings *Pyrénéisme* into the Modern Age.

1926   Cames and Sarthou climb the Grande Aiguille d'Ansabère with artificial aid. The revolution begins.

1933   The North Face of the Vignemale, climbed by Barrio and Bellocq of the newly-formed *Groupe Pyrénéiste de Haute Montagne,* inspires a rash of hard climbs made possible by the growing use of artificial aids.

1949   Clos and Jolly take to the North Face of the Vignemale in winter, and succeed in a single day. Other winter ascents of similarly difficult summer routes become almost commonplace.

1953-54   The Ravier twins, Jean and Pierre, establish themselves as the most talented climbers seen in the Pyrenees with several demanding early routes. In the years that follow, countless new and exciting ascents are made of an extreme nature. With their dramatic routes on the Piton Carré and Grande Aiguille d'Ansabère - both in 1954 - the Age of Extreme Climbing opens.

1956   With Jean Ravier and Claude Dufourmantelle's classic two-day route on the Tour du Marboré's North Face, *Pyrénéisme* leaps ahead.

1957   A five-man rope makes the first ascent up the awesome South Face of the Tozal del Mallo.

1960   Bescos and Montaner complete the challenging traverse of the four main summits of the Pic du Midi, in winter. As a result, winter climbing of an extreme nature is given a boost. In the two decades since, a remarkable number of hard climbs have been created under the hazards of snow and ice, thereby providing a greater element of uncertainty - and subsequently increasing the scale of challenge - to all-year-round activity.

1965   Paul Bouchet joins the brothers Ravier in creating one of the finest, and most difficult, routes in the whole range when, on 17th and 18th September they force the North Face of the Embarradère Pillar.

With this example of modern enterprise as the yardstick by which progress may be measured, *Pyrénéisme* pushes forward into the 'seventies and 'eighties as a never-ceasing search for the next great challenge. The mountains, meanwhile, remain as gracefully aloof as ever, inspiring with their elegance, and offering assorted delights to those of ranging degrees of commitment.

*

The double-headed Forcanada dominates the sterile wastes of the Valleta de la Escaleta.

PART THREE

The Mountains

Aiguilles d'Ansabère.

'There is something almost unearthly about the high mountain landscapes of the Pyrénées. You have no gentle foreground to diminish the savagery of the mountains. Your very valleys are too high for trees or any but Alpine flowers. You are in the mountains of the moon - on a crust that is already growing cold. It is the fantastic landscape of a dream. Around and above rise black peaks, mirrored beneath in the deep blue of some still mountain lake'.

Harold Spender

Pic d'Arriel (see page 61)
Photo: Pete Smith

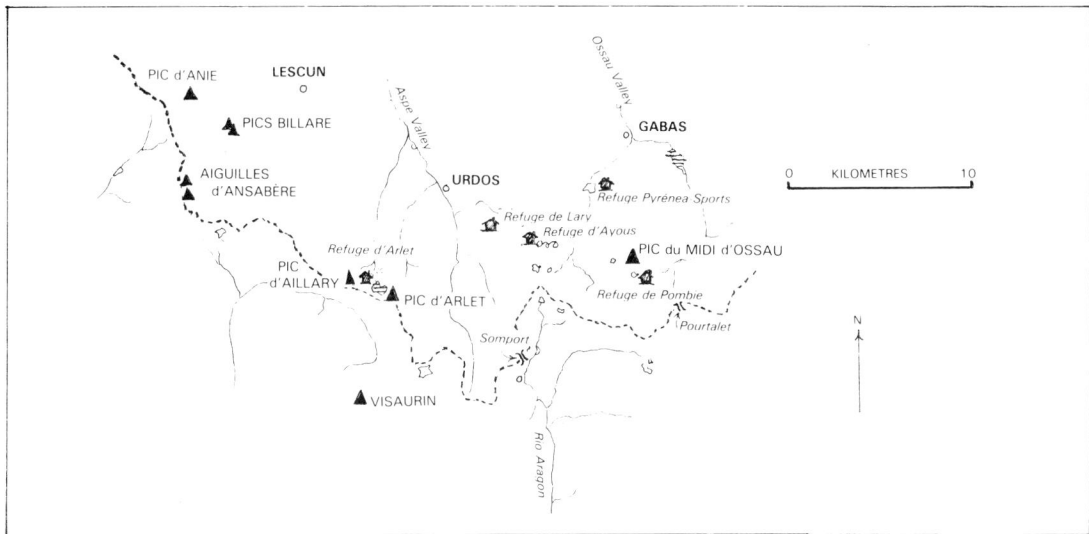

PIC d'ANIE

LESCUN

PICS BILLARE

Aspe Valley

Ossau Valley

GABAS

AIGUILLES d'ANSABÈRE

URDOS

0   KILOMETRES   10

Refuge Pyrénéa Sports

Refuge de Lary

Refuge d'Ayous

PIC du MIDI d'OSSAU

Refuge d'Arlet

PIC d'AILLARY

PIC d'ARLET

Refuge de Pombie

N

Somport

Pourtalet

VISAURIN

Rio Aragon

THE WESTERN HEIGHTS

So distinctive are the soaring white limestone peaks of **Ansabère** hidden above the left bank of the Aspe Valley, and so lush and gentle their spreading pastures and forests, it is difficult to comprehend that beyond them to the south lies a veritable desert of barren, shadeless rocks, apparently as lifeless as the mountains of the moon.

These are the first of the High Pyrenees, the first mountains to draw the climber with their magnetic pinnacles, their shapely groups of individually placed peaks arranged with perfect symmetry as if specifically to entice the mountain lover with their siren-like lure. They gaze out, one upon the other in serried ranks, to the green dipping knolls of the nearby foothills, and beyond them still to the plains where the countless rivers that drain these heights feed the land, and in so doing spread the goodness of the generous mountain uplands to vineyards and cornfields so far removed from the world of overhangs and slopes of primitive scree.

The Aspe Valley rises near the Col du Somport, that easy port of entry into Spain, and is headed by a semi-circle of bright, dazzling mountains clutching slender aprons of snow; the Cirque d'Aspe. These are walkers' mountains; the forest glades below them holding shepherds' huts, the glades linked by winding paths of great charm. As the valley grinds northward the forests become more dense, the walls rise steeper while the river thunders in its rocky bed; and the more impressive summits grow reserved, seductively shielding their more alluring aspects somewhere off to the west. To reach them requires an excursion out of the valley itself, a diversion up to a hillside shelf of great sublimity where sits a thick, stone-walled village seemingly as ancient as the mountains themselves. Lescun.

Lescun commands a magnificent panorama, as perfect as imagination could produce. Its prospect is one of rich undulating pastures leading to a backcloth of staggering, jagged peaks. Meadows abound, cut here and there, stooked or baled into parcels of hay around antique barns smelling of cowdung and drying grass, with chuckling brooks sidling through their shallow courses and woodlands ahead, beyond the checkered meadows, and beyond still and above the forests, the sparkling limestone pinnacles appearing for all the world like a Dolomite fairyland.

Above the village and to the north-west, a mule track beckons through sloping pastures to allow access to Pic d'Anie (2504m.), the most westerly of the peaks to reach two and a half thousand metres. By its height it is significant for it marks a boundary of the High Pyrenees. All the country

Aiguilles d'Ansabère

to the west of it is Basque land; green moulded hills and valleys of pastoral benevolence, great tracts of beech forests and villages of a solid character. Their mountains offer, in the main, outings of pedestrian simplicity, with now and then a route of a more strenuous quality. These hills and well-dressed mountains fold themselves persistently off to the far distant ocean; they have an attraction all their own, a quality of permanence; mountains and valleys to explore at leisure, in the tranquility of autumn years.

Pic d'Anie, marking as it does the introduction to high mountains, is a fraud; a somewhat shapeless, waterless limestone mass rising over a chaotic wasteland and demanding little more than a long walk to attain its upper limits. Even the views from here, although extending far, have little of the dramatic to lead the eye, despite the proximity of some of the range's finest peaks upon whose heights promises may be fulfilled.

Guarding the Ansabère cirque from Lescun stand twin peaks, the Grand and Petit Billare. They rise with certain dignity from the forests, and block Pic d'Anie from view. While they may be climbed with ease from the Anaye valley, the Ravier twins, with Bouchet and Grenier, established an exacting route up the East Face of the Petit Billare in October 1966, thereby offering additional challenge to the hard men who come here with their eyes set fast for the airy pinnacles peeping from the south-west.

It is to these pinnacles that the climber is irresistibly drawn. From Lescun the approach is made along a gentle lane with tangled hedgerows and over one or two streams and into the dark, cool forest with mountains growing ever higher along the edges, and ahead there beckons a landscape rich in mystery and generous with its promise. The forest track is traded for a narrow climbing path which opens into a clearing, and quite suddenly the mountains are there, all around, with steeply sloping pastures shaded here and there by broad-leaved trees ... and a vision of exquisite loveliness.

Ahead, the glorious sight of the Aiguilles d'Ansabère, stabbing above the distant beckoning ridge, is sufficient in itself to reward an already delightful approach. It is one of those mountain vistas of which dreams are made; it represents the savage nature of the heights, yet at the same time excites with the pure majesty of upright rock, a delicate symbol, a composition of soaring height and plunging depth, of dazzling white above a foreground of dappled woodland. Nowhere else in the length and breadth of the Pyrenees is there a comparable scene; nowhere else does a mountain eminence so completely impress itself with such effect upon the imagination. The Aiguilles d'Ansabère are unique.

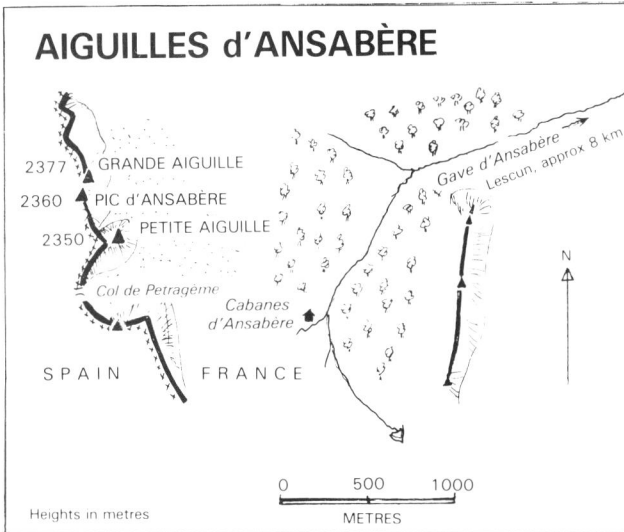

AIGUILLES d'ANSABÈRE

2377 GRANDE AIGUILLE
2360 PIC d'ANSABÈRE
2350 PETITE AIGUILLE
Col de Petragème
Cabanes d'Ansabère
Gave d'Ansabère
Lescun, approx 8 km
SPAIN FRANCE
N

0 500 1000
Heights in metres
METRES

The Aiguilles d'Ansabère

The higher of the two pinnacles, the Grande Aiguille (Aiguille Nord), has a tragic history. On June 24th 1923 Lucien Carrive, a strong and agile climber with several respectable routes behind him, partnered the young but promising Armand Calame in attempting to make the first ascent via the West Face (*Voie du Surplomb*), which is somewhat shorter than the other exposed faces. It was a brave attempt, heroically conceived but horrifying in its undertaking, for on the ascent Carrive faltered at the crux where he slipped, and the rope broke. Shaken badly by his companion's death, Calame nevertheless continued alone to the summit, but whatever grim satisfaction he experienced on this bitter-won peak was destined to be brief. The broken rope was fixed for an abseil descent, but it had been considerably shortened in the accident and Calame, too, slipped and fell to his death.

With its understandable reputation for severity, the Grande Aiguille became the focus of attention among the more ambitious of *Pyrénéistes*. Three years after the wretched first ascent, Marcel Cames and Henri Sarthou successfully found an alternative to the Calame-Carrive fissure by turning an overhang with their historic use of an 'enormous rod of iron'. This, the first major climb in the Pyrenees to use artificial aid, set a precedent, and now a number of incredible routes adorn this, and its neighbouring peak, made possible only by the acceptance of direct aid climbing techniques.

The glorious North and East Faces, so clean and polished in the morning light, display themselves openly and tantalisingly to those approaching through the pastures of the Ansabère Valley. So provocative are they that it is only natural for the extreme climber, shouldering a hefty rucksack containing a jangle of hardware, to experience a surge of excitement - tempered by a certain foreboding - with the prospect of getting to grips with their secrets.

On the North Face a long, shadow-hugging diedre is the dominant feature. In the 'thirties it was the scene of competition and much rivalry involving a number of abortive attempts by members of the newly-formed GPHM, led mainly by the indefatigable Henri Barrio, but the mountain stubbornly resisted every assault until 1954. Then Jean and Pierre Ravier, with Guy Santamaria, entered the arena, and the route which they created *(North-East Diedre)* effectively consolidated the Age of Extreme Climbing in the Pyrenees, and at the same time firmly established the leading position of the Ravier twins among the ranks of modern *Pyrénéistes*.

Fifteen hours of concentrated effort, together with forty or fifty pitons, were required to complete this strenuous route (T.D. sup., with passages of A2 and V sup.) which is some 300 metres in length, and it says much for the persistence and expertise of the first ascentionists that the line of their success had defeated so many talented pioneering craftsmen, so many times, and over such an extended period.

Nearby on the East Face, which rises from the screes to a broad, smooth slab base, then continues in its upper section which is scored by a great couloir that disappears under the summit, another superb route has been produced. On the 5th and 6th October 1957, a young and artistically vigorous rope comprising Patrice de Bellefon, Raymond Despiau, Claude Dufourmantelle and Jean Ravier, spent fourteen hours of actual climbing before the summit was reached. The Face, some 350 metres high, contains one or two notoriously crumbling sections, but on the whole the rock is good, enlivened by a series of cracks, narrow chimneys and overhanging roofs. In 1933 Barrio had attempted the central diedre of this face, but without sucess. Thirty-two years after, on on 16th and 17th September 1965, Hervé Butel and Jean Ollivier managed to complete the route, finding a number of Barrio's rusted pitons still in place.

*

The Petite Aiguille d'Ansabère (Aiguille Sud), rising so abruptly from the cleft of the Col de Pétragéme, is a most elegant spire; but upon close inspection this elegance is clearly only temporary, like a misted illusion, for the limestone suddenly announces itself as being most fragile and while it rises steeper and steeper it threatens to unbalance, to topple slowly outward, crumbling as the angle narrows until the scattered screes fill the air with their ancient dust. But even this is an illusion, a fantasy orchestrated by the sun glancing against this vertical obelisk. The mountain is doomed, as all the mountains of the Pyrenees are doomed. Daily, hourly, their time advances as moisture insistently nibbles at the porous rock. The moisture which nourishes life also immobilizes in frost, expands as a solid to splinter the vulnerable blocks. The fine white limestone, eternal and so magnificently barren as it appears from afar, grants life to numerous plants, and the plants in return aid the mother mountain's eventual destruction. Reluctantly, yet with certainty, the flakes of decaying stone fall from their lofty buttresses as predictably as do the tanned leaves of autumn depart the valley trees. Nothing can halt this persistent decay. Nothing can prevent their ultimate ruin. The mountain's mortality is no less than that of the stray butterfly that alights for a fleeting moment upon its splintered summit.

Fragile and doomed though the Petite Aiguille may be, it stands today as a temptation to climbers of ambition and nerve who find themselves drawn to its flanks. In the late winter of 1970, Baudéan and Garrotté took up its challenge and completed their ascent in fine style, but as they made ready their descent a severe storm enveloped the peak. So dramatically did conditions deteriorate, and so swiftly, that the descent turned into a nightmare. Garrotté somehow fell, and was killed. As for Baudéan, he was left stranded, hanging from the rope for nearly three days before rescue came.

The easiest route (*Voie Normale,* AD with pitches of III) suffers from abundant stonefall danger, and has one or two sections of unpleasantly threatening, unstable blocks. First climbed by Lacq and Naud in July 1926 it has never become a popular ascent route on account of its great objective dangers. The South Face, on the other hand, has a very fine route of about 200 metres in length (graded TD, with pitches of V and of A2) on mostly good rock. It was worked through in June

*Petite Aiguille d'Ansabère
(Aiguille Sud).*

1958 by the Spanish pair of Montaner and Vicente, and follows the line of a great chimney that is eventually blocked by an overhang.

The classic route of the Petite Aiguille is the Spigolo South Face (*Spigolo Sud*, TD sup., sustained with pitches of V and A2), an essentially artificial route completed only after numerous attempts were made in the years betweeen 1957 and 1967. The single-minded determination of Raymond Despiau, using siege tactics through the month of July 1967, gradually reduced the difficulties one by one. Between 10th and 15th, with A. de Boysson, and later from 18th to 21st with J.C. Lucquet, Despiau bolted and pegged his way stubbornly towards the summit. Then, after a month's respite, he returned with Patrice de Bellefon to finish the route over the period of 22nd and 23rd August. On the same day that the route was completed, Jean Oscaby, Jean-Louis Perez and Tony Sarthou made the second ascent and cleaned a number of pegs from it, taking fourteen hours in all. This Spigolo South Face is 350 metres long, involving a lower section of free climbing before the upper 200 metres are tackled with bolts in position, though widely spaced, and most of the belays taken uncomfortably in etriers. A route far removed from Pyrenean traditions, but one which symbolises the direction taken by the modernists who would deny the existence of 'inaccessible' pinnacles.

*

Eastward from the white peaks of Ansabère there unfolds a country of immense charm and tranquility; moulded uplands whose contrast of felt-soft pasture and tumbled screes, of silent tarn and encircling ridges that echo to the mournful cry of choughs, leads insistently towards the ragged heartland of the range that swells in a mass of blue haze upon the fluted horizon.

South of the watershed here the limestone wastes are traded for green-turfed valleys edged with lines of cliffs. In summer the valleys seethe with insect life, but in winter, when the driving snows cake every hollow, the mountain crests rise in stature and offer outings of charm amid a matchless purity. The peak of Visaurin, being the highest of the Aspe group - though some way south of the Aspe Valley - makes a day's pleasure in either season when approached from the north across the frontier. The French slopes, too, with their rocky cirques and deep, thrusting valleys; their scattered tarns and simple *cabanes,* reward those who would seek the delights of an uncluttered landscape.

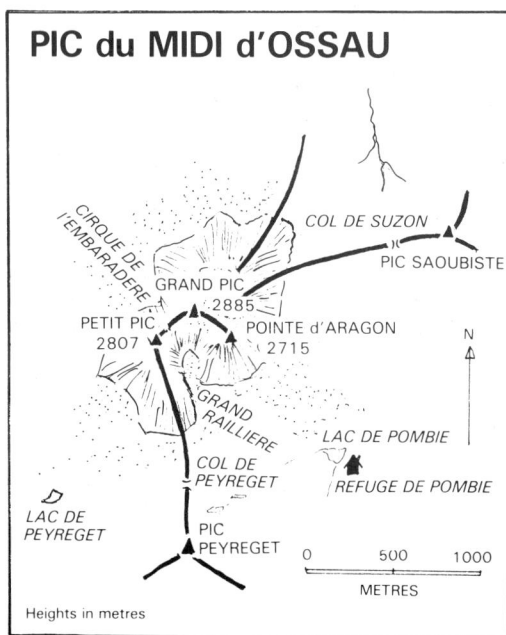

PIC du MIDI d'OSSAU

Heights in metres

Pic du Midi d'Ossau

The deep trench of the Aspe Valley is walled to the east by reluctant heights knuckled here and there by minor valleys rich in luxuriant vegetation. The peaks themselves refuse to bully, they sprawl above boulder slopes, untidily linked by dipping ridges and a series of accessible cols. The country which they protect is worthy of further exploration; it is a country that has been known and loved for centuries, and one that is dominated by the peak affectionately known by those who live in its shadow, as Jean-Pierre.

The Pic du Midi d'Ossau is a truly magnificent peak, and despite the absence of either glacier or lengthy field of permanent snow, it has the classic components of a great mountain. Long ago its icefields retreated, leaving behind a landscape of perfection, trading névés and blue chasms of crevasses for the luxury of herbaceous pastures where shepherds now tend their flocks and clustered tarns reflect the surrounding heights.

It stands quite alone, aloof, isolated from its nearest neighbours, gaunt and somehow savage upon its high plateau with massive walls of pale granite bursting out of the meadows. Flowers colour the snaking valleys, while the screes nurture lichens and harbour resilient life in the form of groping tentacles of alpenroses and bright cushions of *androsace*, contrasting the seemingly lifeless mountain '... whose roots are in the vast forests of Ossau and whose crest is in the sky'.

Even by Pyrenean standards its altitude is modest, yet the unique profile which it displays, and the impressive manner by which it dominates the landscape, combine to invest it with a stature surpassing that of many higher mountains found elsewhere in the range. Every face presents a challenging prospect. From each of the idyllic valleys that pave its approaches the mountain

Pic du Midi d'Ossau

appears supreme, a time-sculptured monument marking the passage of the centuries through numberless seasons; by the rough caress of constant winds, the blistering of nightly frosts and by the scorching influence of a southern sun. It rises from the screes in immense buttresses riven by darkened gullies and systems of cracks, while the craggy ridge is divided into a brace of distinct summits; the Grand and the Petit Pics, the two separated by a deep cleft known as La Fourche, creating thereby the double-pronged silhouette that is the Pic du Midi's unmistakable signature, and recognisable as easily from the terraces at Pau as from the summits of innumerable peaks at the centre of the range.

From the rock climber's point of view it is a gem of a peak. There are probably more routes adorning its flanks than on any other Pyrenean mountain, while the *voie normale* by way of the north-eastern shoulder offers a delightful scramble. The modest walker, too, has a number of opportunities for excellent outings in the vicinity, and in particular with a fine tour of the valleys that surround it, with ever-changing vistas unfolding as the walk progresses. Add to these its convenient access and a most comfortable hut - the Refuge de Pombie - and it is easy to understand how Jean-Pierre has become one of the most popular of all Pyrenean mountains.

*

In view of its rather formidable appearance, and the apparently impenetrable walls that guard its upper reaches, it is a little surprising that Francois de Foix should have even considered making an attempt to climb it back in the misted recesses of 1552. The account of this attempt, however, makes it clear that others - possibly the ubiquitous isard hunter - had ventured some way onto the mountain before him.

' ... he (de Foix) ascended as far as a place where he found the lairs of wild goats, which he saw running in large herds over the steep rocks ... (and) having gone still further, he observed a number of the nests of eagles and other birds of prey; ... Up to that point, they had found marks blazed on the rocks by people who had been up there before; but then they saw no further path ... (and) he made his way by a fresh route, with the help of the peasants whom he had brought with him ... When the rock resisted their endeavours, they made use of ladders, grapnels, and climbing irons (and) by this means he got as far as a place where they no longer saw any trace of wild beast or bird, though they saw birds flying about lower down; nevertheless, they were not yet at the top of the mountain, (but) in the end, he got to it, or within a very little distance of it, with the aid of certain hooked sticks.'

Two hundred years later the Pic du Midi d'Ossau had unarguably received its first ascent, for a military engineer by the name of Junker visited the neighbouring valleys in the course of his surveys and made an entry in his notebook (20th March 1787) to the effect that he had seen a 'triangulation turret' upon the summit. It later transpired that the ascent had been made by an unnamed shepherd from the Aspe Valley, '... who accomplished it at the demand of the geographers Reboul and Vidal'. Another shepherd, Mathieu, took part in the second ascent which was achieved on the 2nd October 1796 in the company of Guillaume Delfau. This ascent was something of a landmark in mountaineering terms, for it was carried out in a purely sporting style and without a smokescreen of scientific pretension. Delfau, it might be added, is not known to have ascended any other mountain, seemingly his ambition being satisfied with this scramble on the rugged Jean-Pierre.

*

When the Heroic age was gathering momentum during the latter half of the nineteenth century, Henri Brulle turned his attention to the Pic du Midi. With his eye for an interesting line he surveyed the North Face in the summer of 1896, and with René d'Astorg, Célestin Passet and Francois Salles, a novel, rambling route was developed. This original route has become something of a standard, a respectable outing of about 500 metres, it runs from the Brèche des Autrichiens and cuts across the face diagonally to the saddle of La Fourche, and from there up to the summit. The modern overall grading of this line is AD, with several individual pitches of III.

The first winter ascent of the North Face came about more by accident than plan. In April 1928 Douglas Busk and his American companion, Caleb Gates, floundered in snow in search of the ordinary route, only to find themselves on the wrong side of the north-east ridge. Rather than spend several more hours ploughing through the snow to reach their originally planned ascent route, they turned to the nearer North Face. Although ignorant as to the start of Brulle's route, they reached the crags of the Brèche at 10 o'clock in the morning and set off up the icy veneer of the slabs. After much scrabbling in chimney after chimney, cutting steps in the hard ice and clearing snow from rubble-strewn ledges, they eventually reached the summit at 5.30 p.m., seven and a half hours after tackling the first of the crags.

*

Besides the major summits of the Grand and Petit Pics, there are two other peaks that are not immediately apparent until viewed from the south; the Pointe d'Aragon, a rock tower separated from the Grand Pic by a narrow ridge, and Pointe Jean Santé, a secondary tower rising from the great moat of scree known as the Grande Raillere. Both have several difficult routes traced upon them, although the Pointe d'Aragon has an easier *voie normale,* an interesting yet strenuous outing involving a rather novel vertical chimney that is totally enclosed. Pointe Jean Santé was named after the creator of its first ascent - solo - in 1927. On its South-East Face, bathed in the golden light of these southern mountains, a sustained route of 500 metres was pioneered on 8th May 1953 by Jean Ravier and A. Armengaud. This *Voie Originale* has, over the passage of a quarter of a century, stood the test of time and become a classic in its own right.

Another classic, and one of the finest expeditions of its kind in the Pyrenees, is the traverse of the four peaks. A long, interesting and constantly varied excursion which demands about ten hours of climbing - including several passages of grade IV, and one short stretch of V. - it was originally linked in its entirety by B. and J. Sanchette in an act of escapist inspiration during the dark days of the Second World War. The traverse begins with the ascent of Pointe Jean Santé via the Pombie-Peyreget couloir, crosses to the higher Pointe d'Aragon, where a superb view shows the imposing South Face of the Grand Pic across the enclosed hollow well of the South Cirque, and then continues along the airy and complicated ridge to the Grand Pic's summit. From the Grand Pic the route leads to the Petit Pic, involving first the descent into la Fourche and then climbing out again beside the eastern arête, and descending from this final peak along the Arête de Peyreget. A complicated, but extremely satisfying expedition which requires a sustained and concentrated effort.

*

Stonefall is one of the major hazards of climbing on Jean-Pierre, but in spite of this the many faces of the mountain have seen an enormous amount of activity since the very dawning of *Pyrénéisme*. As each stage of development came along it was on the Pic du Midi that techniques were tried and perfected. As one generation succeeded another the established routes were dismissed in favour of fresh explorations, and Jean-Pierre bore the brunt of ambition.

During the 'thirties Robert Ollivier and Roger Mailly of the GPHM began fully to exploit the vast potential of the walls of the mountain with routes of surprising ingenuity. Their West Face of the Petit Pic (1934) was won with a single peg; it was followed a year later with an attack on the North-West Face, a line which resisted them once, but finally relaxed its defences under their determined return which was aided by the use of a dozen pitons. With unabated enthusiasm they continued to storm the walls, developing the North-West Face - again of the Petit Pic - in 1936, and on 14th July 1938, the North Buttress of the Grand Pic (TD), a 700 metres long outing with many strenuous pitches.

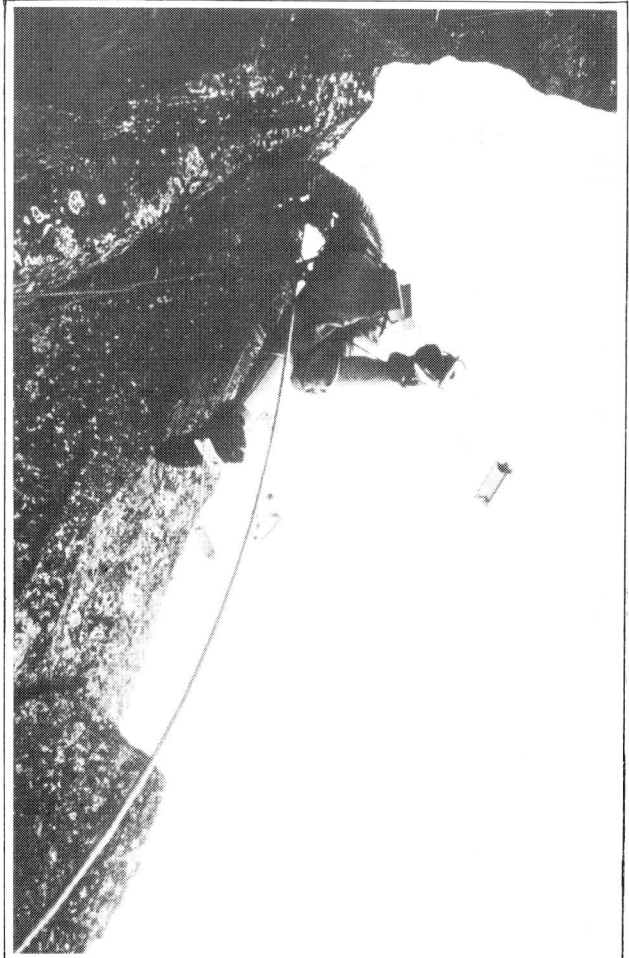

Raymond Despiau in action during the first ascent of the South Pillar of the Grand Pic du Midi d'Ossau, July 1959.

Photo: Ravier.

The winter ascent of the Pic du Midi by way of the South Cirque in February 1939 - by Aussat and Cazanave - was another of the highlights in its rich history, and Marcel Jolly maintained interest there throughout the late forties and early fifties until the emergence of the Raviers. As they found full expression for their enormous appetite for hard climbing, ever more difficult lines began to lace the walls with increasing momentum. The South-East Face of Pointe Jean Santé (1953), North Buttress of the Petit Pic (1956), and the South Pillar of the Grand Pic (1959) are just three of the exacting routes in which one or both of the Ravier twins played a prominent part. This last, involving Jean Ravier, Patrice de Bellefon, Raymond Despiau and B. Grenier, was an exhilarating expedition that demanded twenty hours of actual climbing, and was pioneered on the 5th and 6th July 1959. The route, though only some 250 metres long, was predominantly artificial (TD sup., with individual pitches of grades V, VI and of A2) broken by stretches of free climbing. It has become one of the accepted classic lines on Jean-Pierre.

Another true classic, but much longer than that of the South Pillar, is the 650 metres of the West-North-West Face of the Grand Pic made in July 1960. Patrice de Bellefon and Sylvain Sarthou pushed their route, which was mainly free, but with some additional artificial aid, from the base of the Cirque de l'Embarradère to the summit of the Pointe de France; one of the hardest and most exacting of lines on the Pic du Midi, it is graded ED inferior, with pitches of V, VI, and A2 and A3.

The most enterprising climb of this, or any other, Pyrenean region, was that of the North Face of the Pilier de l'Embarradere, a most advanced route of some 400 metres assiduously undertaken by the brothers Ravier with Paul Bouchet throughout the 17th and 18th July 1965. This abrupt, sullen, shadow-clutching wall, dwarfed perhaps by the protective shoulders of both the Grand and Petit Pics, had been overlooked by so many of the past masters of *Pyrénéisme,* awaiting the combination of cool confidence and expertise that marks the quality of genius. The difficulties of this route are sustained throughout. (ED, with numerous passages of V, V.sup., and one of VI, and of A2 and A3.) The vertical shaft, cold and uncompromising, demands rigorous antics of a somewhat acrobatic nature. It stands as a monument to modern *Pyrénéisme,* a reminder that mountaineering here, as elsewhere, is an activity that thrives on the search for greater challenges, and the development of means - both technical and physical - by which to overcome them.

*

The Pic du Midi d'Ossau is the playground of the Pyrenees. In the summer the vast walls of the mountain echo to the sound of peg hammers at work; and to the clatter of falling stones, a sobering hint that even the seemingly solid, rust-coloured granite of this much-trodden peak has its suspect ledges and gullies, as further witness the great slopes of scree.

The tranquil valleys, seen slumbering below in idyllic pastures from the summit, will rarely be wandered in solitude. Since the formation of the National Park their secrets have been advertised openly, their paths improved, their flowers protected. Isard roam in arrogant disregard, keeping their distance but watching the antics of climber and walker alike with obvious disdain. They move across the screes in large protective herds, picking amongst the rocks for intermittent nourishment, leaving the lower meadows knee deep in wild iris to the lizards and the frogs.

From the crystal ox-bows of the Bious river to the last minute hold on an exposed buttress, this mountain they call Jean-Pierre contains something for everyone; top-grade climbs for the committed *Pyrénéiste,* low-key scrambling for the man with lesser ambitions, and a walking circuit that is among the finest of its kind. A mountain, indeed, for everyone.

*

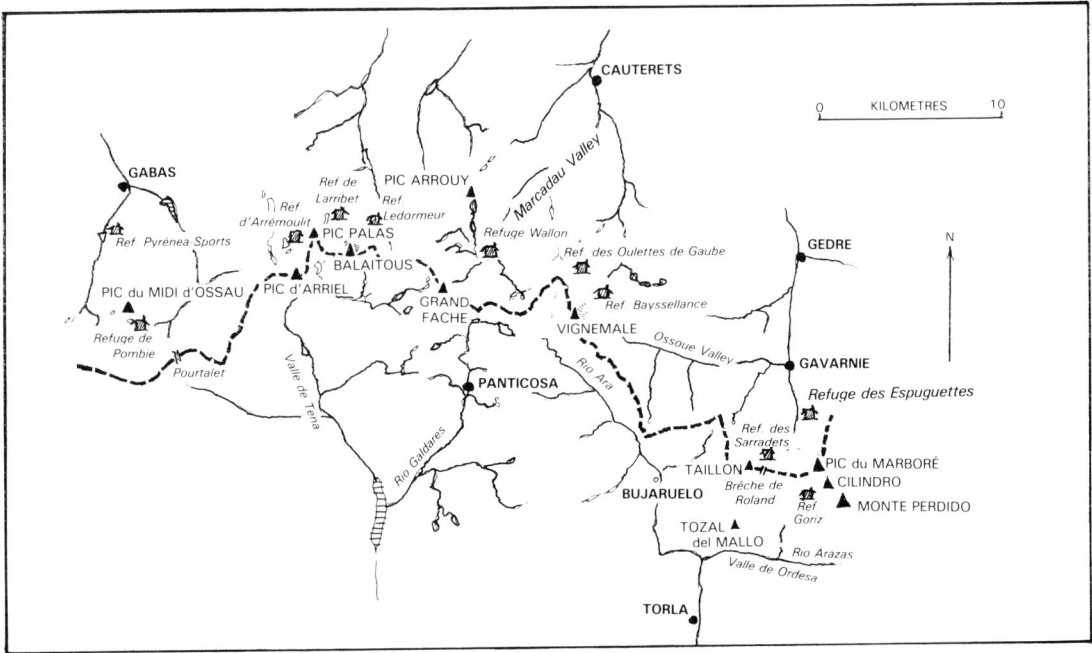

OSSAU TO GAVARNIE

In direct contrast to the gentle pasturelands and abundant forests that carpet the approaches to both the Ansabére cirque and the dramatic Pic du Midi d'Ossau, the high country that swells east of the Ossau Valley is a barren wilderness, a turbulent landscape of discarded boulders and ice-gripped tarns, of defiant looming summits and splintered crests.

The valleys which make tentative inroads on this vast region of savagery begin with a brave show of smiling meadow and silver stream, but all too soon the encircling ridges frown in shadow and replace the attempted pastoral elegance with sinister glacier-smoothed rocks, and chutes of grey scree, but for all that it is a worthy patch of mountain-land containing several grand peaks of a somewhat austere majesty; Pic Palas, Pic d'Arriel and Balaitous, Grande Fache and Pic Falisse, and the four main tops of the Vignemale. Glaciers survive, the first to be found on approaching from the west, and scores of glacial lakes. The ridges and summits of these mountains reveal the rough fretwork of nature's artistry; they are coarse and uneven, they are unfinished. It is a harsh and uncompromising arena for mountain adventure, but it is in this very harshness that the essence of its appeal lies. It casts its challenge well.

Beside a cluster of solemn tarns on the western perimeter of this wilderness there squats the Refuge d'Arrémoulit, backed by the misleading slopes of Pic Palas, and confronted across the ice-calving waters by the apparently short North Face of Pic d'Arriel. It is a scene of disquieting enchantment, quite unlike any other to be found in these ever-varied mountain fastnesses. 'The barren ridges, the vast heaps of tumbled rocks, the melancholy, deserted lakes - all seemed to form together the scene of some gigantic disaster, some terrific upheaval'.

On the Pic d'Arriel are one or two moderate ascent routes that depend for their ease and safety on the stability of the snow. In winter, or at the start of the season, this peak adopts a new dimension, presenting in its gullies and verglassed slabs a completely different aspect, and the routes become elevated as serious undertakings.

*

Col du Palas.
Photo: Pete Smith

When Peytier and Hossard were exploring these desolate acres in the first quarter of the nineteenth century they were quite understandably confused by the rugged and bewildering terrain. As a result of their confusion they climbed the pyramid-shaped Pic Palas under the impression that they were on the Balaitous, and it was not until they reached the summit - with the fine view of its loftier neighbour - that they discovered their error. Their ascent route is today adopted as the *voie normale*, an interesting scramble on the northern ridge.

Pic Palas has a dignified silhouette; symmetrical ridges rising steeply to a conical peak. It is a peak that dominates a landscape of lifeless rock and wintry tarn, of screes and boulders and slips of permanent snow. It plunges, in the south, to the Lacs d'Arriel by way of a tortuous bowl of mountain debris topped on either side by '... ugly, precipitous gullies'. South-eastwards its slanting ridge forms the limits of the long projecting North-West Arête of the Balaitous, while from the west it rules the Arrémoulit lakes with its sentry-like position.

The South-West Arête, which slopes down to the saddle of the Col du Palas - by which a westerly approach is made to the Balaitous - offers an ascent route of some charm. It was pioneered in 1913 by the brothers Von Martin from Germany, and crosses a subsidiary summit which now bears their name. This route, which has a couple of passages of grade IV climbing in it, is about 350 metres from col to summit, and has the modern overall grading of AD superior.

Another route that has achieved the status of a classic outing, is that of the South-East Arête rising from the notch of the Port du Lavedan. This was made first in 1937 by Robert Ollivier, Arruyer and Petitjean, although Russell had suggested its appeal seventy years earlier, but from the summit, where the views are of great scope, the eye may not ignore the vast ridges and the extraordinary plunging West Face of the Balaitous.

*

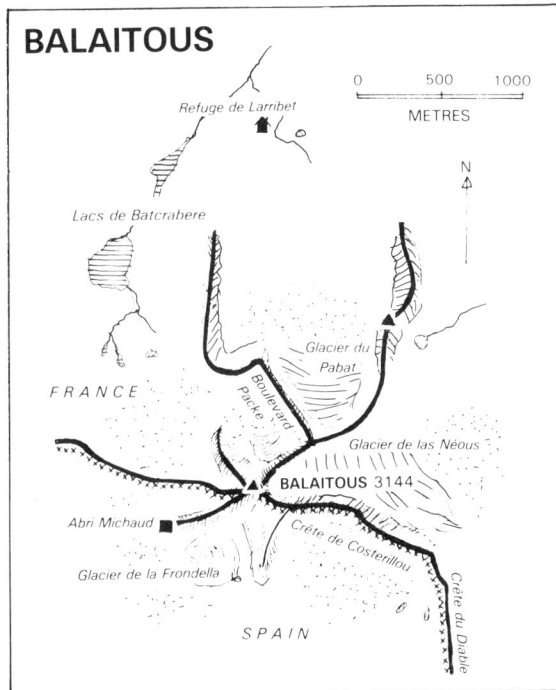

Balaitous

'The Pic de Baletous,' wrote Packe in the first edition of his guide, 'is the highest mountain in this part of the chain; but it lies so completely away from the route of the ordinary traveller, that the Eaux Bonnes guides seem quite at a loss as to its exact whereabouts.'

Defended on all sides by massive ramparts, and locked in by the swollen ridges of other peaks, the Balaitous commands the wildest and least accessible portion of the whole range. So remote is it that several of the early attempts to claim its summit failed even to reach the lower slopes. The surveyors, Peytier and Hossard, who made the first ascent in 1825, only did so after encountering numerous difficulties of access, but their route information - and, indeed, even the acknowledgement of their ascent - was lost for almost forty years, and Packe's ascent in 1864 was as much an act of pioneering as was the original. It was not until he actually stood upon the summit where he found a cairn, that he knew for certain that it had been climbed before. 'As for the difficulties he encountered', said Russell, some years later, 'they may be measured by the fact that he wandered for seven days on and almost all round the mountain before setting his foot at last on its real summit'.

Balaitous - showing a section of the long Costerillou Ridge (right).

Packe's first attempt was made in 1862 by way of the North Ridge. He set off along the pleasant Vall d'Azun with his guide, Jean Pierre Gaspard, of Arrens, and spent the night in a rough shepherds' *cabane* not far from the present site of the Refuge de Larribet, '... on an elevated basin affording a scanty pasture, at the foot of the northern glacier of the Baletous'.

His comments with regard to the night's lodging in the *cabane* are typical of those recorded by many of the pioneers of mountaineering of the period, both here and in the Alps.

> 'The three shepherds, the occupants of the cabane, returned late that evening, and found us already installed, and preparing our supper over a fire made from their fuel ... Wine is a luxury they never indulge in on mountains, and a pull at our bottle was considered an ample recompense for our night's lodging ... I would willingly have preferred sleeping *sub Jove*, but it would have been a slight to their hospitality; so we lay down all five of us shoulder to shoulder, as tightly packed as sardines in a box; and what with the fleas, who concentrated all their energies upon me, the smell of my companions, and the want of fresh air, I passed an indifferent night, and gladly hailed the approach of day.'

Packe and Gaspard started out from the *cabane* at 5.15 in the morning, but then lost much time in **crossing and recrossing the rocks that form the western wall of the Pabat basin.** (This wall rises as the Crête de la Garanère to meet the longer Fachon crest at the Cap Peytier-Hossard, where the converging ridges lead directly to the summit of the Balaitous). Once on the Garanère ridge they moved steadily along its south-western edge - now known as the *Boulevard Packe* - where they found that '.... the main difficulty is getting from this upon the pic, which can only be done by crossing its western face above the glacier, which is excessively precipitous'. Some time was spent here seeking easier ground as an alternative way of progressing.

'... one spot (on the ridge) appeared to me to present so much risk that I declined attempting it, as also did my guide, for whom I offered to wait if he liked to make the attempt to reach the summit, and so reap the honour to himself... The highest point we reached I computed (as) 9,954 feet, (and) the summit must have been full 400 feet above us.

'The view from this spot was, of course, very inferior to what it must have been from the summit ... The most striking features, however, were the glaciers that stretched at our feet on either side of the arête on which we were standing, that to the east being still a very fine specimen of a Pyrenean glacier, which has left its tokens all down the valley, having once extended as far as Arrens ... We set up a pile of stone, a trophy of our defeat, which is visible from the cabane below, and returned by the road we came; but in passing the foot of the western glacier incurred some risk, from the artillery of granite rocks that came bounding down at intervals, as the sun's rays demolished the ice props on which they rested.'

A year after Packe's attempt John Ball came to the Pyrenees and also tried to find a way to the Balaitous's resisting summit. His attempt was likewise doomed to failure, but in 1864 Packe returned once more with Gaspard intent upon finding an alternative to the *Boulevard Packe*. This time they chose to spend the night, not in the shepherds' *cabane,* but beneath one of the great blocks of granite - named the 'Tour d'Arribet' - offering a rough shelter about an hour below the hut.

Their successful ascent led them through '... the savage gorge of the Bacradére, which forms a sort of cirque'. Passing the string of tarns they climbed the snow and ice slopes which swept from the lofty ridge at the head of the cirque, and joined the ridge at the Col Noir. This ridge is the long arête that links the Balaitous with Pic Palas, and once upon this the difficulties began. Packe's guide - second edition - outlines the problems: 'Mount first (from the large rock used as the 'breakfast stop') NNE. over a couloir of loose débris, and at the top of this turn more to the right (east), and climb upwards as best you can, clinging to the obelisks of dislocated rock... A little higher, it is better to take to the south side of the arête; and, finally, a couloir of rather slippery *schist,* terminating in an awful precipice, leads to the summit'.

Ten days after Packe's ascent, Russell repeated his route - by the western aréte - and later reviewed 'this threatening and proud peak' with the following comment:

'... after five journeys up or down this terrible arête, and thirty-seven years of Pyrenean ascents, I still think it is the most perilous *mauvais pas* of the whole chain. It has long ago been given up for easier *couloirs* on the north-western side of the formidable precipices which surround the whole of this Pyrenean 'Cervin', and the perils of the Balaitous are a thing of the past. Ladies have climbed it, although neither cables nor chains have as yet profained it. It has never been dishonoured!'

The summit of the Balaitous, reigning supreme as it does over this tortuous region, inspires a profound respect for the pioneers who first charted these heavily-guarded sanctuaries. It offers a wild panorama of distant peaks and hinted valleys and glaciers, 'but far more impressive... (is) the vast chaos of bare ridges and mountain heights lying all silent and lifeless in the light of the sun'.

Henri Brulle made two spirited winter attempts on its ridges, but it was the brothers Cadier who, attracted by its very wildness, chose to make extended campaigns among its many shattered arêtes and noble faces. Among their more notable routes are those on the face of Batcrabere - in 1908 - and the fine series of explorations made by George and Edouard in 1913 on the Costerillou ridge.

In the thirties there was considerable activity, with pioneering efforts made by Lamathe, Le Breton and Senmartin - on the North-West Arête - and Le Breton with B. Sanchette making the descent of the bristling Costerillou ridge. The Crête du Diable, which extends that of Costerillou to the south, had earlier been explored - in 1927 - by Arlaud and Abadie, and one of the most serious undertakings of this massif was the linking of the three main ridges in one glorious traverse. This was initially achieved on 17th July 1938 by Roger Mailly and Barré, an expedition requiring about twelve hours of concentrated effort. On the Tour de Costerillou - originally named Tour de George Cadier - a hard North Face route was pushed through in 1956, an exposed line rearing above the 'huge crevasses of its eastern glacier'. This Costerillou wall holds a number of difficult routes, and there is still ample scope for climbing of an exploratory nature here, as elsewhere on the battlements of this, the most uncompromising of Pyrenean mountains.

*

The Crête du Diable expires on the summit of Pic Cristail, and in turn this plunges down to the little col of the Port de la Peyre-St Martin. It was here that in days gone by shepherds from both sides of the frontier - the pass marks the international boundary - used to gather to settle disputes over 'cattle-lifting'. It was also frequently used by smugglers trading chiefly in silk and tobacco, the pass being an easy crossing point while at the same time offering various ways by which to reach the main centres of trade.

Continuing eastwards the landscape maintains its barren appearance; bleak and inhospitable mountains cluster over blackened tarns, but then streams appear, and the first of the smiling flowers, and one by one the mountains show their vegetated lower slopes and distant valleys smile under the sun; and there below, where creamy cascades bellow and streams join forces to become a river of substance, the Marcadau valley projects itself with all the colour, fragrance and tranquility that makes these Pyrenean heartlands so welcoming.

The upper reaches of the valley broaden into rich meadowland sliced by the lazy meanderings of the Marcadau river, spattered with flowering plants and stunted pines, pocked with weathered boulders long jettisoned by the surrounding mountains. These peaks do not frown with solemn faces as do those around the Balaitous, they stand back a little shyly, offering a tender courtship,

The Marcadau valley. Left to right: Port du Marcadau, Pic Falisse, Grande Fache.

particularly so when they blush in the reflected glow of a rising sun. The Marcadau becomes an oasis of light.

These are not climbers' peaks, it is not climbers' country. The Marcadau Valley offers the charm of a mountain idyll, the river with its trout sparkling through gentle pastures, the mountains and side valleys giving opportunities for pleasures of a pedestrian nature. The Grande Fache attains three thousand metres, but it appears much less significant than its altitude might suggest. Yet altitude is nothing, comparisons are unworthy, for every mountain and every mountain valley has its own specific charm. The Marcadau's is to be found in its colour and tranquility.

North of the Wallon hut there lies another confusion of misplaced tarns and desolate hollows with sombre peaklets here and there affording exercise of a somewhat agile character. On the Aiguilles du Pic Arrouy above the Lac du Pourtet, for example, a number of sudden, jagged needles have encouraged activity, and the traverse of the two main aiguilles that rise above the col makes a pleasant diversion offering pitches of V and even V superior to contend with, but the climber with an eye for an interesting line need never be limited in these mountains, yet at the same time it is understandable that certain peaks command the attention of all ambitious or prospective *Pyrénéistes*. Few have a greater natural appeal than the shapely giant which looms above the nearby Gaube valley, the Vignemale.

*

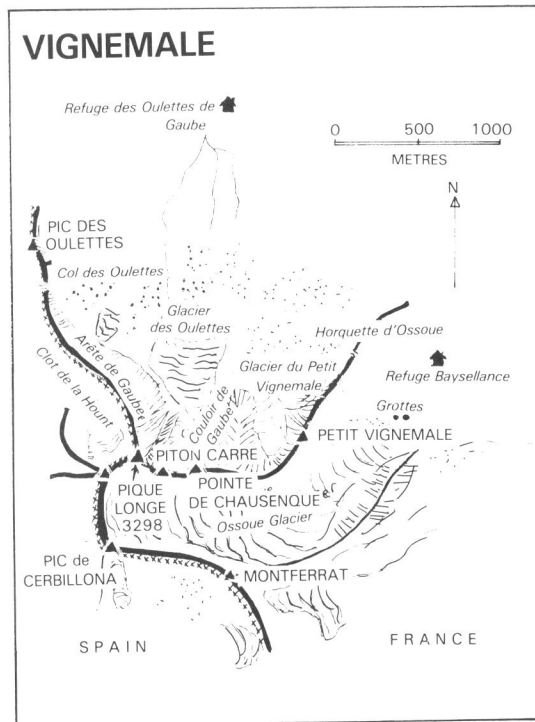

The Vignemale

From every side, save that of the south - the direction from which the early ascents were made - the Vignemale appears regal, the supreme monarch of all it surveys. From the north-west, on the Col d'Arratille above the upper reaches of the Ara Valley, the high curving crest of the Clot de la Hount, with its sweeping snowfield and ice-locked couloirs, reveals itself with dignity. From the heights of Gavarnie, from the Taillon or Perdido or Marboré, 'the noble eastern face' dominates the horizon with its sprawling glacier draining into the beckoning verdure of the Ossoue Valley.

Out of the glacial levels of scant meadowland at the head of the Vallée de Gaube there bursts the

Vignemale North Face
Pointe de Chausenque, Piton Carré, Pique Longue.
Couloir de Gaube divides Piton Carré from Pique Longue.

great North Face of the Vignemale in a show of arrogance. It is an impressive face; polished by time here, coarsely hewn there, riven in places by deep seams and systems of slender cracks leading to a high conical summit that is often wrapped in cloud streamers from the west. This face is one of the finest rock walls of the Pyrenees; over eight hundred metres of forbidding precipice from lofty summit to the aggravated contortions of its glacier below. A face which rules the tight cirque of strutting, straining, perfectly-moulded slabs that comprise the North Faces of Petit Vignemale, Pointe de Chausenque, Piton Carré and the main summit of the Vignemale itself, Pique Longue.

This is a truly magnificent landscape, a stark contrast to the splendour of down-valley forest, meadow and sparkling lake, but in such contrasts lies the essence of these mountains. It is a compelling image of basic simplicity, and to the climber this cirque offers in its austere beauty the challenge of vertical activity tempered only by the difficulties of the routes it offers.

After the harrowing experience suffered by Cazaux and Guillembet during the first ascent by way of the Ossoue Glacier, all the early climbs on the Vignemale required a long approach from Gavarnie, crossing over into Spain to the *Serbigliana* - the valley of the river Ara - from whose slopes the route lay. This was a relatively difficult, complicated route enlivened by a short chimney. In the summer of 1838, when Anne Lister made the first tourist ascent, she had to squeeze her way through this chimney - 'so narrow that the body can scarcely enter' - wearing a complex of capes, shawls and petticoats, with all sorts of tapes and loops with which to tie up her skirts whenever necessary. Above this, the 'Col Lady Lyster' leads to the upper snow basin. 'Then begins a fatiguing and monotonous walk of upwards of 2 hours, cutting steps as you go along, in a series of short zigzags up the steep *talus* of ice and snow'. The rock peak of the summit is reached by an easy scramble.

Year in and year out this was adopted as the *voie normale,* and it was not until the fears of glacier travel were put into true perspective that the Ossoue Glacier route became acceptable. Then Russell began his infatuation and the Vignemale's popularity and fame were assured. It became one of the classic ascents in the Pyrenees, '... the one followed by Cauterets bathers who play at 'heroism'; said Henri Brulle, adding; 'it is, however, quite capable of becoming troublesome towards the end of the season. I know it by experience having once floundered, when descending along its left bank, into a trecherous crevasse, out of which my two companions, both experienced mountaineers moreover, were unable to extricate me, no matter how strenuously they pulled the rope'.

Brulle's desire for novelty and challenge was rewarded by the success of his rope in the Clot de la Hount couloir, on 12th August 1879, which presented the Vignemale with climbing of a more adventurous quality, but it was in the Couloir de Gaube that the most prestigious climb of the century was created.

Henri Brulle, Jean Bazillac, Roger de Monts, Célestin Passet and Francois Bernard Salles comprised the pioneering rope that forced the passage of this '... great ice couloir (which) cleaves (the Vignemale's) dark and inaccessible ramparts' on August 7th, 1889. Brulle's tireless enthusiasm was the driving force behind this ascent; he had studied carefully the problems likely to be faced - 'The last bit especially was particularly puzzling', - and had been haunted by its possibilities. Passet's supreme mastery of difficult rock and ice-work made his contribution invaluable, and in high spirits they set to work at 8.40 in the morning.

'The bergschrund gave us much trouble', wrote Brulle. 'Beyond we advanced rapidly, in spite of the slope, thanks to the good condition of the snow, but little by little the slope increased alarmingly; ice succeeded snow, and the ascent became very severe. Near the top of the couloir we came upon a really diabolical obstacle. It was a great boulder, hemmed in between the two rock walls, slightly overhanging, about 5 metres high, and covered with a thick coating of ice. We spent there two terrible hours, in an intense cold, and unable either to turn or to force the passage.

At half-past three o'clock on the evening, we had to come to a decision, Célestin determined to make a last effort, and this time he won the day, thanks to a very light and well balanced ice axe from Grindlewald which he had luckily borrowed from me. I still remember with what anxiety we were watching his slow progress, whilst stoically receiving the pieces of ice-pavement flung about by the ice axe, which bespattered our heads and hands, at the imminent risk of hurling us down. With what joy did we see him at last reach the top of the wall! ... The remainder of the couloir, always very steep, was carpeted with stalactites of ice, where natural steps and handholds greatly facilitated our ascent. At last, after seven long hours of obstinate struggle spent in the freezing shade of this dismal gulf, we emerged on the upper névé plateau, where we found a dazzling and comforting sunshine, happier than Dante, who, in escaping from hell, had only seen the stars.'

The couloir did not receive a second ascent for 44 years, and today, some ninety years after Brulle's and Passet's superbly executed route was established, the ascent of the Couloir de Gaube is still regarded as an outing of some consequence; 600 metres of mixed rock and ice and snow, steepening to 60° or more in its upper section, and the verglassed block which forms the major obstacle giving a grade IV struggle to overcome.

The Arête de Gaube, the rather fine north-west ridge of Pique Longue, is another classic route established early in the new century. Rather long, but consistently interesting, it overhangs a section of the North Face before airily rising in slabs to the summit. It was in 1908 that Jean d'Ussel, with the guides Castagne, Courtade and Salles, first completed the route, while in 1967

Lechene and Sebben made an exhausting addition to it by first climbing the 500 metres of the North Pillar, a route which included the great diedre that it is found near the foot of the vast north wall.

During the thirties, members of the GPHM scanned the forbidding shadows of these virgin walls, and on 8th August 1933, Barrio and Bellocq pushed the first route up the North Face of Pique Longue *(Voie Classique),* starting at its ice-washed base, and finishing more than 800 metres later on the summit; the longest unbroken wall in the Pyrenees, an arena for adventure in a truly grand setting. Numerous new routes and variations have been made in the years since, but nothing can detract from the many and varied qualities of this original line. It remains a true classic.

Also during 1933, across the cirque, Jean Arlaud, with Souriac and Lescamela sharing his rope, explored the possibilities of the Aiguilles des Glaciers, and subsequently made its first ascent. Pointe de Chausenque received a bold assault via the North-West Buttress - from Boyrie and Simpson - in July 1945, and then, four years later, Jolly and Clos came up with their astonishing winter ascent of the Vignemale's North Face.

This tightly-knit cirque of grand north faces continues to attract the elite of *Pyrénéistes*. Hard routes abound; North Face and North Buttress of the Petit Vignemale, North Face of Pointe de Chausenque, North Face of Piton Carré, and numerous demanding lines that have been traced on Pique Longue's great face. Limitless appear the prospects for further exploration on these walls, and the lines already established offer outings of a very special quality. Add to these the unique nature of the setting, and it is easy to understand the Vignemale's undeniable attraction.

At work on the North Face of the Vignemale - the first ascent in 1964, of one of the hardest routes - the Dièdre Nord.
Photo: Ravier

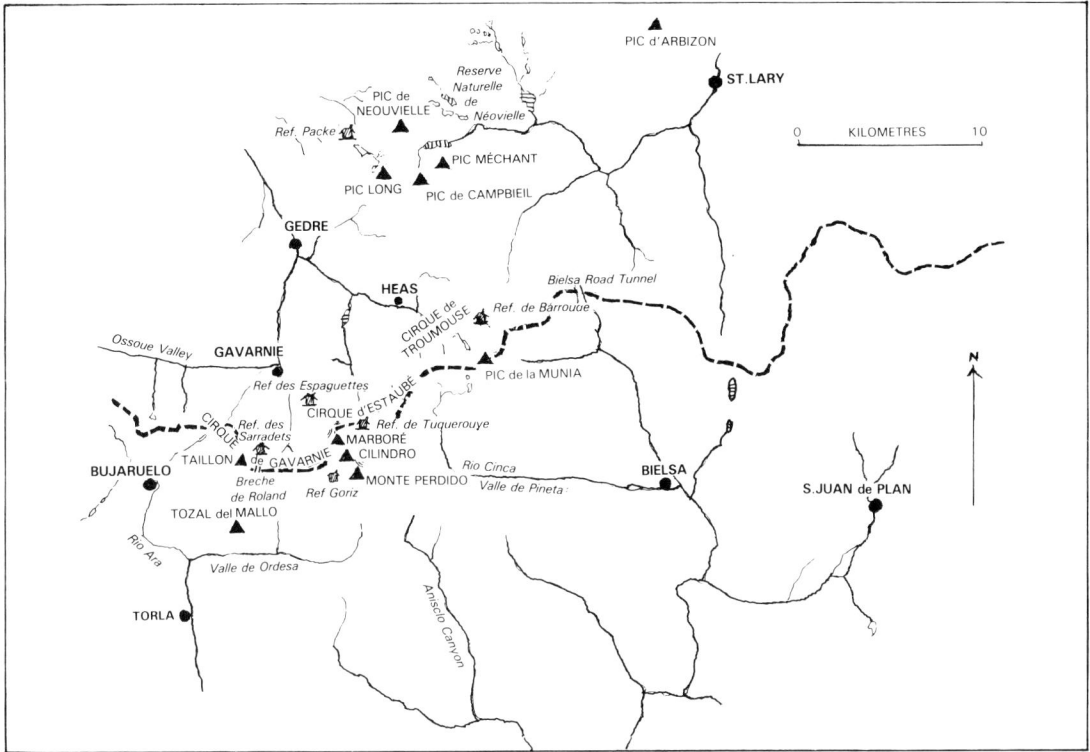

Map labels:
PIC d'ARBIZON
Reserve Naturelle de Néovielle
ST.LARY
PIC de NEOUVIELLE
Ref. Packe
PIC MÉCHANT
PIC LONG
PIC de CAMPBIEIL
KILOMETRES
GEDRE
HEAS
Bielsa Road Tunnel
CIRQUE de TROUMOUSE
Ref. de Barrouue
Ossoue Valley
GAVARNIE
Ref des Espaguettes
CIRQUE d'ESTAUBÉ
PIC de la MUNIA
Ref. des Sarradets
CIRQUE
Ref. de Tuquerouye
MARBORÉ
CILINDRO
TAILLON
de GAVARNIE
Rio Cinca
BUJARUELO
Breche de Roland
Ref Goriz
MONTE PERDIDO
Valle de Pineta
BIELSA
S.JUAN de PLAN
TOZAL del MALLO
Rio Ara
Valle de Ordesa
Añisclo Canyon
TORLA
N

FRENCH CIRQUES – SPANISH CANYONS

Gavarnie

'Of all the possible Pyrenean centres', wrote Brulle, 'the most perfect is Gavarnie'.

Packe and Russell both endorsed this view, adding their belief that it was, in Pyrenean terms, the headquarters of mountaineering. It is not difficult to see why, for no other village is more ideally situated among high mountains; from no other Pyrenean centre can one leave the comfort of a valley hotel and be involved in a major climbing route within the hour; from no other mountain community in the whole length and breadth of the range does such a staggering highland panorama so openly reveal itself to the visitor.

The idyll of such a scene has its draw-backs. Daily throughout the season coachloads of tourists wind up the long, narrow road from Lourdes to spill into the streets of Gavarnie as part of the pageant of a centuries-old pilgrimage. The soft tranquility of mountain pastures is traded for blaring hooters and the constant babble of voices, and as a consequence Gavarnie's economy is understandably based almost entirely on this predictable trade. Yet despite this daily assault nothing can diminish the grandeur of the scene as presented from the outskirts of the village.

'It is at once a mountain and a wall', wrote Victor Hugo. 'It is the most mysterious edifice of the most mysterious of architects. It is the Coliseum of nature ... Picture to yourself this magnificent silhouette ... It is a long dark wall, every perfection and every inclination of which is marked by lines of snow, every platform of which is covered with a glacier. Near the middle are two great towers. One of these, which is towards the east, is square and turns one

71

of its corners towards France. The other, which is near the west, seems to be less a tower than a sheaf of turrets. Both are covered with snow. Towards the right are deep breaches, deep notches cut into the wall like two vases filled with clouds. Finally, at the western extremity, and still towards the right, is a kind of enormous border, puckered with a thousand tiers, and presenting to the eye, in monster proportions, what would be called in architecture the section of an amphitheatre ... in a word, a thing of perfection - great beyond expression, serene even to sublimity.'

All this has a lacework of truth in it, the graphic romance is inspired by a landscape of untarnished brilliance, but surprisingly, Hugo fails to mention the countless ribbons of cascades that add a certain grace and movement to the scene. In spring and early summer, in particular, the sparkling falls dazzle in the sun to enhance these otherwise awesome mountain walls. With an element of poetry, Hippolyte Taine drew his reader's attention to them, and thus presented his eulogy:

'The streamlets of water come by thousands from the highest layer, leap from step to step, cross their stripes of foam, wind, unite and fall by a dozen brooks that slide from the last layer in flakey streaks to lose themselves in the glacier at the bottom.'

He then concentrates his attention on the Grande Cascade, a spout which bursts from its hidden shelf in the south-eastern corner of the cirque below its clustered peaklets.

'It falls slowly, like a drooping cloud or the unfolding of a muslim veil; the air softens its fall; the eye follows complacently the graceful undulations of the beautiful airy veil. It glides the length of the rock, and seems to float rather than to fall. The sun shines, through its plume, with the softest and loveliest splendour. It reaches the bottom like a bouquet of slender waving feathers, and springs backwards in a silver dust ... No stir is in the air; no noise: no living creature in this solitude.

*

Before mountaineering scrutiny uncovered the vast potential for climbing upon the massive walls of the cirque, there was one notable outing that was made by the more adventurous of visitors to Gavarnie, and that was to the very frontier with Spain at the Brèche de Roland. It was almost a

Gavarnie: Cascades streaming from the walls of the cirque.

CIRQUE de GAVARNIE

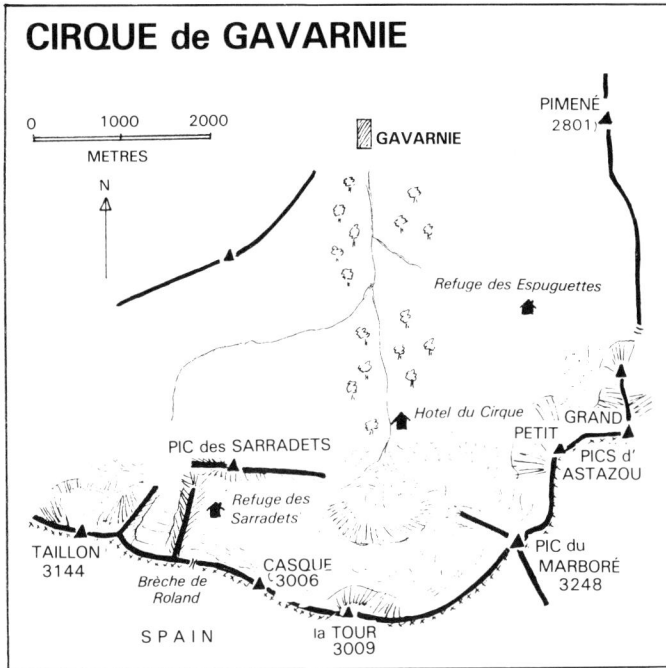

prerequisite of any Pyrenean visit, a highlight of 'heroic' mountain explorations; it was a lure to the romantically inclined who had warmed to the legend of Charlemagne's retreat, and of Roland's sword that was held responsible for this huge gash in the high limestone ridge; and above all it allowed the energetic tourist to venture into the otherwise forbidden world of lofty mountain wastes.

In the early eighteen hundreds one such tourist was T. Clifton Paris, who rightly said '... the grandest scenery of these vast solitudes is alone accessible to the pedestrian'. However, the glacier draped immediately below the Brèche proved to be just one 'vast solitude' too many:

> 'This dizzy labour (ascending the glacier) is generally effected by the traveller with a guide on each side, who have their feet armed with *crampons,* and are furnished with hatchets in order to notch the slippery surface. I essayed the snow with my feet, looked at the stupendous gateway so provokingly near, and then down the huge slope of smooth ice, which went down and down, and grew steeper and steeper, until it was lost in the hideous precipices of the Circus. The sight was too appalling: I could not summon sufficient resolution to attempt the passage, which was in distance about a quarter of a mile, and wisely, I think, abandoned it, considering that I was without *crampons* or any knowledge of the proper mode of effecting it. To understand all its terrors the place must be seen; once slip, and you are gone for ever past all human aid: the death is too frightful for contemplation.'

*

Gavarnie was early adopted as the classic mountaineering centre. Not only was the cirque - with its clustered summits topping three thousand metres - right on the doorstep, there was the Vignemale, accessible in six or seven hours to the west, and Monte Perdido across the frontier. Numerous ascents could be made from a base in the village; it had a 'rough inn' - in the early days - but very soon two or three hotels were opened to accommodate a growing clientele; and it had the finest guides of the whole Pyrenees. In 1883 the C.A.F. constructed its refuge below the Brèche de Roland, and scope for mountaineering - and travel in wild mountain country - was consequently enlarged even more.

When *Pyrénéisme* was developing from the slumbering apathy of a constant repetition of *voies normale* into a lively search for climbing 'problems', it was to Gavarnie that the pioneers turned. On the walls of the Gabietous, on the Taillon and the 'finger' of the False Bréche and the narrow cliffs that form the gateway of the Bréche de Roland, routes were explored. On the curiously shaped Casque, on the Tour and the Épaule, lines were traced, as were the walls of Marboré and those of the Pics d'Astazou.

One of the earliest of the classic routes to be produced was that of the Couloir Swan, the vast diedre that splits the 'open book' faces of the Grand and Petit Astazou. Here, Francis Swan and Henri Passet enjoyed a somewhat harrowing assault in 1885. The Pailla glacier was troublesome even before they reached the Couloir, with open crevasses making the approach a delicate affair. Then a great avalanche fell, but it seemed then safer to advance than to retreat, and at last the route was successfully negotiated.

Two years later, Jean Bazillac, Roger de Monts and Célestin Passet created their novel Cascade Wall route. This line began at the very base of the cirque's vast cliff-face, '... particularly attractive, very steep, but not really bad in dry weather'. The weather, on this route, is of particular importance, for:

'At about two-thirds of its height one comes to a 'traverse' ... At first it is a narrow cornice on which falls a cascade which seems nothing, but when it flows down your neck and at the same time you feel it escaping on your feet you seem to be walking under Niagara. Immediately after comes a steeply inclined 'Platte', with a great precipice below, and under this you have to worm yourself on your knees, hanging on by the top of your fingers.'

On the Petit Pic Rouge de Pailla, Henri Brulle, with Réné d'Astorg and Célestin Passet, was in action in 1894, making a new route from the north.

'The last bit', said Brulle, 'is one of the hardest I have ever encountered. On a rock wall, to which I only clung precariously, Célestin stood on my head, then on my hand and arm, as on a bridge, and thus supported he managed with great difficulty to haul himself up.'

Gavarnie, with the Grand and Petit Astazou behind. The Couloir Swan divides the peaks.

The Pic des Sarradets- rising behind the Brèche de Roland Hut, makes an ideal training ground with numerous short rock problems.

The 'Heroic Age' developed around Gavarnie where ' ... it is not difficult to select a course sufficiently wild among the mountains in any direction'. Brulle and the Passets were active almost everywhere upon these peaks, arêtes and faces, and after twelve years of concentrating almost exclusively upon the exploration of the cirque's great heights, Brulle confessed that '... we have not yet exhausted its resources, and few of our best performances have been repeated'. In addition to those already noted, he made the first ascent of the Petit Pic d'Astazou by its north-western arête in 1892, and in 1895, with Célestin Passet once more, he forced the North Face of the Taillon. These represent only a handful of the exciting developments that effectively lifted Gavarnie's reputation as a true climbing centre.

*

In the decades since Brulle's stirling work opened the walls of the cirque to the climbing fraternity, numerous new and ever-harder routes have been established. The terraces of perpendicular rock have received the continued close scrutiny of main-stream *Pyrénéistes* searching for prospective fresh lines and variations of classic, long-respected climbs. In winter, too, when the cirque gleams under its glaze of ice, even the very hardest of summer routes have been repeated, with Raymond Despiau among the more forceful of winter activists.

In 1961, Patrice de Bellefon and Sylvain Sarthou made the first winter ascent of the wall of the Grande Cascade, Crête des Druides and Arête Passet, an active encouragement to the hard men to create winter routes of a dramatic and serious nature. The most demanding of Gavarnie's major routes, - that of the North Face of the Tour de Marboré, pioneered by Claude Dufourmantelle and Jean Ravier, in September 1956 - was repeated as a full winter epic in January 1973 by Despiau, Louis Audoubert and Francis Tomas, who spent four bitter night bivouacs upon the face. In early March 1978, the entertaining, but extremely exposed '*Voie de l'Overdose*' - Grande Cascade - was created over a three-day period by Michel Boulang, Serge Casteran, Dominique Julien and Rainier Munsch. The momentum continues.

*

The Cirque de Troumouse

The Cirques of Estaubé and Troumouse

Immediately to the east of Gavarnie there runs the lovely valley of Estaubé, blocked in the south by its own cirque, '... less imposing, no doubt, than that of Gavarnie, but with crests which afford fine and sometimes hard scaling'.

It was through this valley that Ramond came in the summer of 1797 on his attempt to climb Monte Perdido, and it is interesting to read his descriptions for, nearly two hundred years later, little has changed beyond the damming of the river near the valley mouth.

'... in silence we contemplated its quiet solitudes. It possesses, at the same time, the calm of the upper regions, and of the secondary grounds. Some mountains which appeared considerable ... astonished us still more by the simplicity of their forms ... The masses, boldly modelled, present smooth, yet striking contours, which no strange accident has caused to pass the limits of the beautiful. All rise and fall in just proportions. Nothing spoils the design both severe and bold; and the colour, too, so transparent and pure, - it is grey a little warmed with pink, - suits equally the light or shade, and softens the contrast between them ... Vegetation flourishes up to the very foot of the rocky ridges ... A little river with grassy banks flows peacefully over a stony bed, and afterwards, further on, it becomes a torrent.'

At the head of the valley, in the crest of the cirque's high walls, two important passes allow access to Spain. The Brèche de Tuquerouye is that which Ramond forced, reached by a steep and icy gully, with one of the oldest of Pyrenean refuges tucked in the wedge of the Brèche itself. Packe was the first to sleep in it, and he described its appearance succinctly: 'Its shape is that of a boat keel upwards, and it is so strongly built of stone and lime cemented with pitch, that it is thoroughly proof against wind and weather'. Russell was not so enthusiastic, and gave it a limited lifespan. However, it is still there, though recently renovated. The other pass lies a little to the east and is reached by a more gentle approach. This, the Port de Pinéde, is an old smugglers' pass, and one that was adopted by many of the earlier travellers in these mountains.

The peaks themselves; Pic d'Estaubé, Montferrant, Pic de Pinéde and Pic du Tuquerouye are prominent, yet their proximity to other, more challenging, heights has had the effect of perhaps reducing their true value, while Brulle and Passet established two routes on the Punta del Forcarral in 1894; and a long and interesting traverse of the ridge connecting the two main passes remains as an outing of great interest. The valley is, in itself, one of such charm that there is a tendency towards complacency, a tendency fed by the sun's drawing of fragrance from the flower-rich meadows.

Pic de Troumouse (left), Pic Heid (right) and Barroude Wall - the eastern side of Cirque de Troumouse.

The Cirque de Troumouse is even larger than that of Gavarnie, and makes the biggest natural cirque in the range; a vast amphitheatre, topped by an almost level summit ridge, and cupping ' ... a wide-spread undulating plateau, of which the rich and fresh verdure contrasts strikingly with the snow-clad ledges of rock'.

The highest of its summits, Pic de la Munia (3133m.), - first climbed by Packe and Chapelle - was explored long ago, and has one or two interesting routes on it, including the *voie normale* which rises to the Col de la Munia and finishes along the western ridge. Jean Arlaud found consolation for his failure in the Couloir de Gaube by forcing a satisfying route on the Deux Soeurs (two sisters) of Troumouse in the twenties, and in 1957 Jean Ravier, with his sister, Lysette, discovered a fine route on the eastern buttress of the Petit Pic Blanc, which overshadows the two Lacs de Barroude; but of more recent vintage are the two difficult lines traced upon the broad North Face of the most southerly of the Troumouse peaks, the Pène Blanque. In 1969 the Ravier twins, with Bonnenfant and Bouchet, established their 500 metre route, which was graded TD, and on 26th and 27th July 1970, Despiau and de Boysson created an even more demanding ascent which involved some delicate moves of V and V sup.

In all the Cirque de Troumouse is a much neglected area, a region of unquestionable character, worthy of the attention of all mountain enthusiasts, while its eastern side plunges via the long Barroude wall to a country equally neglected.

*

The Néouvielle Massif

North of the Cirque de Troumouse the *Parc National des Pyrénées* terminates in the nature reserve of the Néouvielle massif. This is a land of granite peaks and blackened tarns, difficult of access and, consequently, little visited away from the high and narrow valleys that shyly encroach its outer limits.

Rare paths, there are, and one or two huts, but the major peaks may only be reached by long approach marches. It is a region of somewhat savage isolation, a mountain wilderness where one may experience the solitudes known to the early pioneers, where hard climbs abound and, on the

Néouvielle Massif:
Left to right-

Turon de Néouvielle,
Pic des Trois
Conseillers,
Pic de Néouvielle.

Pic Long, the highest mountain set entirely in the French Pyrenees, a dramatic North Face leers its challenge with an almost arrogant austerity.

Ramond explored here during his Revolutionary exile; de Chausenque climbed Pic de Néouvielle in 1847, and has a pass named in his honour, and the Pic Long received its first ascent from the Duc de Nemours and Marc Sesquet. There was a long period of inactivity in these regions until Roger Mailly and Robert Ollivier came in search of blank walls on which to practice their craft. In 1933 they studied the fine North Face of Pic Long which rises steeply from the Lac Tourrat in bands of granite and broad icefields, and their resulting ascent was a difficult line which skirted the upper icefield before scoring directly up to the summit itself. The face sweeps almost 600 metres to the lake, a severe yet tantalising piece of architecture, and it is not unnatural that since its initial ascent a number of equally demanding lines have been traced upon it.

Of the other principal summits of the region - Turon de Néouvielle, Pic Badet, Pic de Campbieil and Pic Méchant - although giving the appearance of complex, or somewhat arduous ascents, each contains one or more easy routes to the summit. Pic Méchant, for example, whose name suggests a certain formidability, falls steeply on its southern side, yet allows an uncomplicated route to be made from these southerly slopes. Of the medium grade routes available here, the northern arête of Pic de Néouvielle offers a long and exhilarating traverse, while on the eastern edge of the Néouvielle region the North Pillar of Pic d'Arbizon holds one of the most difficult routes in the Pyrenees. The mountain, of no great height, stands above pleasant green pastures, but Paul Bouchet and the brothers Ravier forced a magnificently bold, almost direct line up the 300 metres of this shadow-spreading pillar on 11th September 1968. It has subsequently become acknowledged as one of the finest of Pyrenean routes, and an outstanding example of the type of challenge that awaits the attentive modern *Pyrénéiste*.

*

The Spanish Canyons

Immediately to the south of the Cirque de Gavarnie there lies a barren highland, a landscape of contorted limestone blocks suggesting in their weathered desolation the terminal stages of mountain decomposition. It is a dry, soulless region; lifeless, monotonous, decaying under the power of an enervating sun. In its savage and decimated acres it broods hostility, it rejects man's fleeting intrusion ... and conceals until the very last moment any possible hint of the glories to be found deep below. And yet there, deep below in the valley of the Arazas river - the Ordesa Canyon - some of the richest scenery in the whole of the Pyrenean range is to be found.

Few mountain regions can match the romantically wild scenery of this dramatic canyon, split as it is by the tempestuous river which drains the south-western slopes of Monte Perdido ... 'With every step you go deeper into enchantment'. The lower reaches, where the Arazas is joined by the Ara as it emerges from its own delightful and picturesque defile, are cloaked with a thick forest of pine, silver fir and beech. The open meadows here, and higher at the valley head, are starred with countless alpine plants, the lower shrubs fragrant, heady, alive with the buzzing of insects on a warm summer's day; but it is the staggering mountain architecture that fully arrests the attention; the wildly coloured castellated rocks, the vast soaring faces of chiselled limestone and the dark, moulded, mysterious ravines. The ochre hues, 'the ruddy pinnacles and bastions towering above the trees for a thousand metres' which seem for all the world like the backcloth to a Dolomite dream.

Ramond had a preview of its wonders after climbing Perdido. Alfred Tonnelle marched through the valley on his whirlwind journey of 1858, but it was Packe to whom credit is due for discovering the true value of its splendours in his explorations of 1860. Not a man to colour his writings with extravagent prose, it is nonetheless easy to detect his enthusiasm for Ordesa upon reading his account of an early visit which formed part of an extensive tour. He and his companions had descended from the Brèche de Roland, 'over the plateau of Millaris' and with some difficulty found their way through snow to the base of the Circo de Soaso. Whilst crossing the upper river, in full flood, one of the party fell in the water and lost his boots which were only later recovered by 'strenuous effort'. Beyond the enchanting stepped cascades known as 'Las Gradas' they spent a cold and uncomfortable night in a rough cave, but the morning held promise:

> '... truly grand is the walk down the valley. First we have a series of cascades ending in one (Cascada Franchinal) which rivals that of the Handeck, with much superior surroundings. Then come the magnificent walls ... rising above the forest zone ... capped with snow. On the left bank of the stream the rocky wall is continuous, but on the right and grander side the precipices recede in deep ravines to the main chain, forming two huge amphitheatres, of which the sides are almost inaccessible - first that of the Cotatoir, and then that of Salarous. By a rift in the ledges of the last it is possible to mount to the snowfields of Excusana, and so to the Brèche de Roland.

> 'Twenty years ago the Vallée d'Arras was scarcely known; it is now becoming a favourite resort as a hunting-ground. It is a noted haunt of the bear and bouquetin ... but for the artist and ordinary tourist it must ever have attractions which will repay a visit when these animals have become extinct.'

*

The earliest climbing practiced around Ordesa was that of the hunter of isard and ibex, ascents made in the pursuit of game. In the two 'huge amphitheatres' alluded to by Packe, a number of ancient pegs are still to be found, placed there by hunters - possibly E. Buxton, whose '*Short Stalks*' includes a section on Ordesa - and which facilitate ascents now, some one hundred years later. The Passets had their mountaineering instincts whetted by scrambles above the canyon, but so dramatic and awe-inspiring are the major faces that loom over the valley, that *Pyrénéisme* had long come of age before any *real* climbing took place here.

It was not until the spring of 1957 that the first major route was created; the vast South Face of Tozal del Mallo capitulating under the determined forces of a rope of five enterprising young climbers.

The south face rises sheer for something like 400 metres out of the darkened forest, glowing in the keen light of a Spanish day. On this face, over two strenuous days, Kahn, Blotti, Dufourmantelle, Jaccoux and Jean Ravier pushed their route with the aid of about sixty pegs. It was a remarkable

Ordesa: the superb South Face of Tozal del Mallo. Illustration by Whymper, from 'Short Stalks'.

achievement, but since then a number of neighbouring lines have been traced, all exposed and of great difficulty on this and the East Buttress. It has become the Spanish test piece.

On the western corner of the Circo de Cotatuero - '... a cirque so wildly beautiful, so different in fantastic grandeur' - there stands a high rock tower, the Punta Gallinero. A demanding route of three hundred metres, on rock similar to that of the Tozal del Mallo's, was made over a three day period - on 15th, 16th and 17th August 1961 - by Alberto Rabada and Ernesto Navarro, thereby showing the scope available for exploitation in this elysian world of verticality.

Again, west of the Tozal del Mallo, the enormous cliffs that comprise the South Face of Mondaruego, leering their challenge to those approaching along the Ara Valley, are no longer chaste and untouched. The central buttress of the long Mondaruego wall received the attention of Escos, Falo, Mustienes and Vicente in May 1964. Over three days they worked their way systematically up these airy cliffs to pioneer a hard, 400 metre route requiring a total of 23 hours of labour. Their route remains a severe test to those who visit this enticing sanctuary of colour and light in search of high quality climbing adventure.

*

Seen from the lofty summit of Monte Perdido the surrounding country has been gouged with deep trenches. Ordesa's canyon is one of these, but to the south the high, gently undulating escarpment appears to have been torn by gigantic pressures of primeval origin. Packe mused on the question:

'To the torrential action of the waters on the porous and somewhat crumbling rocks of the Upper Greensand I believe these singular gorges (Ordesa and Anisclo) owe their origin. Possibly the waters permeating the rock formed subterranean galleries, which in time fell in, and were enlarged by the stream incessantly cutting its way ...

Whether or not this be the true explanation of the singular formation of these rocks I leave it to others to determine; but whether for science, scenery, or sport, I am certain none will regret a visit to these magnificent and unfrequented valleys that lie south of the Mont Perdu.'

The Anisclo Canyon - the valley of the Rio Vellos - is even wilder than that of Ordesa; narrow, seemingly impenetrable, thickly wooded in its lower reaches and entered from above by a slender path that plunges steeply down the wall of the ravine. It was in the late 1870's that Franz Schrader pursued a detailed exploration of the gorge - although it remains comparatively little-known even today - and Packe chose to revisit it on one of his final pilgrimages to the range.

'Starting at five,' he wrote, 'we at once plunged into the deep gorge of the Rio Vellos, which may well compare with an American cañon. Forcing its way through this rift in the mountains for twenty kilometres, the river at last issues near the village of Escalona. For two-thirds of the way the pedestrian may, with difficulty, descend, keeping the bottom of the gorge, but for the last five kilometres it is absolutely impracticable ... For the first two hours our way lay through a virgin forest of box, yew, beech, and silver fir, many of them dead through age and prostrate upon the ground. In places the walls so overhang the stream as all but to bar passage; in others they recede in terraces, rising one above the other, and supporting on their ledges impossible fir-trees. Here and there for a few yards there is a more open turfy glade, but it is not grass but strawberry beds that carpet the soil, producing fruit the size and flavour only to be attained under a Spanish sun.'

Torla - with the cliffs of Mondaruego marking the entrance to the Ordesa canyon.

Monte Perdido

'Since names were first given to mountains', wrote Ramond of Monte Perdido, or Mont Perdu, 'never was one better named.'

From the northern side of the watershed Perdido is something of a 'lost mountain'. A few isolated summits reveal its position, but from many more it is hidden by the crowding frontier peaks, a briefly glimpsed dome of snow, an extension of a cloud-bank perhaps. From the entrance to the Estaubé valley it becomes visible; 'It is very apparent and nevertheless not very noticeable to those who are not on the look-out for it'. Elsewhere, in the north, it remains beyond detection and, consequently, in the early days of Pyrenean exploration there was no small amount of confusion as to its exact position. From the south, however, it is less of a mystery. There are countless distant towns and villages tucked among the contorted sierras from which the snows and gleaming icefields of Perdido may be viewed shimmering like some transient formation of bleached cumulus above the rolling highlands.

It may well be that the essence of Perdido's enigma lies in the fact that it is seen either from the isolation of distance, or not until one's nose is actually rubbed against it.

MONTE PERDIDO

FRANCE

Refuge de Tuquerouye

SPAIN

PIC du
MARBORÉ
3248

Lago Helado de
Marmoré (Lac Glacé)

CILINDRO
3325
Collado del Cilindro

N

Lago Helado

Refugio Goriz

MONTE PERDIDO
3355

```
0        500      1000
```
METRES

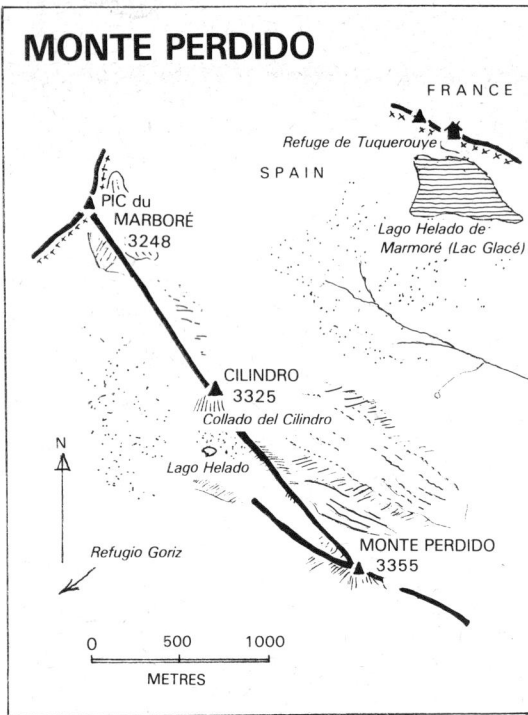

Monte Perdido is a huge limestone hulk of a mountain, the third highest in the range, and it dominates an impressive landscape. With the canyons of Ordesa and Anisclo radiating spoke-like to the south and south-west it looms its massive hub, rather barren and comparatively unimpressive, but south-eastwards there stretches the glorious valley of Pineta with imposing limestone walls down which spray delicate ribbons of cascades, and from here the lofty snows suggest something of the dramatic which may only be fully appreciated from a closer inspection. The mountain's full value is apparent once the upper glacial basin, suspended above the Pineta cirque, has been reached. From there the North-East Face is seen to best advantage; a scene of glacial tiers undercut by banks of gleaming séracs and ribs of seamed rock leading up to the hint of a distant fine summit. A mountain worthy of further exploration.

North of Perdido, and separated from it by a deep col, stands the curiously box-shaped Cilindro, which in turn leads to Pic du Marboré, the major summit of the Cirque de Gavarnie. To either side of Marborè the frontier curves in great amphitheatres, each in turn divided by long, north-projecting ridges. Monte Perdido is thereby ably protected by the castellations of its surrounding peaks and by the depths of its aromatic valleys.

*

Ramond's first attempt to scale Perdido was made in August 1797 in the company of his regular companion and guide, Laurens, and a largely incompetent party of thirteen. The 12th August dawned fine and full of promise as the expedition left the barn at Héas in which they had spent the night, and shortly after, as they entered the Estaubé glen, they had their first view of the mountain they sought.

'It consists of an oblique and blunted cone, and glistens with the eternal snows which rise above the high walls of the valley ... I pointed it out to my young companions,' wrote Ramond, 'who, seeing it so clearly, thought themselves already nearing the end of their journey.'

However, it was to take between four and five hours just to reach the head of the valley, and once there they met shepherds who advised the crossing of the Port de Pinéde as the only practicable way over the cirque's walls, '... which seemed to tower up to the very skies'. Ramond was not warmed with the prospect of this diversion, and boldly took to the tumbling cascade of ice which filled the couloir before him.

'We were obliged to step on to the snow and face the threatening *couloir* at the top of which we expected to find Mont Perdu. At first this was a mere game; the snow had a good consistency and a moderate inclination; and we all went on with all the confidence which experience of mountains gives. But we had not gone fifty steps when the inclination increased; and we could see that it continued to do so.'

Not only did the slope steepen considerably but the snow turned to ice, and the party - with the exception of two who descended - put on their 'cramping irons' and had recourse to use their

North-East Face of Monte Perdido.

'hatchets'. For an hour or so they made reasonable progress, but as the couloir became yet steeper so the party grew more tired and concerned for their safety. Two of the party attempted to climb the rocks at the side in preference to the ice, but without success. 'There was really nothing to fear,' said Ramond, 'except the discouragement of the party'. He continued, sensing that the top was not far, and giving encouragement to the faint-hearted by his example.

'The only question now, was how to triumph over an obstacle beyond which our imaginations showed us the top of Mont Perdu. We gathered up all our remaining strength. We mutually animated and encouraged one another. At each step that we took, we saw the distance lessening. The breach which had long been hidden from us by the edge of the glacier, reappeared in gigantic proportions, and already we felt the cold wind which rushed through the great opening. We hastened on, we pushed forward, and, out of breath, we reached the desired point. An exclamation of delight was uttered by all; but a deep silence succeeded at the sight of a new world, of the depths which separated us from it, of the glaciers which girded it round, of the clouds which covered it; a frightful and yet sublime spectacle by which our senses seemed over-powered.'

Rather than find themselves within striking distance of Perdido's summit, Ramond's party were astonished to discover that they were not yet even on the mountain at all, and instead, there before them the great face revealed itself in all its ice-caked grandeur. 'It signified nothing that I had seen it a hundred times at a distance; it appeared to me more fantastic than ever.'

'Cut out by the same scissors which have fashioned the flights of the Marboré, it presents a succession of steps sometimes draped in snow, sometimes covered with glaciers which at times overflow and pour themselves one over the other in large and motionless cascades, even to the borders of a lake of which the surface, still frozen, but freed from the snows,

Monte Perdido, rising above the Circo de Soaso at the head of Ordesa's canyon.

shone with a quiet brightness which heightened the dazzling whiteness of its banks.

'This lake, the desolate area in which it reposed, the mass of ice which bounded it on the south, the black walls which surmount it, the Cylindre and Mont Perdu towering up into a stormy sky, and that rocky, naked, and rugged enclosure, from one of the battlements of which we were contemplating the most imposing and frightful scene in the Pyrenees; all and everything defied comparison.'

The attempt ended here; Ramond and his companions were forced to return by way of the Port de Pinéde, but with the freshly-gained knowledge of Perdido's true defences he planned a second expedition to take place a month later. This attempt was more carefully planned, and the party much less cumbersome than before. It consisted of Ramond, Mirbel and Pasquier - who had both taken part in the first attempt - a Monsieur Dralet, Judge of Auch, and three guides; Laurens and Mouré - who also had been on the previous expedition - and Rondau. They spent the night in the shepherds' *cabane* at the head of the Estaubé valley, and at daybreak began the ascent of the couloir which would lead once more to the Bréche de Tuquerouye. Here the ice they encountered was even more solid than before, so much so that even the iron points of Ramond's alpenstock made little impression in its surface.

'It was like ascending a ladder of ice. There was no possibility of zigzagging, and so mitigating the steepness of the gradient. The angle of inclination continually increased, and the precipice continually grew more profound.'

The couloir continued to tax their strength and skills, and after two hours they had still only surmounted the easy portion of the route. They came to an arête, 'sharp as the blade of a knife, and separated from the rocks by a wide space that opened before us like a funnel'. Rondau led this section.

'A dozen steps carved in the ice took us on to this *arête;* but we had to knock away the cornices, and test the ice with heavy blows from our sticks, to assure ourselves that it would bear our weight. In this way we succeeded in advancing thirteen steps in twenty minutes, balancing ourselves on the slippery track, with precipices to right and left and behind us.'

A rest was called during which Ramond dropped his spectacles into a crevasse; he found himself wondering at the ease with which '... a feeble insect plays about ... where I have to hold on'. He studied the route ahead, grew concerned over his companions and their ability to advance, but then with determination resumed the climb.

'At every instant this ridge exposed us to fresh perils. Twice we were stopped by projections of rock which barred our path. We could neither go up nor down, but had to worm our way round them, at the risk of losing our balance and falling. Presently we found that we could follow the *arête* no further, and had no place of refuge except the rocks which we had at first supposed to be inaccessible ... Here, however, we had to hoist ourselves up from step to step. The first man was pushed up by the man beneath him. Once safely anchored, he, in his turn, gave the other a hand. The risks, in the two cases, were at least equal, even if the disadvantage did not rest with the latter, for those who were ahead could not make a false step without endangering the rest of the company, or loosen a bit of stone without sending it flying over the heads of the others. For my part, I was hurt rather badly by one of these falling stones, as I could only stiffen myself and let it hit me, my position not allowing me to get out of the way.'

This final piece of climbing took more than an hour, and it was during this that Ramond realised the summit of the 'lost mountain' was again to be denied him. Leading, he had turned to those beneath him and detected upon their faces '... a sort of sadness, produced by their long anxiety'. With characteristic concern for the safety of others in his care, he ordered a retreat.

Ramond then left the Pyrenees. He turned his back on the mountains to pursue his career among learned men in dusty rooms far away from glacial heights where only the isard roamed in freedom. It was to be five long years before the opportunity presented itself for a return. Monte Perdido still remained aloof, but Ramond's energies and ambition were no longer sufficient to be reigned to arduous, and quite possibly unproductive, adventures. As a compromise he called upon his old friend, Laurens, to accompany Rondau in seeking a route on his behalf.

On 7th August 1802, the two guides joined forces with a Spanish shepherd and actually completed the route to the summit, their ascent being made by way of the Col de Anisclo and the southern slopes. Ramond, thankful at last of the positive outcome, repeated the route three days later in the company of Laurens and his brother, Palu.

*

To the early Pyrenean adventurers Monte Perdido became a respected and much-prized outing. From Gavarnie it was accessible through the Brèche de Roland, with a night spent in the Spanish *cabane* of Gaulis which Packe described as '... a nest of filth'. Then, in the early 1860's, the Passets discovered the Brèche d'Astazou which gave '... far more genuine snow and glacier scenery, and occupies about one-third less time (than the rather circuitous Brèche de Roland route) so that travellers who have an invincible repugnance to camping out or sleeping in a small smoky hut can, if so minded, return to Gavarnie the same night'. Henri Brulle even managed to climb both Perdido and the Vignemale in the same day '... without having missed any of the meals at the hotel'. Even accounting for the direct access allowed by the Brèche d'Astazou it was a remarkable achievement.

After Ramond's pioneering effort it took a further eighty years before a new outlook among the *avant-garde* consolidated attention upon the broken and aggravated ice-face of the lost mountain. In 1888 the Comte Roger de Monts, after several preliminary attempts, succeeded in making the first ascent of the steep and dangerous North Face. His route, '... which every true ice-man will be happy to face', gained the lower glacier at its southern extremity by way of a rock scramble which made it possible to avoid the very real danger of ice-fall from the treacherous but gleaming séracs. The upper glacier was barred by a second, and even more formidable, ice-fall whose séracs were found to be impassable, and it was only by very careful and exhaustive exploration that a way was found from the 'grand plateau' to a low rocky spur beyond the glacier's snout. By climbing to the right of this spur, and thereby avoiding a difficult bergschrund, it became possible to mount the steep snowslopes which in turn led to the high wall of grey limestone lining the summit cone.

Célestin Passet was the leading guide on this exciting break-through, and the success of the venture was heavily dependent upon his great perseverance and cool-headed competence. But such was the unpredictable character of this face that on three separate occasions he attempted to repeat the climb with Henri Brulle, but each time the attempt was foiled by dangerous conditions above the 'grand plateau'. Eventually, however, Brulle and Passet did succeed in repeating the North Face, a route which Brulle was convinced was becoming more and more arduous.

> 'Several times', wrote Brulle, 'we found ourselves in great difficulties. The climb began on such steep slopes of ice that notches for one's hands were quite indispensible, the rope being useless and remaining on Célestin's shoulders; and, as he never cuts large steps, there was plenty of personal labour left for the others. Then came a complicated and dangerous region of séracs and crevasses, where the rope was an absolute necessity.'

After more than two and a half hours of work they were approaching the central, or 'grand' plateau when they found their way blocked by an enormous crevasse, '... as long and as wide as a boulevard'. This was only a part of their problems for before them there rose a wall of ice, '... absolutely disheartening, for it was vertical and its crest overhung'.

> 'Célestin himself, who, however, never recedes or yields when a problem of this kind has to be solved, was getting cross, and as for myself,' said Brulle, 'I felt very humble, when I heard scarcely disguised allusions to the mania and folly of certain tourists, who only care for mountain *casse-cou*.

> 'But nothing is perfect in this world, not even a wall of ice. After long researches Célestin discovered a kind of pillar, slightly detached from the ice cliff along its entire length. It was our only chance. So with infinite precautions we crossed a mass of broken blocks which formed inside the crevasse a series of more or less secure bridges, and Célestin, always the *'Deus ex machina'* between a dark abyss and a threatening sérac, managed to overcome, with his usual pluck, the thin and perilous crest of ice.'

Brulle, spearheading the Heroic Age, made a good many assaults on Perdido's challenging faces - he made at least seventeen complete ascents - and created a fine route of his own on the North Face, in 1896. He summed up his activities in vivid prose:

> '... an ascent of Mont Perdu in January, and others, in powdery snow up to one's neck, in freezing hurricanes, or in the calm serenity of the full moon, have left both my friends and myself the most delightful memories.'

*

Though the glaciers have withdrawn somewhat since the days of Ramond, and of Henri Brulle, the North Face of Monte Perdido retains its charm. The ice-polished basin at its feet is as wild and as barren as any region of these mountains, but the rearing bands of fretted ice which loom so threateningly above impress with their untamed and unpredictable grace. The routes which past masters so persistently laced on icefield and lofty wall of rock remain as respected outings for the modern *Pyrénéiste,* while a more recent challenge has been seized upon the great buttress that forms the left hand wall against which the glaciers abut.

This Esparrets buttress is a broad, roughly triangular block that is topped by the mountain's eastern arête, while its lower cliffs plunge to the grassy levels of the tranquil Pineta valley some two thousand metres below the summit. When viewed from the balcony leading off the upper reaches of the Pineta cirque into the glacial basin, the buttress appears to be broken into adequate terraces, yet the south-facing flanks impose problems enough, and it was on these that the Ravier brothers, Jacques, Jean and Pierre, spent two strenuous but rewarding days in August 1973 creating a superb mixed route. It is a route that enjoys the great variety of mountain scenery to be found in these quarters; from the splendid green pastures that give the Pineta its quality of tranquility and colour, to the graceful snows of Perdido's frosty breast by way of the airy buttress of tanned limestone; a route of imagination and diversity of form.

*

By its ordinary route from the FEM's Goriz refuge, the ascent of Perdido demands little more than a stiff, four-hour scramble. From the confines of the Bréche de Tuquerouye the sudden vista of snow and ice frozen in a motionless cascade is a revelation of impressionable impact, sufficient in itself to induce a sense of awe, an experience similar to that of Ramond in the balmy days of pioneering almost two hundred years ago, and from the summit an immense panorama of great complexity spreads itself on all sides. This bewildering, often dramatic, sometimes sullen country reveals itself in its many tones. Distant peaks, comforting in their recognition, invite further inspection. Others, anonymous and obscure, jostle in moulded massifs, while near at hand the gaunt cliffs of Cilindro offer prospects of a number of difficult routes. Far off, to east and west, lie beckoning summits jutting with snow-laden shoulders rank upon rank above barely-hinted valleys, until the warm southern breath of baked sierras and orange groves sets the horizon to recede into an uncertain imagery. Then only the cool glacial breezes of the threatening icefalls below form an awareness of the true identity of this, the lost mountain.

*

The summer grazing hamlet of Viadós,
situated below the vast West Face of the Posets.

The privately owned 'Refugio' here, allows much
wild country to be explored.

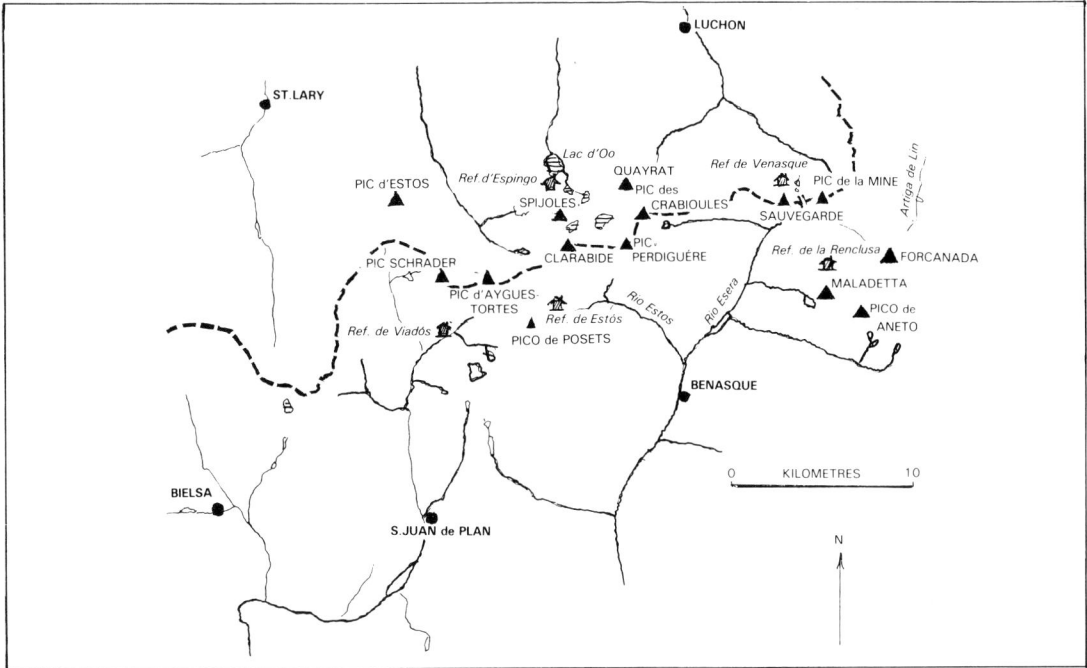

The Heartland map showing: LUCHON, ST.LARY, Lac d'Oo, Ref. d'Espingo, QUAYRAT, Ref de Venasque, PIC de la MINE, Artiga de Lin, PIC d'ESTOS, SPIJOLES, PIC des CRABIOULES, SAUVEGARDE, PIC SCHRADER, CLARABIDE, PIC PERDIGUÉRE, Ref. de la Renclusa, FORCANADA, PIC d'AYGUES TORTES, Rio Estos, Rio Esera, MALADETTA, Ref. de Viadós, Ref. de Estós, PICO de ANETO, PICO de POSETS, BENASQUE, BIELSA, S.JUAN de PLAN, KILOMETRES 0 10, N

THE HEARTLAND

The Frontier Heights

The frontier crest maintains its high average altitude throughout the central portion of the High Pyrenees, broken here and there by lofty passes - 'ports' - and crossed by no road at all between the Portalet above the Pic du Midi, and the Bonaigua to the east of the Encantados. There is, it is true, a brace of tunnels - those of Bielsa and Viella - and other proposed road links, but at the present this serrated crest retains a certain wild dignity, and in particular along that section which runs between the Cirque de Troumouse and the northern projection caused by the Vall d'Aran; an austere and savage grandeur.

With its noble collection of 3,000 metre summits guarding the frontier - Pic Schrader (Grand Bachimale), Clarabide, Gourgs Blancs, Seil de la Baque, Perdiguére, Crabioules, Maupas and Pic de Boum - there stretches the longest continuous portion of the whole frontier, a distance of about 30 kilometres. Linking these sometimes desolate peaks by way of straining ridges are several similarly provocative mountains that protect haunted corries and ice-bound tarns; Spijeoles, Quayrat, Lézat. Naked peaks, shadowed ports and coldly sinister draperies of reluctant snow and ice. A region of sullen mystery.

When Ramond crossed the Port d'Oo in his travels of 1787 there were even then cairns to show the route, and the Lac d'Oo already had become a favourite scene for the more adventurous of Luchon's spa visitors. Packe invested 'the beauties of this exquisite scene' with a touch of romance, too: '... the Lac d'Oo ... a deep dark basin of most cold clear water, fed by the ice streams from the mountains, and shut in on all sides except the north ... by precipitous rocks. Only at midday does the hot sun kiss its waters; and only at midnight does the pale moon glimmer on their bosom'. It is in the upper regions - 'amid very wild and snowy scenery' - that the semi-frozen tarns, with their tumbled-scree walls and glacial smoothed rocks, reveal their frosted origins. Long-released from the grip of ancient ice-fields, the mountains and their misted hanging valleys neverthless appear reluctant to dress themselves with the foliage of neighbouring massifs swelling

Lac de Portillon d'Oo
taken from Packe's 'Guide to The Pyrénées'.

a little south of the watershed. They remain aloof, inert, untouched save by the whispering vapours that daily stream with the rising and sinking of the sun.

Franz Schrader brought his mapping table, his ice-axe and his ambition, and explored the mysterious Aygues-Tortes and the Gourgs Blancs. Emile Belloc added his name to the region's exploration in the late nineteenth century, and Dr Jean Arlaud opened up the faces and ridges with routes in advance of his day. Among these were the arêtes linking Pic Lézat with the two Crabioules summits - a delightful traverse first completed with Charles Laffont in 1921 - and the West Face of Lézat, in 1926. In the forties several ropes concentrated on the many unexploited facets of these remote highlands; the western buttress which forms the wall of the Abadie-Arlaud couloir on Pic Lézat, was forced in the summer of 1942 by a four-man team; but at the fore-front of the major developments here was the Luchon guide, Francois Céréza. Céréza created new and difficult routes on the faces of Pic de Maupas, on the Grand Dièdre of Pic des Spijoles and the West Face of Quayrat. He revived interest in this central portion of the chain and inspired a new era of advanced climbing, establishing at the same time a limited reputation amongst the post-war *Pyrénéistes* on behalf of the frontier peaks.

With Céréza's undoubted example shining a spotlight upon the prospects available for exercise of a challenging nature, Couzy and Georges responded with their prestigeous 1948 route on the North-East Face of the high, conical eastern summit of Crabioules, a climb of technical interest in an austere setting. Then, in 1949, a seven-strong party tackled the long and ever-interesting arête that runs from the Aiguille de Clarabide to the Fourche, thereby demonstrating once more that these lofty ridges in themselves supply ample worthy diversions.

With the advent of extreme climbing in the fifties, the Raviers turned to the West Face of Quayrat - the face that had been pioneered by Céréza seven years earlier - and created a hard line of their own; this, in 1955. They similarly attacked the broad South Face of the little-known Pic d'Estos, which stands a little north of the watershed near the head of the Louron valley; and also established a novel outing by first climbing to the east summit of Clarabide by way of its northern buttress, then traversing the remaining two summits and the shattered western ridge. This last route combination which was made in 1970, though not excessively difficult, has the quality of variety and sustained interest which elevates so many of these mountain courses. But to the south the barren, cluttered slopes fall towards the colour and fragrance of the delightful Estos pastures, and then, beyond the glimmering stream, rise again to the broad, swelling heights of the Posets massif.

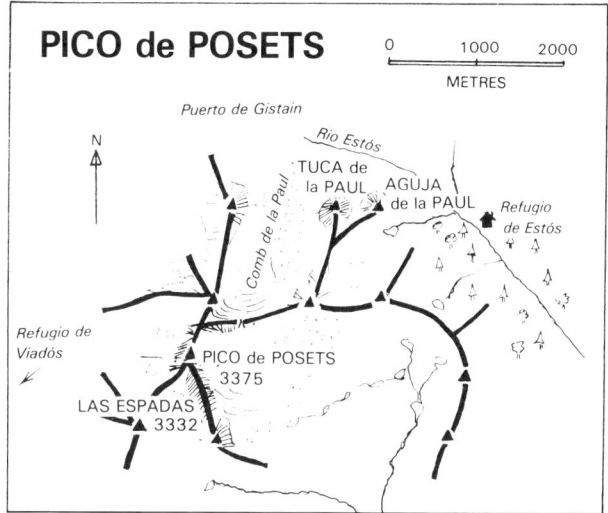

PICO de POSETS

Puerto de Gistain

Rio Estós

Comb de la Paul

TUCA de la PAUL   AGUJA de la PAUL

Refugio de Estós

Refugio de Viadós

PICO de POSETS
3375

LAS ESPADAS
3332

The Estos valley, which moats the Posets.

*The shattered
North Ridge of the
Pico de Posets.*

Posets

Bounded to the west by the lovely Cinqueta valley and to the north and east by the splendour of the Estós, the Posets massif is a swollen region of high straining ridges and encircling hollows, of cradled snowfields and weary glacial remnants; and sudden thrusting peaklets upon which the climber may find sufficient attraction. The grassy valleys with their sparse forests, their silver streams and foaming cascades contrast to a degree with the stark heights and the betraying rock of its crests. And between pastureland and summit ridge there lies a ' ... majestic desert of huge boulders, eternal snows, and frozen ponds.'

When Halkett, that most elusive and little-known of all the pioneers, achieved the first ascent of Pico des Posets on 6th August 1856, with Redonnet and Barrau as his guides, it is probable that his route led initially from the Estós and by way of the Valle de Perramo and the high col at its head in order to attack the summit cliffs from the south-east. This would have been the same route taken by Behrens on the second ascent, some three weeks later, - also with Redonnet and Barrau, - and by Charles Packe who was third to reach this, the second highest summit in the range. In those days the ascent was often preceeded by a night spent in the simple shepherds' hut situated roughly halfway along the Estós valley, and about which Packe wrote scathingly:

> 'The Cabane de Turmes is a rude stone cabane on the right bank of the stream, but the weather must be very bad indeed before you are driven to take shelter in such a smoke-grimed, filthy den.'

In the 1860's and 70's Packe and Russell were both drawn to the vast solitudes of the Posets where they bivouacked on numerous occasions, either alone or together, exploring by day the hidden tarns and unknown peaks, while '... enjoyable would be the reunion for the evening meal, and the story of each day's adventures.' Their explorations achieved a good number of fresh approaches on the main peak, as well as first ascents of several of its satellite peaklets. in January 1880 the Comte de Monts and Célestin Passet made the first winter ascent, but it was not until shortly before the Great War exploded across Europe that climbs of a more inovative character were worked out in various corners of the massif.

Henri Brulle spent the early summer of 1914 in the company of his son Roger - who was to lose his life in action in 1918 - among the many hitherto untouched pinnacles of the Perramo glen. They worked, too, on the peaks south of the Espadas ridge, climbing Pic de las Espadas by the southern arête and on the same day made the first ascent of Tucon Royo. This was virtually Brulle's Pyrenean swan song for, having rectified the poor maps of the area, and having created at least six new routes, war called a halt to adventures of a self-imposed kind, and he gave his energies in turn to the Red Cross.

It was Jean Arlaud, and members of his *Groupe des Jeunes,* who focused attention on the Posets when war gave way to a gentle calm. The main summit, Pico des Posets, was treated to several fresh approaches; from the south, by way of the 'triangle' formed by the junction of the two southerly ridges, in 1922 with d'Espouy and Maigné; by the North Face, in July 1927, and the West Face with Grelier, in 1935. On the secondary peak of Les Espados - first climbed by Louis le Bondidier, curator of the Pyrenean museum - Arlaud pushed new routes in 1924 and '27, but such was his enormous enthusiasm for the massif that hardly a corner exists without a route of his having been established there. The granite aiguilles that stand sentry-like above the Estós, and the shattered limestone and schistose ridges that hourly eject their waste down clattering gullies, have all been systematically devoured by the searching eyes of the GDJ.

The summit of Posets has the reputation of the finest view in all the Pyrenees. Standing in the very heart of the range, and unencumbered by crowding peaks of equal size, it certainly encompasses the very broadest of panoramas. Packe was enthusiastic about the contrast of glaciers close to hand and the distant yellow cornfields of Plan, and perhaps it is this contrast, more than the vastness of the scene, which gives it its individual character.

> 'Full in front', says Packe, 'a glorious view of abrupt mountains and snowy cols, from the Clarabide to the Perdiguére, and beyond this the menacing peak of the Sauvegarde, with the well-known ports of Venasque and Picade. To these succeeds the ponderous mass of the Maladetta, with the silver Pic de Nethou ... To the south the barren mountains of Aragon rise range upon range, till distance softens their ruggedness into a blue outline.' Harold Spender wrote of '... a sea of mountains ... fifty miles broad, tumultuous and anarchic, and yet motionless and at rest ... It is just a crowd of mountains.'

A crowd of mountains it may be, but each has its own peculiar charm, each its own sense of enchantment, and the Posets no less than any other.

*

The Maladetta Massif

Before Ramond's visit to the Esera in 1787 no-one had given serious consideration to climbing among the countless attractive peaks which make this one of the most delightful of all the regions south of the frontier. The Romans had discovered the sulphurous waters of the Baños de Benasque - then known as Vescelia - on the western slopes of the massif, and for centuries the high notch in the frontier ridge - the Port de Venasque - had been used for trade and in times of war, but the mountains themselves were seen in a different light than as a venue for adventure. Ramond was to alter all that. In the Alps the beginnings of mountaineering had given witness to the first ascent of Mont Blanc, and a fresh attitude was dawning. Ramond had already been fired with an enthusiasm for mountain exploration, and on the heights of the Maladetta this enthusiasm was to be confirmed without doubt; it was here that he translated de Saussure's dedication into Pyrenean terms.

> '... as we ascended the Penna Blanca,' he wrote, 'we beheld the enormous mass of the surrounding mountains unfolding itself; but ... all our attention was taken up by a very majestic summit which rose from the chaos behind us. From the heights of the rock, this summit may be seen in all its grandeur, covered with eternal snows, surrounded with large bands of ice, and overtopping every thing. It is the Maladetta; a mountain reputed inaccessible.'

The Maladetta, Mont Maudite, the 'accursed mountain', lies to the north-east of the Posets massif across the green moating valley of the Esera; a massif of considerable breadth and great charm and containing a high granite ridge of some 7 kilometres, hung with glaciers, sliced with dancing streams that drain hanging valleys, and adorned with glistening tarns. It contains no less than fifteen summits in excess of 3,000 metres and culminates in Pico de Aneto at 3,404 metres the highest peak in Western Europe outside the Alps, with the single exception of Mulhacen in the Sierra Nevada.

A secondary group, that of Mulleres, is welded to the massif to the east of the Aneto peak by a lateral ridge that dips to the Coll de Salenques, rising and falling in a simple amphitheatre to create the valley-head of the sterile wastes of the Valleta de la Escaleta.

Contained to the north and west by the curving pastures of the Esera, to the south by the equally charming Valhiverna, and to the east by a deep wilderness sliced by the hidden valley of the Noguera Ribagorzana, the Maladetta offers a mountain landscape of rare perfection.

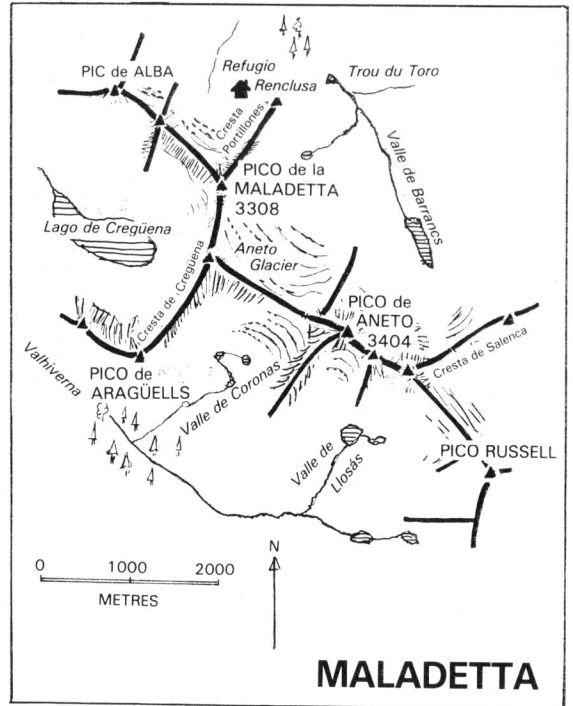

MALADETTA

Viewed from the north, as the climber emerges at the Port de Venasque from the shadowed confines of the French slopes, a broad panorama presents itself; the great bulk of the massif rises in a steady sweep of between a thousand and 1,600 metres above the valley, from stunted pines to the mouldings of graceful hollows sculptured by the action of glaciers long since shrunken to the flowing white napkins from which rises the long spine of granite. The granite spine has been blasted and broken into individual peaklets of varying qualities, but the most prominent feature is the long northerly ridge - known as the Cresta de los Portillones - which effectively divides the two main glaciers of the massif's northern slopes. Here lies one of the curious contradictions of the range; for the western icefield - the Maladetta Glacier - spawns the infant Esera which tumbles to the valley to flow west, then southwards, to the plain of the Ebro and eventually east to the Mediterranean; while the melt-waters of the eastern glaciers - the Aneto, together with the Barrancs and Tempestades icefields - grow to a considerable stream which plunges in a broad cataract out of the Plan de Aigualluts into an indolent hollow, best known as the Trou de Toro. From here, the waters then flow by courtesy of a subterranean passage beneath the limestone mass of the Tuca Blanca, emerging in the Vallée del Joeu as the Garonne, the most important river of south-west France, which waters the vineyards of Bordeaux on its journey to the Atlantic.

*

Before Ramond's visit the heights had received scant attention. The tranquil pastures of the Esera were nourished by the melting snows of summer, and threatened by avalanche in winter and in spring; to the peasant mind the naked rocks and solemn glaciers were indeed 'accursed', they held nothing of value. Ramond recognised this:

> 'The Maladetta has no accessible pastures: the izard inhabits only its lower region: the neighbouring valleys offer communications which render the ascent of its rocks unnecessary. It might therefore have been reputed inaccessible, because neither the shepherd, nor the hunter, nor the traveller, have any interest to examine whether it be otherwise.

The fine western ridge of the Maladetta.

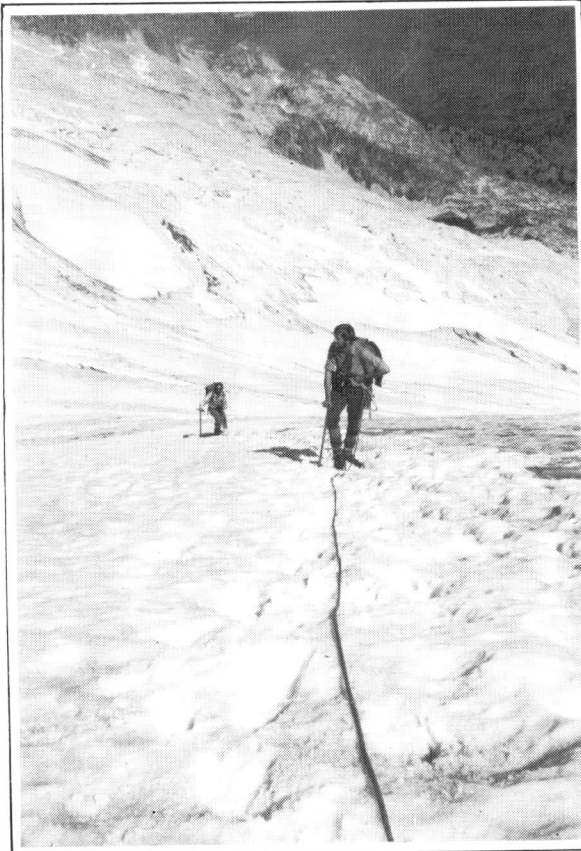

On the Aneto Glacier.

'The situation, the volume, the height and ices of this mountain, made a very lively impression upon me, and determined me to verify the pretensions which it might have to the title of inaccessible.'

Ramond and his party sought a route from the Plan d'Estan up to the snout of the Maladetta Glacier. They made their ways separately, Ramond remarking on the variety of flowering plants, describing with a lively prose the ever-changing face of the mountain; but only one of his guides Simon, joined him at the glacier, the other '... had been obliged to stop from vertigo and sickness.' Pausing only to study the glacier from its terminal crevasse, Ramond then continued his ascent alone, having no alternative but to turn Simon back since his 'cramp-irons' had been left with the second guide.

'I was obliged at first to keep along the borders of the glacier, and afterwards to ascend a part of it. I avoided it as much as possible, because its declivity was considerable, and its ices so hard as scarcely to give way under my cramp-irons ... Above this glacier, and at some distance from it I found a smaller one partly buried under the snow. I was obliged to pass over one extremity of it. Its inclination was greater

95

The short east face of the Pico de la Maladetta.

than that of the first, but less than that of a third, which I met with much higher up, and which is the last to be perceived in this region. Upon this last I stood as on a roof, and the sight of the precipice about me was most alarming. But when I reached the snows above it, my situation was still worse, for the snows are ever more moveable ... and when the inclination is considerable, the danger of their giving way is very great.'

The danger did not last long, and Ramond reached the base of the long ridge - probably below Pico de Alba. Clouds were by now streaming across the mountain, obscuring large portions of the ridge. He climbed on.

'These rocks were easy of ascent, but of a most frightful appearance. The eye finds no repose on any side, and rapid declivities only are to be seen, which plunge into the abruptest precipices.The earth seemed to fly beneath my feet, as I was advancing into the storms of an angry sky ... and the clouds of this region, retained by the mountain ... were struggling at present to pass the summit, and invade the north. I could see them rising from the bottom of the vallies like the swellings of an ocean ... and sometimes rolling on high in the atmosphere, and formed over my head in whirlwinds, could perceive them escape the barrier of the mountain, surround me with their mist, and bound upon the wind over the declivities below me.

'According to my estimate, I must now have been at the summit of the mountain, or at a little distance from it, but I could go no further so as to verify my situation ... Alone, and in a spot which the foot of man had never trodden ... I seemed to command the world.'

Ramond's pioneering effort, conducted mostly alone and in conditions that were far from ideal for such exploratory solo scrambling, was a considerable achievement. It is not known exactly where, along that splendid crest, he reached. He had not attained any major summit, of that we may be sure, but it has been assumed that the Collado de Alba, itself over three thousand metres above the sea, was won for the first time. Without doubt this outing did much to further whet his appetite for climbing, and in consequence Pyrenean activity was given a definite boost.

*

Frederic Parrot's great trans-Pyrenean ramble of 1817 revived interest and attention on the

*Pico Maladetta (left) and the western summits
from behind the Alba Crest. (Ramond's 1787 ascent route)*

Maladetta's icy, untrodden summit. He arrived in Luchon on September 25th, and there sought the services of Pierre Barrau as his guide. Four days later, after having spent the night in the crude shelter of the Renclusa - three walls of piled-up stones beneath an overhanging rock - they made their attempt.

The Maladetta Glacier was found to be heavily crevassed and with a light covering of snow, yet here their ways divided for a time. Parrot, having crossed the glacier direct, found a snow bridge over the bergschrund, but once over this he was confronted by a difficult rock wall. '... the rocky mass,' he wrote, 'constituted an impossible obstacle to an isolated individual.' Accepting the situation he made a traverse to rejoin Barrau below the Collado de la Rimaya. From there it was only a matter of seeking the easiest route up the rocks guarding the summit itself. Their success came with surprising ease; a major peak won without any substantial problem, thanks to the combined experience of both Parrot and his guide.

In those early days and, indeed, for a good many years to come, the rope was rarely used. Even for the crossing of crevassed glaciers its protection was shunned. In consequence accidents were bound to occur. In August 1824, Pierre Barrau was again bound for the Pico de la Maladetta under the patronage of two young engineers, Eduard Blavier and Eduard de Billy. Upon the glacier they found their route barred by a vast crevasse. Barrau probed the snow to one side, only to find that here the direction of the crevasse had made an undetected turn. The guide sank unchecked through the flimsy snow cover beyond hope of rescue. His remains, incidentally, were discovered in 1931 - more than a hundred years later - only a couple of kilometres from the site of his disappearance.

*

The death of Barrau was to have a profound effect upon the attitudes of climbers within the Pyrenees for a number of years. Glaciers and snowfields were to be avoided wherever possible; fears and prejudices gained further fuel when Cazaux and Guillembet plunged into the *Grande*

Approaching the summit of Aneto: behind - the Cresta del Medio, Maladetta and Portillone Ridge.

From the summit of Aneto: Mulleres Group and Forcanada.

Crevasse on the Ossoue Glacier, and the memory of these two isolated incidents was in part responsible for the devious route taken by the first men to gain the summit of Aneto.

It was in July 1842, that Albert de Franqueville and the young Russian officer, Platon de Tchihatcheff, joined forces in Luchon to organise an expedition determined to find a successful route to the summit of the Pyrenees. On 18th July they set out with their guides; Jean Argarot and Pierre Sanio, and two isard hunters, Bernard Ursule and Pierre Redonnet. That night, a night of wild storm, they spent at the Renclusa, and in the morning made their way to the Collado de Alba. From the col they descended to the lovely Cregueña tarn, then climbed out of the steep glen via the Collado de Cregueña in order to reach the Valhiverna. In that valley they passed the night in a squalid *cabane,* leaving with relief at daybreak to explore their mountain from the south.

Unable to avoid all the icefields, they emerged at the Collado de Coronas to be faced with an ascent of a very steep slope of snow which led directly to the airy blocks of the Pont de Mahomet. At 9 o'clock on the 20th July, 1842, Aneto had been won.

Four days later Tchihatcheff - jubilant and enthusiastic - returned to the summit, but this time his route led directly across the broad Aneto Glacier from the Renclusa, the route adopted now as the *voie normale.* His companions on this occasion were Laurent, Redonnet, Ursule and Sanio.

*

Aneto became a popular ascent, and the number of visitors to Luchon who made the excursion through the valley of the Pique to the Hospice de France, and then over the Port de Venasque, increased annually. In 1858, the youthful Alfred Tonnelle entered the Esera. On the 16th July, he made the ascent of Aneto - the 34th - and caught sight of the double-pronged Forcanada gracefully dominating the Escaleta. He went away for a while to explore elsewhere, but returned to climb Sacroux on 27th July, and Sauvegarde on the 29th. Forcanada beckoned, and with Pierre Redonnet as his mentor he entered the tortured wastes of the Escaleta on August 1st.

An attempt from the west failed, but on discovering a col in the southern ridge - later to be named Collado Alfred in his honour - a possible route showed itself. After an exciting scramble, and the crossing of a ridge '... like the Pont de Mahomet' Tonnelle and Redonnet stood upon the summit. Two months later the young poet had returned home to die of typhoid.

More than Aneto or Maladetta or any of the summits of that grand massif, it was to the Pic de Sauvegarde that the majority of visitors were drawn. Not a towering peak of individual character, it nevertheless offers a superb viewpoint from which to study the Maladetta and even the Posets massifs. It is, in a way, the 'Brevent' of the Pyrenees, standing above the Port de Venasque on the frontier ridge, and offering a short scramble from the port itself.

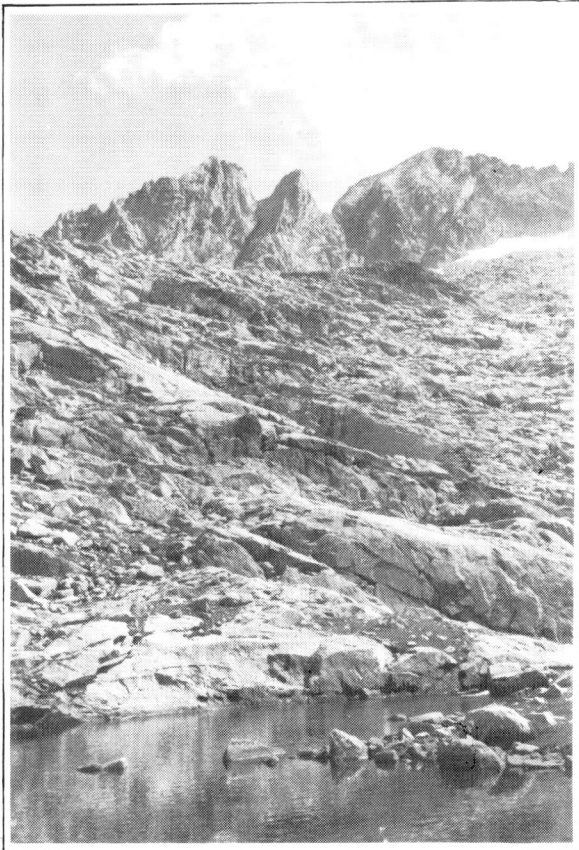

During one of his earliest visits to the range, in 1859, Packe was accompanied by Archdeacon Hardwick who slipped, whilst descending the Spanish slopes of the Sauvegarde, and was killed. Some time after this accident a path was cut on the southern side of the Port de Venasque to the summit, and an enterprising Spaniard installed there to levy a tax of one franc on all who used it.

Pico Forcanada (2881m)
at the head of
Valleta de la Escaleta.

Packe was responsible for opening the uncharted corners of the Maladetta for climbing. He wandered everywhere around the massif, probing the mist-shrouded corries where nestled silent tarns, taking measurements from rocky belvederes and making the first ascent of countless peaklets; his observations forming the basis of the first detailed map to be drawn of this region. Often he travelled alone save for the companionship of one of his dogs, sometimes he had with him fellow enthusiasts from England, and at times he was joined by Russell.

Russell similarly created new ascents there, and his memory lives on with a peak (3205m.), a brèche and a cluster of tiny pools bearing his name.

Henri Brulle found one or two rocky spires upon which to exercise his passion, and the brothers Cadier maintained an interest in the early years of the new century, as did the Viscount d'Ussel, but once again it was the splendid determination of Jean Arlaud that led to routes of a higher standard being established.

Arlaud's routes displayed true virtuosity; they ranged from the rather long traverse of the Cresta dels Estatats - which runs from Pico Estatats to the Pico de Aragüells - to the ascent of the Forcanada by its eastern arête. He climbed the North Face of the lofty Pic de las Tempestades, North Face of the neighbouring Margalida, the South-West Face and Arête of Pic Russell, the aiguilles that separate the Llosas and Coronas amphitheatres, and North Face of Aneto. In four glorious days in the summer of 1930, he created major new routes from the GDJ camp beside the Cregueña lake. On 27th July, he climbed the Tuca Blanca via the Tuqueta arete, on 29th Pic Maudit - Maldito - by la Diagonal, and on 30th, laced the 'crest of the fifteen gendarmes' on Pico de Alba. It was a period of great productivity, an era of sustained activity in which Arlaud's *Groupe des Jeunes* played a leading role.

*

The Maladetta, and the neighbouring massif of the Mulleres, are not, on the whole, rock climbers' playgrounds. Climbs there are, but they do not seriously challenge the superiority of the Pic du Midi or the Vignemale or Ansabère regions. Only the North Face of the Forcanada - climbed by Jacques, Jean and Pierre Ravier, with P.Bonnenfant in 1969 - offers routes of any length and of serious difficulty. What the climber does find of considerable appeal is the fine choice of swelling arêtes that grant traverses of great interest amid the most enchanting of landscapes. Such outings may be undertaken with a wide range of settings and with the possibility of numerous variations and diversions. With so many lofty crests departing from the main granite spine to create intimate cirques and little-visited hollows, the options are vast indeed.

As early as 1882, Brulle, Bazillac, and Célestin Passet recognised the wealth of possibilities and undertook a spirited traverse from the Tempestades to Pico de Alba, crossing over the summits of Aneto, Maldito, Maladetta and its western peak; from start to finish - at the Hospital de Benasque - a total of fourteen hours. In 1912, Jean d'Ussel, with Castagne and Haurillon as guides, made the first crossing of the Tempestades arête; ten years later Arlaud and Laffont claimed the Salenques arête, and in 1934, Ollivier and Wild linked the two to create a major traverse (AD sup.) of about seven hours duration on delightful granite.

By virtue of its height, and the broadness of its terrain, the Maladetta makes winter, too, an ideal season for activity upon its flanks and airy summits. Aneto received its first winter ascent from Roger de Monts as early as 1879, with a second shortly after from Maurice Gourdon, but yet again it was Arlaud and his companions from the GDJ who took the lion's share of pioneering laurels in the 1920s and early '30s.

*

While the impressive heights, the glacial draperies and alluring ridges of the surrounding mountains offer an undeniable attaction to the visiting climber, the valleys themselves that receive the benediction of their waters and their protective shelter, respond with a wealth of flowering plants and a rare sense of tranquility. For two centuries mountain travellers have expressed a certain wonder at the perfection of the upper sanctuary of the Esera.

Ramond spoke of the streams '... uniting with each other in the meadow, the one descending from the snows of a high valley, ... the other ... rolling in long cataracts.'

J.D. Forbes wrote of '... bare rocks with only scattered pines, savage in the extreme.'

Harold Spender considered it to be one of the most deserted valleys in Europe, describing it as '... the valley of silences, where sounds neither the voice of man nor the rustle of woods, nor any murmer of waters, but only the Esera creeps modestly along.'

For centuries nature was left to her own devices, only the shepherd's influence intruded and the pastures with their tiny pools and their terraces of fragrance remained quite unspoiled by the transient passage of climbers in search of exercise. But ours is an age that is geared to the domination of man over his environment, and the Esera can no longer be seen as a sanctuary of peace and unchecked perfection. A road, bulldozed from the south, has brought with it the spoils of urban prosperity; the clutter and waste of lowland man, the shame of modern civilisation. Here, beneath the dazzling snows of the highest of all Pyrenean mountains, among the flowers and withered pines, beside the bubbling streams and the curious hollows that devour immature rivers, the climber and the man in search of the last of nature's fortresses will find a lesson that must be learned ... before it is too late.

The Esera can teach it.

*

The upper reaches of the Esera valley.   *Photo: Keith Sweeting*

Tuc de Saboredo (2840m) left,
Agulle d'Amitges (2665m) right.

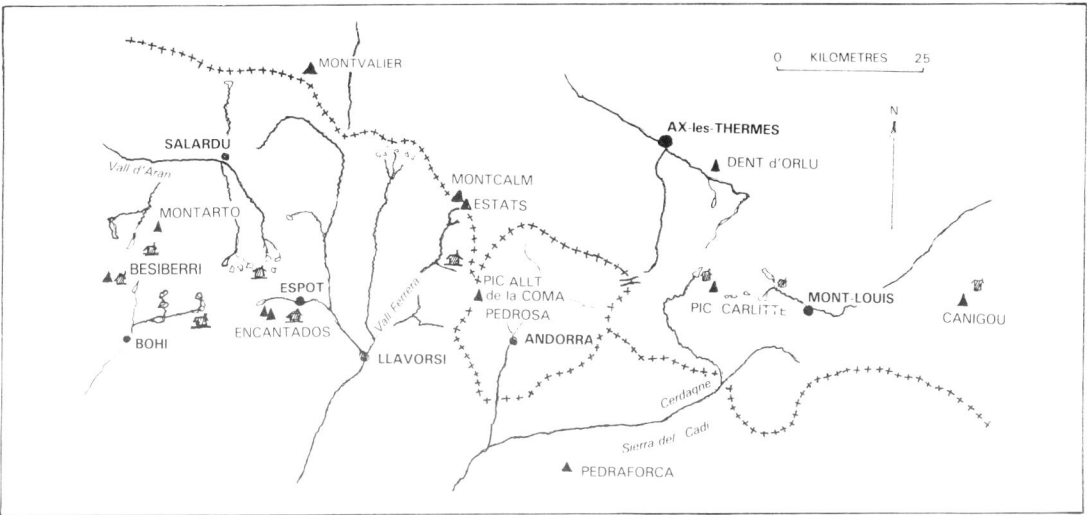

THE EASTERN HEIGHTS

After the Posets and Maladetta massifs the mountains gradually lose height, and with it a certain amount of their grandeur. Those glaciers which remain are seen to be insignificant draperies, and all but the most elusive pockets of snow drain away as summer adopts its air of Mediterranean brilliance. And yet, in many ways, this eastern sector of the range retains a spell of enchantment; the splendour of its fragrant valleys attracts both botanist and walker alike, while there are specific peaks of unarguable magnetism that lure the climber with their pleasing, seductive promise. There are isolated aiguilles and frowning gorges, granite wastelands lit by the golden fire of flowering broom, semi-arctic tarns unaccountably frosted in the full-bodied warmth of July, pine woods and pastures alive with the shrill buzzing of cicadas eased into eloquence by the sun. Wild boar shuffle uneasily through the trackless forests. Heavy bellied and somewhat inelegant, ptarmigan remain undisturbed under cover of low-growing shrubs. Villages, eyeless and deserted, cluster here and there in remote corners, abandoned to the winter storm and the unchecked ravages of the strangling briar. Rivers, swollen streams, and vigorous mountain torrents rip and roar down their ancient courses, gouging dark defiles where the diffused spray encourages a primitive vegetation.

From Aneto to the sea, massif succeeds massif, each with its own individual character. If their summits, on the whole, lack the questionable distinction of advanced altitude, the complete highland landscape does not withold diversity of form or colour, and the idyll of a number of these regions, scarcely altered since first they rose alarmingly from the depths of that limpid sea to be dressed by the seamstress of Time, protect their secrets from man. It is a region of colour, of grace, where the mouldings of hill, mountain and valley are brushed with a mellow dignity. The eastern heights, whilst offering in certain areas all that the tourist eagerly seeks, at the same time maintain upland valleys and rock-girt, brooding peaks where the foot of man rarely treads. It is a sector rich in its contrasts.

*

Aigües Tortes/San Mauricio

Eastwards from the deep valley of the Noguera Ribagorzano there lies a wild, chaotic landscape of discarded tarns and barren screes, of dark woodlands and sun-bleached crags; a landscape of delight, little-visited and mysterious. Above bewildering deserts of scattered boulders, scoured and

103

polished by lost glaciers and now coloured here and there by gnarled alpenroses, rise several peaks whose ascents are worthwhile; and the green valleys that form its limits and make tentative inroads on the very edges of the wilderness, offer attractions of their own. The northern boundary, for example, is the broad and sunny Vall d'Aran, whose pleasant checkered meadows and crowded grey villages are almost unique among the Pyrenees; while to the south stretches the Noguera de Tort, the valley of Bohi. Here, in three small villages, are to be found four lovely examples of early Romanesque churches, but higher, up-stream beyond the woods and ancient, troubled moraines, the valley is lost among its parental heights, it opens as a huge bowl protected by a crescent of rocky peaks where the tarns and jaunty ridges mark this no-man's land of obscure mountains. Trout rise of an evening from the glassy lakes, and on the mountains themselves flowers colour the ledges with their seemingly delicate blooms.

Packe was among the first to explore the area, but then only cautiously, keeping mainly to the western edges. In 1860, according to Russell, he '... passed into Catalonia, explored the Montarto, and scaled one of its many peaks, or rather 'teeth''. Seven years later he visited it again, and climbed one of the summits of Besiberri. Russell, too, made the ascent of the Pic d'Avellaners - which he referred to as Besiberri West - in 1869, but neither completed their explorations. 'At that time,' wrote Russell, 'the topography of these lost regions was veiled in such mystery ... that Packe himself might have had difficulty in explaining his route of ascent.' Franz Schrader travelled through the area after Packe and Russell, as did Maurice Gourdon, but so extensive, and so wild is it, that large pockets remained locked in anonymity for many decades after these initial pioneering efforts had been digested.

Towards the eastern limits the twin summits of the Encantados, formidable-looking as they rise from the pine woods that surround the lake of San Mauricio, are conveniently reached from the village of Espot. According to the legends of the locality, two shepherds once were tending their flocks on a Sunday morning when they heard the summons of Espot's church bells calling them to worship. Ignoring the call they were turned instantly to stone, and today they stand in grey solemnity demanding, in their own muted fashion, the attention of rock climbers. First to heed their call was a Franco-Spanish rope comprising Fontan de Négrin, Isidre Romeu, Raphaël Angusto, Francois Bernard Salles, and Bartholomé Ciffre who, on 29th August 1901, climbed the higher of the two summits. The following year Henri Brulle, René d'Astorg and Germain Castagné pushed

The high ridge of Besiberri commands a rugged, but charming landscape.

*A rock climber's playground. The twin
Encantados peaks dominate the landscape.*

the first route to the Petite Encantat, considered by some as one of the most difficult of the major Pyrenean summits, but one whose routes are susceptible to stone-fall.

Though the Encantados- or Encantats - are the best known and perhaps the most attractive summits of the region, they give their name to a distinct area; the Sierra de los Encantados, the Enchanted Mountains, and this they truly are. '...these terrible mountains called the Encantados, eight and nine thousand feet of jumbled rock, with high lakes where no footfall comes, and enormous chasms brimmed with mist, and torrents that plunge from inaccessible cliffs and fill the air with ice-cold spray ... the traveller will know the meaning of awe when he comes to the Encantados.'

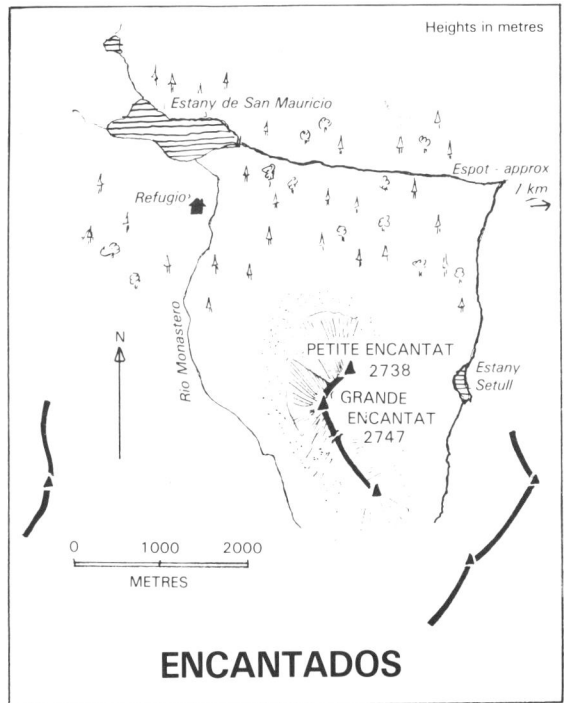

105

Aiguilles de Trevessany, in the Montardo wilderness.

Louis Le Bondidier, who had made several first ascents in the heart of the range, studied the North-West Arête of Besiberri in the summer of 1905, and succeeded in making its first passage; but here, as elsewhere among the Aigües Tortes, Montardo and San Mauricio region, it was the influence of Jean Arlaud, operating from the lakeside GDJ camps of the twenties and thirties, that saw the development of the long ridges and short but demanding faces of these peaks. In 1926, he had a bumper season. As one of a rope of six he made the north-south traverse of the Besiberri peaks; an excursion that was destined to become one of the classic routes of the area. He was active on the Aiguilles de Trevessany, whose solid granite gave a number of invigorating lines; and then the North Face of the Gran Pic de Peguera. On another occasion he found success on the lower of the Aiguilles de Ratera, as well as pointing out numerous possibilities to the members of his eager group.

The region, enchanted and enchanting, gives rise to so many possibilities. With their lakes and woods and wild, hollow cirques, the mountains contain their appeal. The thrusting needles of the Agulles d'Amitges offer difficult routes. The Gran Pic de Calomes, '... a noble mountain,' has an airy east ridge of granite balanced between precipitous slopes. The Pic de Coma lo Forno, at the southern end of the long Besiberri ridge, grants encouraging views over the whole country; views which at long last give logic to the apparent disorder of the tarn-spattered wilderness below.

Everywhere, the tarns, the little cradled lakes so typical of the Pyrenees in general, and here in such evidence to bring relief to a sometimes sullen corner, to sparkle reflections of peak or turf-soft bank, linked one with another by a thread of silver. They complement the woods and stark, brazen crags, and help create an image of tranquility. Yet in many instances the more accessible lakes have seen the manipulations of man. Some have been dammed for hydro-electric purposes, and when their waters are drained there remains a scene of dejection; mud lying naked to the sun, and half rotted trees in the midst of decay. But so numerous are the tarns, and so wild the terrain, that he with the will to wander is bound to find adequate compensation around the next corner, or over the next pine-topped bluff. And then in winter the whole country offers a majestic landscape for touring by ski, with the additional challenge of some aggressively demanding climbs to be had, and the traverse of one or two lofty ridges.

*

The Vall d'Aran holds no great peaks of its own. This is country for walking in, for the study of a delightful flora, for visiting the many side valleys that have attractions of their own, where hillsides are tended and the dancing streams drain hidden tarns. And north of the frontier ridge the mountains sweep down into narrow, steep-walled valleys, heavily forested but with pastures cut from their basins and above the tree line, dotted now and then with stone built hay barns, the slopes grazed by sheep that appear for all the world from a windswept ridge like so many distant maggots.

It comes, then, as something of a surprise to find that a little north of the frontier there stands a mountain, not three thousand metres high, that boasts a broad and spectacular East Face all of 800 metres from base to summit, a face offering an exposed and delicate route to match some of those better known farther to the west.

Montvalier was climbed, according to legend, in the 5th century by Saint Valier, and resembles in appearance the much-lauded Pic du Midi d'Bigorre. From the valleys that provide access it is often hidden from view, but '... its advanced position ... renders it conspicuous from nearly all the plain of the Haute-Garonne, and the number of points from which it can be seen sufficiently evince what a panorama it must command.' Packe, whose second edition of his *Guide* includes details of its ascent, continues: 'Though a mountain of only the second rank, it is impossible to persuade the peasants of Ariége that it is not the highest point of the chain.'

Packe's route was a long and strenuous ramble from the village of Seix, south of St.-Girons, where reasonable accommodation could be acquired. It led through the darkened gorge of Estours, cold in the early morning, and then up into the bright shining hillsides that come sweeping from the rather austere heights of the mountain itself. He crossed the Col de Cruzous, ignoring as he did the horrors of the eastern face's precipices, and made the final scramble from the west. In this manner Montvalier provided a pleasant day's exercise, but of more recent times the faces, sombre yet alluring, have attracted *Pyrénéistes* of another order.

The North-East Face, with its 600 metres of cold forbidding rock, was won in 1967 by the guide Maruzzi, some ten years after an attempt by a rope of three men had been overwhelmed by a tragic accident.

In 1970, Louis Audoubert led the first North Face winter route, and the following year he returned again with the East Face in prospect. On 29th and 30th September, 1971, he inaugurated the superb *voie du Trou Noir,* sharing his rope with Marc Galy, Alain Blassier and Monique Rouch. A fine, somewhat exposed route, this, it has been graded TD inf., and boasts several individual passages of IV, and one of V, and has since become regarded as one of the recommended classics of the Eastern Pyrenees. Thus, rather unexpectedly, the heights east of Aneto do present the occasional challenge worth the pursuit of ambitious rock men, while at the same time modestly concealing their more alluring and provocative aspects behind a facade of forest and delicate pasturage.

*

The Noguera Pallaresa rises near the head of the Vall d'Aran. After making a curious diversion it flows southwards through the high country to make its tortuous way among the baked sierras, eventually to discharge into the Mediterranean. A little south of the Bonaigua Pass it becomes swollen by the streams that flow out from the Encantados; and shortly after, where Llavorsi lines its banks, receives the accumulated waters that come rushing from the wild highlands to the east; that patch of empty country which separates the Aigües Tortes and its enchanted mountains from those of Andorra. A vast stretch of lonely and lofty mountains furrowed by dark, flashing ravines; of dense forest and glittering lakes, all under the patronage of the highest of all Catalan summits, Pica d'Estats.

*

*Estats Montcalm.
The Sotllo valley.*

Estats and Montcalm

A number of deep green valleys, largely unsung and wandered by few, pave the way to the remote crests that mark the international frontier. The Vall de Cardos, until the coming of hydro-electric engineers, was seemingly as untouched as on the day of Genesis; its upper tarns and spray-filled gullies and tumbling brooks visited only by the isard from one year to the next. Now rough tracks lead enticingly upward, where the clearings are bright with spring flowers, where the air is rich with the scent of new-mown hay and damp turf, and the lost villages of Spain lie far below, unbelievably small, unbelievably distant.

The Vall Ferrera is clothed with thick, resinous forest, its stream forging in alternate stretches of wild foaming cataract and indolent shallow, its upper levels showing felt-soft hillside and rambling mountain. Above the north bank of the stream, and protected by the converging hills on either side and a tangled vegetation below, the charming acres of the Sotllo valley lie tranquil in the sun. Here, in a calm spangled idyll, the sweeping ox bows of the trout stream trace a level plain with cotton grass dancing in a stray breeze. Light and feathery cascades dash the rock walls with their distant echo, and above the natural carved steps of the valley lie the attendant tarns to reflect the blank south-westerly face of Pica d'Estats.

Estats (3143m) is the most easterly of all Pyrenean three thousand metre frontier mountains. It blindly surveys this region of lost valleys from a high, curving ridge which makes for a fine traverse or two, linking as it does several of its individual summits above a distinctly savage area of discarded boulders and channelled scree. The last remnants of glacier persist in protected corners, and one or two ice-choked pools retain a sense of arctic desolation. Yet the ridge itself remains mostly snow-free throughout the summer; bare rock to contrast the luxury of turf and tarn of the lower slopes.

A little to the north-east of Estats broods the '... huge flattened dome' of Montcalm, an unattractive peak when viewed from the south, but one which is usually taken in the same outing as the Estats, requiring little more than half an hour's walk one from the other. From these two summits the views of the surrounding country are indeed spectacular, ranging over Andorra, off to the Maladetta, the rolling heights of Spain and the low-lying plains of France washed with a sea of forest green.

During their cartographic surveys of the eastern portion of the High Pyrenees in 1827, Coraboeuf and Testu climbed to both summits, took readings of the neighbouring peaks, and left a cairn behind. Two years later de Chausenque followed with an ascent of his own, made from the Granges d'Amperrot to the north. From here Montcalm appears a much more respectable mountain, and one that earned an early reputation for a certain majesty which was built upon by successive travellers; travellers, it might be added, who cared less for mountain heights than for pedestrian journeys in more accessible valleys.

Packe recommended the ascent to follow from the north, mostly by de Chausenque's route, but he also suggested that a route could be found from the east by '... the gorge and rocks of Riufred' although it would invariably take longer than a direct attack via the *cabanes* of Pujol and Subra. At the turn of the century the Viscount d'Ussel made a point of studying the less hackneyed slopes of Montcalm, and as a result climbed it by the Riufred wall.

While neither Montcalm nor Pica d'Estats offer important or challenging routes to climbers in search of sport of a demanding nature, their mutual charm lies as much in the remoteness of their approach as in the richness of their summit panoramas. Twin peaks, significant only from a distance, they nonetheless capture a certain flavour of solitude and tranquility; their valleys, their gleaming tarns and blossoming levels contain pleasures of their very own.

*

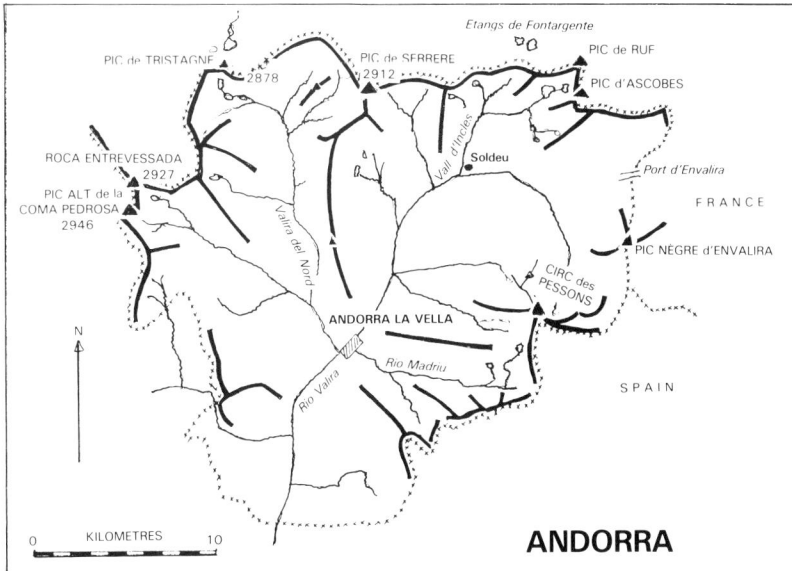

ANDORRA

Andorra

The tiny mountain-locked principality of Andorra is bordered by several delightful stretches of country; the valleys of Ferrera and Tor in the west, and those that feed the Aston in the north among them. In his classic, rambling handbook on the Pyrenees, Belloc was extravagant in his praise for the upper reaches of that valley which cups the Etang de Fontargente - the lake of the silver waters - on the French side of the ridge which blocks the Vall d'Incles, but there are a number of similarly enchanting corners tucked conveniently well away from centres of tourism and industry, and these remain for the man with a rucksack and a tent to discover for himself.

None of Andorra's summits reach the three thousand metre mark, the highest being that of Pic Alt de la Coma Pedrosa (2946m.), but the long curving ridges that make such an effective border, maintain a regularly high average altitude with the lowest pass - Port d'Incles - nestling at 2,252

Andorra:-
The Vall d'Incles.
Port d'Incles on
the left.

metres. The one single exception to this lies in the south-west of the country where the Valira's weighty torrent has cut a deep and narrow defile, and it is here that Andorra breaks into Spain. Elsewhere rise the welcoming mountains, carved here and there by sometimes dark and steep-walled valleys, with flower-spattered glades and glittering waterfalls; sometimes with sweeping, tended pastures, now and then with gaunt crags and boulder-strewn little amphitheatres.

It is a country that long suffered the lethargy of the south. It had been isolated with self-imposed discipline from the economic advances of the rest of Europe and, with the influence of Spain's ancient traditions, found it difficult to emerge from a stupor of mediaeval peasantry. Not so very long ago its economy relied upon tobacco growing, smuggling, sheep and cattle farming and, to an extent, to the working of iron foundries. Yet when change came it came with a headlong rush and the bounty of unchecked tourism swamped all other considerations, so that today Andorra's main central valley is a sacrifice to the brash commercialism of Western Europe, its ancient crude stone houses overshadowed by towering concrete hotels and glaring neon-lit stores. However, it is still possible to escape these horrors, and once away from the Valira the mountains and their valleys have much that remains unspoiled; the peaks have their rugged facades, the valleys their colour and distinctive flora.

*

Early travellers to the Eastern Pyrenees often avoided Andorra since their journeys were mostly limited to the French valleys, and a diversion into the principality would involve a somewhat arduous walk over one of several high passes. Those who did make the effort, however, invariably remarked firstly upon the primitive living standards of the population, and secondly upon the richness of its flowers and the simple grandeur of the mountain scenery. Almost one hundred and fifty years ago, the Hon. James Erskine Murray came this way and recorded the impressions which he received on his rambles.

'From Urdino to Canillo, the pedestrian will find it a toilsome stage; but the beauty and aspect of the mountains will encourage him on his journey. We spent several hours in crossing the ridge of mountains which separate these two villages. The mountains upon the Canillo side of the ridge are covered with the finest pasture ... and the valley of Embolire at their feet produces as fine crops of grain as I ever beheld.'

Elsewhere he was deeply impressed by the wild flowers:

> 'Their profusion was such, and their various tints and colours so beautiful, that in stepping among them I almost felt that I was committing sacrilege.'

Although Packe concentrated the greater part of his efforts to climbing and exploring in the centre of the range, he made one or two journeys through Andorra in order to increase his overall knowledge of the Pyrenees in all its variety. He made few ascents here, contenting himself to finding ways over the frontier ridges. In those days, before the roadway over the Envalira, the traveller on foot was likely to enter from France across the Port de Soldeu, or the Port Dret a little farther to the north. From these two passes '... Andorra looks ... a wild and rugged country,' and contrasts the 'formidable, black, ragged range of peaks which guards the frontier of France.' Nowadays, the main road which slices the country whisks countless thousands of tourists from the Envalira to the fleshpots of Andorra La Vella in a constant stream of exhaust fumes. It follows the ancient mule track that served as the principality's major highway for centuries, and about which Harold Spender wrote in 1898:

> 'It was generally about three or four feet wide; sometimes there had been efforts to clear it of stones, and even now and again to level it ... Small problems arose now and again when we met other mules loaded with hay ... for the path sometimes runs high above the stream bed, and nothing intervenes to save the mule in case of a slip down the steep and precipitous bank towards the stream.'

Forty years later litttle had changed, and it was not until Les Escaldes that the path became a road, and '... there was a sort of smell of 'modern developments''.

The mountains here held little attraction for mountaineers who preferred to seek the challenge of those loftier and more defiant peaks farther to the west, and local Catalan climbers were mostly left to explore on their own. Many of the summits demanded no more than a pleasant grassy walk, on others moderate rock work was required. One of the finest of Andorran peaks, Roca Entre-vessada (2927m.), supplied rock for climbing, as did Pic de Pessons which commands a very fine little amphitheatre of tarns and waterfalls, and above the gaunt and barren Vall de Juclar with its lichen-patterned boulders, the Pic d'Escobes on the frontier ridge.

This is a country for the mountain walker rather than the climber in search of the last great problems. The high valleys retain charms of a tranquil nature and there are countless ridge walks that may be attempted without the encumbrance of a rope. But, as in all mountain regions, there will always be the surprise crag, the defiant gendarme bristling with promise. The

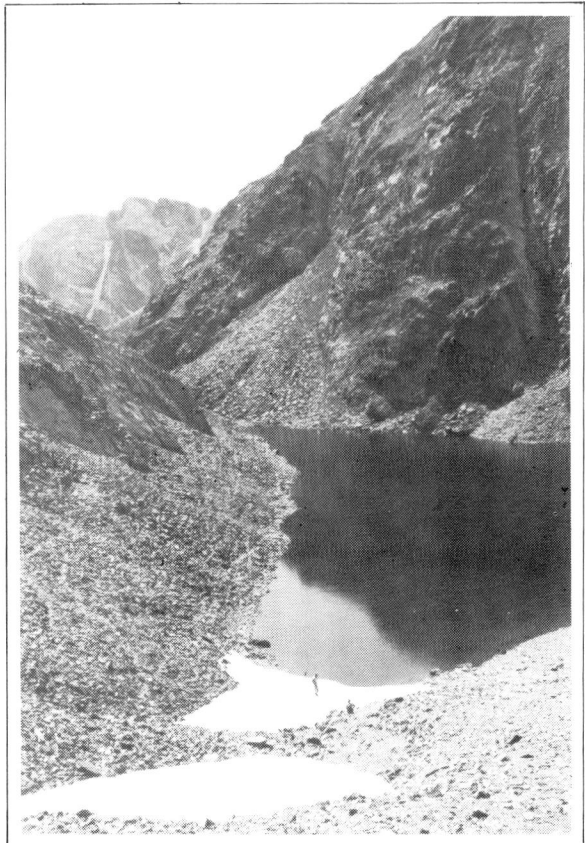

Beneath Andorra's highest mountain, Coma Pedrosa, lie several trapped tarns.

multi-day tour of Andorra by its frontier ridges is a circuit worthy of consideration, a circuit likened to the traverse of the Cuillins, only half-a-dozen times as long and one that is seldom completed.

And when winter descends on mountains and valley alike Andorra opens its doors to the modern downhill enthusiast, while away from the beaten piste there are peaks that may be tackled on ski with the silence of a resting landscape and the brilliance of unchecked distance as the lure.

*

The Carlitte Massif

From the eastern ridges of Andorra's heights an attractive display of peaks and valleys spreads itself away in the north-east. Unlike the heart of Andorra, unlike the downland hills of the Cerdagne, the Carlitte massif is truly wild country; a rugged, high plateau from which a number of granite peaks swell, sometimes bleak and austere, sometimes compelling in the non-conformity. They offer few temptations to the climber seeking extreme lines, and in this they are similar to the mountains of Andorra, but there the similarity ends. Rather they are mountains to repay the attentions of the modest scrambler, the man to whom a day's exercise on unmarked and unsung crags grants satisfactions of a less-demanding nature. There are, no doubt, pitches to be found of all grades of difficulty, but primarily the Carlitte is a massif to explore at leisure, best from a wilderness camp set beside an isolated tarn with only the trout for company.

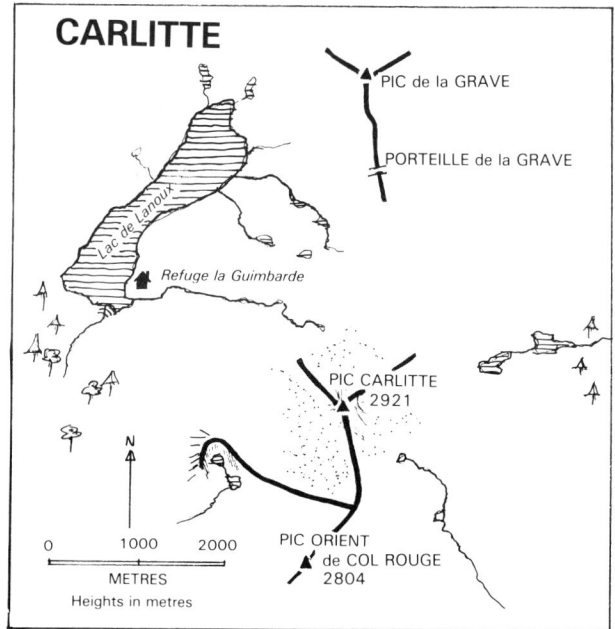

CARLITTE

PIC de la GRAVE

PORTEILLE de la GRAVE

Lac de Lanoux

Refuge la Guimbarde

PIC CARLITTE
2921

N

0   1000   2000
METRES
Heights in metres

PIC ORIENT
de COL ROUGE
2804

Both Packe and Russell scratched at the region in the 1860s. They climbed Pic Carlitte (2921m.) by different routes; Packe, in his own inimitable style, gaining as much satisfaction from the discovery of a dwarf wallflower among the schistose rocks of the summit, as in the manner of the actual ascent. Their attentions strayed to neighbouring peaks, but little could be found to divert their affections from the higher peaks in the centre of the range, and the area was left for others more fully to discover. Consequently the 'heartland' remained *terra incognita* for some time. There were no guides in this eastern sector of the Pyrenees beyond the occasional fisherman prepared to forsake the pleasures of an indolent stream for the ascent of an inhospitable mountain, and then rarely other than the Pic Carlitte itself. Indeed, at the turn of the century it was difficult to find someone at any of the neighbouring villages who even knew which of the mountains was Pic Carlitte. There was little, then, to lure the adventurous climber of a century ago from the obvious possibilities of the Pic du Midi, or of Gavarnie, and even today the untamed centre of the massif, where collections of tarns lie cradled in the hollows of all but the highest ridges, remains little known and generally unrecorded.

Packe and Russell both returned in due course for a brief reminder of the massif's wild interior, and Packe made at least two further ascents of Carlitte, on one of which he took the young Haskett-Smith along. 'This imposing but not difficult peak,' he wrote, 'the highest in the Eastern

North of Pic Carlitte, the ridge forms a strange plateau - the Pla du Carlit.

Pyrenees, rises abruptly from the east shore of the Lac Lanoux.' It has become a popular excursion, but no less worthy for the number of enthusiasts who find their way to its summit. Difficulties are minimal and the views from the ridges are vast and justifiably applauded. The panorama encompasses the heights of Andorra to the south-west, with the Pics Négre standing out well with their fretted edges appearing rather more seductive than on closer inspection; the broad checkered meadows of the Cerdagne with its wall of the Puigmal sprawling green and friendly to the south, while in the east the distant Canigou rises among a welter of swollen heights. Near at hand the surrounding countryside appears sullen, '... savage and desolate, not a tree in sight,' with other peaks suggesting opportunities for scrambles of a similar nature.

On the flanks of the massif stretch valleys of immense charm, each of which offers access to the rugged interior. On the west the valley watered by the Lanous river comes down the slopes of Pic Carlitte and the long Col Rouge ridge in pastures gay with birches and golden broom, from transparent lakes and silver trout streams. At its mouth, below the Col de Puymorens, spreads the untidy village of Porté offering limited accommodation to those who would concentrate their energies on this corner of the mountains. From the north, the wooded Vallée d'Orlu climbs from the elegant boulevardes of Ax-les-Thermes into hidden recesses of the massif, and thereby presents a grand introduction to landscapes of shattered, spiky peaklets growing ever higher and more bewildering as the path advances. Along this valley come climbers with an eye for the impressive Dent d'Orlu (2220m.), a South Face of enormous attraction, rising from the woods with an air of brazen honesty. The eastern limits of the Carlitte region are bordered by that cool basin of the upper valley of the Aude known as Capcir. Formigueres, a winter resort, allows an approach to be made along the curving Lladure, whose tributaries spring from an idyllic spattering of tarns around the eastern slopes of Pic Peric. And from the south, the infant Tet draws the walker through forest glades and pastures lush with flowers, to emerge into a landscape of mountain and moorland and yet more dazzling tarns and graceful corners of upland wilderness.

It is, then, on its sloping eaves, a country of fragrance and of colour. The interior, by contrast, is quite barren and savage; '... a sterile waste of granite sprinkled with mountain tarns.' At one moment there are dwarf pines and flowers, the mountains rising shapely, snow dressing their

Pic Peric, from the Lac de Bouillouses

sheltered faces; then the path tops a rise and ahead '... is a vast treeless waste, covered with scanty grass and scattered with masses of stones of every size, ranging from granite blocks to small fragments. No words can describe the melancholy solitude and forlorn destitution of those vast denuded Pyrenean deserts.'

*

At the turn of the century a modest bout of mountaineering fervour saw an attempt on the Dent d'Orlu by Jean d'Ussel, and in 1905 Prosper Auriol, a leading member of the CAF's Canigou section, made the ascent of both Pic Carlitte and Pic Peric on ski, with Marcel and Henri Spont. Of the many remaining peaks of the massif each received its share of attention in the years that followed, but it took the brothers Ravier to bring a modern emphasis of *Pyrénéisme* into the area. During the 29th and 30th May 1966, Jean and Pierre Ravier accompanied Grenier and Bouchet in establishing the 900 metre South Face route on the Dent d'Orlu. With this climb, an entirely free route with the overall grading of TD, and with several pitches of V and V superior, climbers were made aware of the possibilities that existed even in this remote corner of the range. The Dent d'Orlu is admittedly something of a rarity, and while sport of a modest nature may be found on assorted peaks; on the Roc Blanc and the Pic Col Rouge, on Pic d'Auriol and Pic Pedrous, it is not so much for individual climbs that the Carlitte massif deserves recognition, as for its challenging tours and lengthy circuits. It is a backpacker's paradise in summer, and during winter, when streams are silenced and the mountains grow in stature above levelled frozen lakes, ski-touring opens the whole region with possibilities for major traverses of peak, valley and low-slung col.

114

Then, as the snows melt with the warm air streams of spring, the bursting flowers that light every hollow and greensward, the miniature shrubs that cling to discarded boulders, and the cushions of fire that burn against the primitive screes bring to this granite wilderness all the fragrance and exuberance of a botanical paradise. Every season has its day.

*

Few would choose the Cerdagne for its mountaineering prospects. This great, sunny plain is the only broad and flat-bottomed valley to be found in the Pyrenees; its scenery unlike any other to be seen throughout the range. At its eastern end it is crowned by the Col de la Perche, and from this point comes sweeping a steady slope of meadows and villages and lines of trees; fields of corn and meadowlands where horses graze, and gentle watercourses born among the crags of the Carlitte or the moulded uplands of the Sierra del Cadi, but now disciplined for irrigation. An open, smiling valley, trapping the sun while clouds boil upon distant peaks, it has a number of side valleys, spreading in from the southern rolling downs, that have for a century and more been applauded for their wealth of alpine plants. The Vallée d'Eyne is among the best of these, and the botanist and mountain walker alike would be well rewarded by a visit. At its head stand the easy Pic d'Eyne (2786m.) and Pic de Finestrelles (2827m.), both offering extensive panoramic views.

Next to the Eyne is the Ségre with its shafted gorge suggesting a fine assortment of climbs to the energetic scrambler driven from the higher mountains by bad weather. And the Puigmal, highest summit along these green, pregnant hills, has been subdued for winter skiing. The main skiing grounds of the Cerdagne are, however, situated on the slopes of the outlying Carlitte region where several villages have recently become adapted to cope with the peculiar demands imposed by an influx of winter visitors. Elsewhere the villages of this most gentle of valleys reveal a distinct sense

Pic Carlitte from the Lac de Lanoux

of contentment, and the whole area has an easy pastoral air about it, a satisfaction wrought by warm bright summers and dry, crisp winters; so different from the true mountain communities whose very existence depends on the whims of turbulent nature.

*

Beyond the Col de la Perche the streams flowing down the flanks of the Carlitte, draining the mountains and easing from their marshes and cold pools, unite to form the Tet, the river whose clear ambition is to flee the heights and speedily find the calm of the Mediterranean. Beyond Mont-Louis the Tet's valley cuts deeply into the mountains whose lower reaches here are again dressed with dark woods, but before long these mountains fall back away from the river, they lounge in a languid complacency until at last they plunge into the sighing waters of the sea.

Cutting a channel through the mountains to the south runs the Tech, and between these two rivers there stands the last peak of distinction, the Pic du Canigou (2784m.).

The Canigou towers over the plain of Roussillon, a bold and ostentatious mountain whose claim to character and substance has the effect of dominating a whole district. 'Like Etna', wrote Élisée Reclus, 'the Canigou is one of those mountains which rise vigorous as masters over a wide stretch of country. From below this grey pyramid, cleft with ravines, streaked with detritus between salient ribs of rock, of every tint, is not a whit less striking in aspect than the Sicilian volcano.' And yet the impression of isolation, which aided the belief years ago of its being the highest in the range, is not a convincing one for really the Canigou is only one section of a long block of united peaks and ridges fanning out in all directions, and a continuing part of that provocative mass which rose south of Andorra as the Sierra del Cadi.

In the valleys orchards run in tended rows. Then come the great forests that have for centuries been an important feature of the area. Above these the open mountainsides lead to the crests with their numerous plants, and the last gaunt cliffs of the summit. Here the ridges form a fine horseshoe with their plunging crags openly issuing an invitation for the climber to choose a line or two.

While the Canigou has long attracted tourists to its summit by way of an easy track, the three hundred metre wall on the north of the Canigou/Barbet arête presents opportunities for those climbers marooned away from the main peaks in nearby Perpignan. One particularly attractive route, and one which has become a respected 'standard' in recent years, is that pioneered by Sala and Bobo in September 1960. It is an elegant line traced on the sinister North Face of Pic de Barbet; three hundred metres of effort with a maximum difficulty of grade V superior, and a certain amount of exposure as an incentive to clean climbing.

*

Beyond the Canigou, beyond the last grey sun-blistered limestone hills there stretches the balmy Mediterrranean with its curving bays and beaches, and distractions of another order. The mountains of the Pyrenees return willingly to the waters of their origin.

*

*Agulles d'Amitges
seen here from the south.*

APPENDICES

*'If the tourist is sufficiently hale and hearty to trust to his own feet ... the interest of pioneering
one's own way will be found not a little to increase the pleasure.'*

Charles Packe

APPENDIX A
Notes for Climbers and Walkers:

Pyrenean mountains are ideally suited to the British climber who has worked his apprenticeship on the Lakeland fells, on the peaks of Scotland, or on Snowdonia's rugged crags. Their extent or range may not seriously rival those of the Alps, but what they do possess is an undeniable air of remoteness, a certain character that defies comparison with any other region. Their virtues are sufficient to repay the visiting enthusiast whatever may be his degree of commitment.

There are several considerations which may face the climber planning to visit the range for the first time: where and what to climb, how best to approach the chosen area, and where to make a base. The foregoing sections attempted to outline the history of mountain activity within the range and subsequently to trace the development of *Pyrénéisme* as a sport, and also to describe each of the main massifs travelling from west to east. Having thus produced a picture of the possibilities each area offers, this section now aims to present one or two items of practical information in an effort to answer some of those questions with which the climber is likely to be faced.

Whilst it is undoubtedly true that the majority of the mountains of the Pyrenees may be ascended without resorting to actual rock climbing techniques, the climber is favoured by as many grand and varied cliffs, faces, arêtes and aiguilles as he could possibly wish, upon which to pursue his sport. Taking the High Pyrenees again from west to east the most important areas for rock climbing are as follows:

1. The Aiguilles d'Ansabère, and on the nearby Petit Billare.
2. Pic du Midi d'Ossau, with a wide variety of routes of all grades.
3. Balaitous - mainly on its airy, shattered aretes.
4. Vignemale, North Face.
5. The Cirque de Gavarnie, its attractive walls and neighbouring peaks.
6. Ordesa Canyon - the main target here being Tozal del Mallo.
7. Monte Perdido's Esparrets Buttress, and one or two walls on Cilindro.
8. Pic Long, its North Face, and the North Pillar of Pic d'Arbizon.
9. Spijoles, Quayrat and Pic des Crabioules, on assorted faces.
10 Forcanada, North Face.
11 Encantados, Agulles d'Amitges and several others in the area.
12 Montvalier, and in particular its East Face.
13 Dent d'Orlu - the South Face.

Other peaks, other massifs have their own specific climbing 'problems' that will become evident to those with eyes to see and the necessary vision to create routes of their own. And away from the main areas that congregate along the watershed and international boundary, there are countless roadside cliffs and river-carved gorges that hold a quite astonishing array of tempting, entertaining lines, but which seldom make headlines. They remain for the visiting climber to discover for himself.

As for snow and ice it should be evident that these mountains can offer very little once winter's bounty has thawed. Only the ice cliffs of Perdido reveal possibilities that may be exploited during the summer. On the Vignemale the Couloir de Gaube's mixed route depends for its feasibility on the day to day conditions of the upper Ossoue Glacier. Elsewhere ice-climbing enthusiasts eagerly await the return of winter's frost. There has been a great upsurge of activity in recent years on many of the harder faces, and in particular on the cliffs of the Cirque de Gavarnie, by *Pyrénéistes* anxious to savour the delights of their mountains coated with icy veneer. In addition to those areas listed above for their rock climbing qualities, the massifs of Posets and of Maladetta offer great possibilities for winter outings of the very best.

It will be appreciated, too, that these mountains and valleys are invested with immense appeal to the walker. Every region is adequately served with paths or cairned routes to enable the rambler to wander in some degree of safety, and at the same time there are sufficient wild corners that will attract the seeker of solitude. For those who are drawn by prospects of lengthy tours from one region to another, this diverse and challenging range could scarcely be bettered. The ultimate in routes of this nature is the *Haute Randonnée Pyrénéene,* the 'High Route' which traverses the whole range from Hendaye in the west to Banyuls on the Mediterranean, in 46 stages. However there are numerous shortened versions, countless variations and massifs galore that grant all the prospects one could ever desire.

*

Centres

Unlike the Alps, where in so many instances the most attractive peaks seem to rise directly behind a convenient village, the Pyrenees reserve their more alluring features away from the scrutiny of hoteliers and tourist agencies. This is one of the range's appealing features; that to get the best out of a visit it is absolutely essential to turn one's back on the comforts of habitation and probe the inner sanctuaries.

Possibly the only French centre - as such - from which the climber may operate, is the village of Gavarnie. As has already been explained, it suffers the indignities of great concentrations of tourists by day, but at evening the village is peaceful, and after a day spent grappling with the pleasures of the cirque's walls, the hotels and bars are not so very different from those of the Alps. There are several small hotels in the village; the best-known of the larger establishments being the historic Hotel des Voyageurs which has seen the comings and goings of all the earlier pioneers; a good hotel, but no longer cheap, it has a reputation to sustain. '... the people who come to the place (Gavarnie) usually go away on the same day, and ... therefore there is some anxiety to please those who stop.' One or two of the houses rent rooms at a reasonable price, and there is now a small campsite at the southern end of the village and, at the end of the mule track at the foot of the cirque, the Hotel du Cirque makes a base for the man who likes to begin hard routes almost from the bedroom door.

Elsewhere on the French side of the watershed, transport is a necessity should a village centre be chosen as a base. Laruns, Cauterets and Luchon each have much to commend them, with hotels, rooming houses and campsites, but they stand away from the major peaks and consequently valuable time is given up to travelling to and from the chosen area. Each has its guides' bureau and equipment shops, but their prime attractions, so far as the active climber is concerned, is that they are ideal for restocking with supplies for the mountains, and they make convenient centres for the less-committed members of the family.

Laruns is attractively sited in a mountain-walled bowl below the Col d'Aubisque, and to the north of the Pic du Midi d'Ossau. From here, too, a long approach may be made to the Balaitous.

Cauterets is a spa town and, to a degree, a winter sports resort. It houses a large National Park centre with a fine display of stuffed animals and birds; and an information desk aimed more at the general tourist than the climber. From Cauterets the road climbs to the south to Pont d'Espagne - which has a small hotel and, a little beyond, camping - from which point paths lead up to the Vignemale's North Face, and south-westwards through the Marcadau valley to the Grande Fache.

Luchon, at the railhead of a minor branch line, is the obvious choice for the Maladetta-bound climber approaching by train from Paris. It is a fashionable watering place with bustling boulevardes, expensive hotels and boutiques transplanted from the classy quarters of Paris.

However, it also has a convenient market, bookshops stocking climbing maps and guides, and access via the Port de Venasque with the Maladetta and, via the Port d'Oo, with the Posets.

At other points along the French slopes there are countless villages and small towns offering limited accommodation. Several ski resorts have of late sprung up in former remote areas, each of which may be exploited by the summer climber and walker requiring comforts not generally to be had in a mountain hut. For the man determined to make the most of his time in the mountains there can be no real alternative to the choice of hut or camp. Of huts there are many; either club-owned or private. And for the camping enthusiast there can be few regions left in Europe that can rival the Pyrenees for their enormous wealth of idyllic wilderness sites. Here again it should be borne in mind that the camper carries with him the responsibility of ensuring that future generations of enthusiasts may similarly experience these wilderness areas in a natural, pristine condition. Each man's waste should be taken with him or disposed of with great care.

South of the watershed Spain, in common with the French side, has very little in the way of real mountain centres from which a climber may satisfactorily operate. Espot springs to mind as the exception, but then there are distinct limits to the repertoire of routes he may attempt. A small village, Espot has ambitions for grander things, and a growing ski industry is at present in the development stage. There are a couple of hotels and a good campsite; one or two bars, simple stores and a newly surfaced road along which the local Land Rover 'taxis' ferry tourists to the San Mauricio lake below the Encantados. These peaks, however, may be reached by an easy stroll from Espot, and are the main attraction of the village. The walker would probably gain more from a holiday based on the village than the climber, though, in view of the approach difficulties of some of the more alluring peaks.

Benasque has its attractions, and although it is expanding fast it retains a character of sleepy pastoral nonchalance. Both the Maladetta massif and that of the Posets stand up-valley from the village, but it would take a motorised hard-man to climb among them from a base there. Benasque, then, is best used as a stocking-up point rather than as a centre in itself, except for the walker who could happily travel out from its hotels for the valley walks, of which there are plenty to appeal.

At the mouth of the Pineta valley, south of Monte Perdido, Bielsa has a delightful village square atmosphere, but it is a crowded little place now that the tunnel link with France is open. It makes a base for botanical tours, but again it is too far from the main summits to offer a real option to the

Espot - village base for the Encantados

climber, but there is the large Parador state hotel, 'Monte Perdido' at the far end of the valley, and this could well be used as a short base from which to tackle Perdido's North Face, or the Esparrets Buttress. However, it is not particularly cheap by Spanish standards.

Westwards, and in the neighbourhood of Ordesa, lies the little village of Torla. Yet again, unless the climber has transport of his own, it is a little too far from the challenging heights to be really convenient, but it may be used as a restocking centre. It has several small hotels, rooming houses, and a campsite a short way up-valley. At the entrance to Ordesa stands another 'Parador', almost beneath the toppling South Face of Tozal del Mallo.

The comments with regard to the development of contemporary ski resorts in France apply equally to Spain. Mostly they are vulgar, expedient, jumbled and ugly. In many instances they fall little short of landscape vandalism, but since they are unlikely to be removed they may as well be exploited by the climber or walker who desires to see something of the country nearby. Thus some hotels will be found agreeable for a short stay, and some of these centres even have self-catering flats which offer a cheaper source of accommodation.

As has already been stated, the very best of the Pyrenees can only truly be appreciated well away from the roads, villages and towns. The climber, the walker, the man in search of the full mountain experience will do no better than to disappear into the heartland, and to unravel its secrets from the simple shelter of a climbing hut, or from the fragrance of a wilderness camp.

*

Further Considerations: The Western Heights

Huts: There are no refuges conveniently placed for climbs on the Ansabère needles, and the village of Lescun is some four hours walk away; consequently rough camping, or foot-of-the-climb bivouac are the only viable solutions.

Farther east the *Refuge d'Arlet* is situated in good walking country. It is owned by the PNP and has 30 places, and has a guardian in summer residence. Between the Aspe valley and the Pic du Midi two huts are useful: *Refuge du Larry* - west of the Col d'Ayous - is a small, limited-facilities refuge, again owned by the PNP; and then the idyllically-placed *Refuge d'Ayous,* set beside its lake that presents a double image of the Pic du Midi dominating the scene. This hut, yet again owned by the PNP, has 35 places and a summer resident guardian. Each of these huts is of more interest to the rambler than the rock man, as is the *Refuge du Club Pyrénéa-Sports* at the northern end of the Bious valley, a little above the Lac de Bious-Artigues. For most of the routes on the Pic du Midi d'Ossau the climber will use the fine *Refuge de Pombie,* the CAF's well-run hut set beneath the mountain's intimidating Pombie wall. It has a resident guardian from mid-June to mid-October, a full meals service in addition to facilities for self-catering.

It should be added that camping is officially prohibited in the vicinity of the Ayous hut, and limited to 48 hours in the neighbourhood of the Refuge de Pombie.

Additional sources of information:

Alpine Climbing, 1971 - includes details of selected climbs on both the Aiguilles d'Ansabère and Pic du Midi.

Alpine Journal, 1975 - an article on the PNP gives information about the Pic du Midi.

Alpine Journal, 1979 - an historical survey covers the main developments.

Climber and Rambler, July 1978 - contains an article devoted to the Pic du Midi.

Climber and Rambler, March 1979 - an article outlines a section of the High Route, and includes the region Ansabère/Ossau

The Delectable Mountains by Douglas Busk (1946) - presents an account of the first ascent in winter of the Pic du Midi.

Les Pyrénées - Les 100 Plus Belles Courses by Patrice de Bellefon (1976) - this book, in
French, is on the same lines as Rébuffat's classic 100 best routes on Mont Blanc. It
includes a number of routes on the Ansabère aiguilles and on Pic du Midi.

Montagnes Pyrénées by J.L. Pérés and J. Ubiergo (1973) - mostly historical.

Pyrénées 1876-1976 by Robert Ollivier (1976) - one hundred years of climbing activity.

Guide Books: Pyrénées Occidentales Vol 1 - Aspe et Ossau, published by Robert Ollivier is the
standard work, in French.

Pyrenees West by Arthur Battagel - Gastons/West Col, 1975 - details moderate ascents and
rambles covering this area.

Walks and Climbs in the Pyrenees by Kev Reynolds - Cicerone Press, 1978 - includes voie
normale on Pic du Midi, plus walking circuits.

Map: The 1:25,000 scale Parc National des Pyrénées No 1 - Aspe Ossau published by the
Institut Géographique National (IGN) covers both the Aiguilles d'Ansabère and Pic du
Midi.

*

Further Considerations: Ossau to Gavarnie

Huts: East of the Ossau Valley, in the wild jumbled country on the approach to the Balaitous,
the *Refuge d'Arrémoulit* squats on the northern bank of its icy lake. A small hut, owned by the
CAF, it has a temporary summer 'annexe' at peak times; some meals provision, with a guardian
during the summer period. To the north of Balaitous the main lodging place is the *Refuge de
Larribet*, about 2½ hours' scramble over the Port du Lavedan from Arrémoulit, but more easily
accessible from the north. CAF owned, it has places for about 35 and a summer guardian. It is the
main hut for climbs on the Balaitous, but the other CAF refuge, that of *Ledormeur,* is a very basic
shelter with minimal facilities.

For climbs on the peaks at the head of the Marcadau Valley, the Touring Club de France has the
Refuge Wallon. This is an old, somewhat rambling building, primarily an hotel, but with simple

*Refuge Bayssellance
one of the oldest
of the CAF's
Pyrenean huts, serves
the Vignemale.*

accommodation adjoining for climbers. A full meals service is available, and the position is an idyllic one.

For climbers aiming at the Vignemale there is the very fine *Refuge des Oulettes de Gaube,* the CAF establishment at the foot of the North Face. With a guardian on hand from the beginning of July until the end of September meals are available, but there is also a room set aside for self-cooking, and spaces for 46 people. Across the Hourquette d'Ossoue the base for walkers on a mountain circuit, and for those attempting the Ossoue Glacier route on the Vignemale, the ancient beehive hut, the *Refuge Bayssellance* is nonetheless well-kept, though simple, with self-catering facilities and meals when the guardian is in residence. About 40 places, and fine views.

Additional sources of information:

Alpine Climbing, 1971 - some hard routes are detailed on the Vignemale.

Alpine Journal, 1975 - information on both Balaitous and Vignemale is contained in the PNP article.

Alpine Journal, 1979 - contains an historic appraisal.

Climber and Rambler, May 1977 - includes a piece about Russell and the Vignemale.

Climber and Rambler, March 1979 - the High Route article outlines the traverse of this region.

Mountain Craft, Spring 1966 - contains a useful summary of the Pyrenees in general, but with specific information related to this area.

Climbers' Club Journal. 1969 - contains an article by Hamish Nicol on Vignemale and Balaitous.

Les Pyrénées - Les 100 Plus Belles Courses by Patrice de Bellefon (1976) - several classic routes outlined, and beautifully illustrated.

Montagnes Pyrénées by J.L. Pérés and J. Ubiergo (1973) - for historic interest.

Pyrénées 1876 - 1976 by Robert Ollivier - major developments.

Guide Books: Balaitous, and Pyrénées Occidentales Vol II- de la Vallee d'Ossau au Val d'Azun for the Balaitous region.

Pyrénées Centrales, Vol. 1.   for the Vignemale.
Each published by Robert Ollivier, with French text.

Pyrenees West by Arthur Battagel - Gastons/West Col, 1975 - covers Balaitous, Marcadau and Vignemale.

Walks and Climbs in the Pyrenees by Kev Reynolds - Cicerone Press, 1978 - gives ascents and rambles in Balaitous and Vignemale areas.

Map: Parc National des Pyrénées No. 2 - Balaitous. This IGN sheet covers the area at 1:25,000

*

Further Considerations: French Cirques - Spanish Canyons

Huts: Gavarnie has two refuges, one of which - *Refuge des Espuguettes* - offers a viable alternative to accommodation in the village. About two hours above Gavarnie to the south-east, this recently opened PNP hut commands a magnificent panorama, is well equipped, has a guardian in summer, and can hold about 56 people. Suitable for climbs on the Pics d'Astazou, Pimené etc. The second hut in the area is that below the Brèche de Roland, *Refuge des Sarradets,* a large CAF building, always very busy. Useful for Perdido, Marboré, Taillon and treks to the Ordesa canyon.

In the Estaubé cirque, the ninety-years old *Refuge de Tuquerouye* squats in the wedge of the Brèche de Tuquerouye with the classic vista of Perdido's North-East Face beyond. This was the first hut built in the Pyrenees by the CAF and it has recently been renovated.

At the foot of the Barroude Wall, on the eastern side of the Cirque de Troumouse, the CAF has

Refuge des Espuguettes above Gavarnie.

centre;
Brèche de Roland,
right
le Taillon,

opened the *Refuge de Barroude,* a small hut with about 20 places. To the north, among the turmoil of the Néouvielle massif, there are one or two refuges, but they are not particularly convenient for the major peaks of the area. The *Refuge Packe* is an old and very small hut, owned by the CAF, and is situated on the west of the region. The privately owned *Hotel de la Glére,* reached from Baréges, gives access to the northern sector. It is less a mountain hut than a hotel, has showers, heating and full meals service.

On the Spanish side, accommodation may be had in the Ara Valley below the Port de Gavarnie at *Bujaruelo,* a rough and historic hospice more suitable for the walker than for the climber on account of its position. Above Ordesa, and convenient for the *voie normale* on Monte Perdido, there stands the *Refugio Goriz,* opened in 1963 by the Federación Española de Montañismo (FEM). It has a summer guardian when meals are available, otherwise facilities are at hand for self-catering. Apart from Perdido, it is also convenient for climbs on Cilindro and Marboré.

Additional sources of information:

Alpine Climbing, 1971 - details and route descriptions of several climbs on Tozal del Mallo.

Alpine Journal,, 1975 - the PNP account referred to earlier continues with brief outlines of Gavarnie, and Néouvielle.

Alpine Journal, 1976 - Peter Steele's 'Pierre Vergez' article includes an account of climbing on the Cirque de Gavarnie.

Alpine Journal, 1979 - historical coverage of major developments.

Climber and Rambler, April 1976 - contains a 'fact sheet' mainly concerning Gavarnie region.

Climber and Rambler, Sept. 1978 - an article outlines the history of Perdido.

Climber and Rambler, March 1979 - High Route information to Gavarnie from the west.

Climber and Rambler, April 1979 - High Route eastwards from Gavarnie.

Mountain Craft, Spring 1966 - Pyrenean summary, with some specifics relating to Gavarnie, and Perdido.

Les Pyrénées - Les 100 Plus Belles Courses by Patrice de Bellefon (1976) - many of the best routes of of the area detailed.

Montagnes Pyrénées by J.L. Pérés and J. Ubiergo (1973) - much of interest covering the major peaks.

Pyrénées 1876 - 1976 by Robert Ollivier - of historic interest.

See also: Schuster's 'Men, Women and Mountains' (1931), Dorothy Pilley's 'Climbing Days' (1935), Irving's 'Romance of Mountaineering' (1935), and Norbert Casteret's 'Ten Years Under the Earth' (1939).

Guide Books: Pyrénées Centrales Vol. I for Gavarnie, Ordesa etc.

Pyrénées Centrales Vol. II for Troumouse, Néouvielle etc., both volumes, with French text, published by Robert Ollivier.

Pyrenees West lby Arthur Battagel - Gastons/West Col, 1975 - for Gavarnie, Ordesa, Perdido and Anisclo.

Pyrenees East by Arthur Battagel - Gastons/West Col, 1975 - for Estaubé, Troumouse and Néouvielle areas.

Walks and Climbs in the Pyrenees by Kev Reynolds - Cicerone Press, 1978 - covers Gavarnie, Ordesa and Perdido for modest ascents and various rambles.

Maps: Parc National des Pyrénées No. 3 - Gavarnie, and No. 4 - Néouvielle. The IGN 1:25,000 series. Necessary for north of the frontier. For the Spanish slopes Editorial Alpina publishes a sheet with brief guide-book, Ordesa, with 1:40,000 scale.

*

Further Considerations: The Heartland

Huts: For climbs on the frontier summits above the valley of Aygues-Tortes - Pic Schrader etc. - the only accommodation available is in the 'hotellerie' of the French Electricity Board's administration building at the power station, 'La Soula' above the Clarabide gorge. This *Refuge de la Soula* offers beds to climbers, with a full meals service at reasonable prices. The *Refuge d'Espingo,* an old hut with spaces for about 60, is situated above the Lac d'Oo, and makes a convenient base for climbs on Crabioules, Quayrat, Spijoles etc. For other frontier summits a little farther east, the CAF's *Refuge de Maupas* stands beside the little Lac d'Enfer to the north of Pic de Maupas. Not normally boasting a guardian its facilities are minimal. And east again, a little below the Port de Venasque, the small *Refuge de Venasque,* also owned by the CAF, has neither cooking facilities nor blankets, but makes an ideal bivouac shelter.

The Posets massif is served by two huts: *Refugio de Viadós* and *Refugio de Estós.* The first is privately owned, open from July to September with places for 40, and a full meals service. Ideal for climbs on the west of Posets, and for long walking circuits. That in the Estós valley, built by the FEM in 1949 and formally used as the main base for exploring the north and east of Posets, has recently been gutted by fire. A rough annexe has been provided, but meals are no longer available, and until such times as rebuilding is done, the best advice is to carry a tent and provisions from Benasque.

The *Refugio de la Renclusa* is situated on the northern slopes of the Maladetta not far from the lean-to used by the pioneers. The Centre Excursionniste de Catalogne (CEC) employs a guardian during the summer period, and then meals may be provided. Self-catering is possible in the annexe - an old and simple hut adjoining. This is the base for the *voie normale* on Aneto, Maladetta, Pico de Alba etc., and consequently becomes crowded in the high season. Places for 75 in the main building, about eight in the annexe.

On the southern slopes of the Maladetta are one or two simple shelters that may conveniently be used for a single overnight stay, but camping is the real answer.

The Estos Valley, base for climbs in the Posets.

Additional sources of information:

Alpine Journal, 1979 - for brief coverage of historic developments.

Climber and Rambler, April 1974 - contains an account of a 'backpacking' trip through the Maladetta and Posets areas.

Climber and Rambler, July 1976 - an article deals with the history of the Maladetta massif.

Climber and Rambler, April 1979 - the second section of the High Route terminates at the Renclusa.

Climber and Rambler, May 1979 - the High Route series deals with the area going east from the Maladetta.

Climber and Rambler, July 1979 - includes an article devoted to prospects of the Valhiverna, south of the Maladetta.

The Great Outdoors, Sept. 1978 - contains a description of the Esera Valley.

Les Pyrénées - Les 100 Plus Belles Courses by Patrice de Bellefon (1976) contains several routes included in this section.

Montagnes Pyrénées by J.L. Pérés and J. Ubiergo (1973) - of historic interest, with some fine illustrations.

L'Aneto et les Hommes by J. Escudier (1977) - is devoted entirely to the exploration and development of the Maladetta.

See also: Spender's 'Through the High Pyrenees' (1898), Schuster's 'Men, Women and Mountains' (1931), Casteret's 'Ten Years Under the Earth' (1939), and Robin Fedden's

'The Enchanted Mountains' (1962).

Guide Books: **Pyrénées Centrales Vol III** covers the frontier peaks; published by Robert Ollivier with a French text.

Posets-Maladetta is a French translation from the Spanish, published also by Ollivier.

Pyrenees East by Arthur Battagel - Gastons/West Col, (1975) - moderate ascents along the frontier, and also in the Posets and Maladetta.

Walks and Climbs in the Pyrenees by Kev Reynolds - Cicerone Press (1978) - details modest ascents and rambles in the Posets and Maladetta, and also Valhiverna.

Maps: IGN maps, scale 1:50,000 for the frontier region include Sheet XVIII-48 (Bagnères de Luchon). For the Posets, Editorial Alpina publishes Posets at 1:25,000 together with a brief guide, and for the Maladetta region, Maladetta Aneto, also 1:25,000 with a guide.

*

North-West Ridge of Besiberri

Further Considerations: The Eastern Heights

Huts: The Aigües Tortes/San Mauricio region has a number of huts scattered throughout; mostly they are very small and lacking in facilities beyond bare walls, a roof and communal bunks. Only two or three have a guardian in mid-season.

Below the north-eastern ridge of Besiberri, the FCM has the little *Refuge de Besiberri,* with room

Refugi de Besiberri (2760m) tucked in a gap in the ridge.

for just half a dozen. At 2,760 metres it is only 250 metres below the summit of Besiberri Nord, and situated above half-way along the ridge between it and Pic Harlé. Ideal for overnight shelter before starting one of the long ridge routes. A little way to the east, and contained in the bowl of the headwaters of the Noguera de Tort, the *Refugi Ventosa y'Calvell* (CEC) is perched above the Estany Negre, with another refugi nearby - formerly owned by the Electricity Board - which is used as an unguarded winter hut. To the north, and nestling below the western slopes of Montarto d'Aran, the *Refugi de la Restanca* will be found by the dammed end of the Estany de la Restanca. Room for about twenty, and minimal facilities, this hut is owned by the FCM.

East of the Montarto lie the scattered tarns of the Circ de Colomers. At the end of the Estany Major de Colomers the CEC has built its *Refugi de Colomers,* with places for about thirty. In the nearby Saboredo cirque another hut, this time owned by the FCM, allows a number of climbs to be tackled; on the Agulles de Saboredo, Tuc de Saboredo etc. This *Refugi de Saboredo,* with its spaces for 14, may be reached either from the Vall d'Aran or from Espot. Delightful walking country.

The *Refugi d'Amitges* is one of the largest in the whole region, and boasts good facilities. With room for 56 it has a guardian from July to the end of September, and is CEC owned. A convenient base for climbs on the Agulles d'Amitges, Agulles de Bassiero, Tuc de Saboredo etc. Reached by an easy trail from Espot. There is a small, privately owned hut below the Encantados peaks, on the edge of the pine woods near the lake of San Mauricio. More a shelter than a mountain hut.

For those walking from the valley of Bohi to Espot, the *Refugi d'Estany Llong,* at the western end of the lake of the same name, offers overnight shelter, with a guardian at times, and hidden in the wild country to the south-east of the Encantados the *Refugi Jóse Maria Blanc* commands the dark waters of the Estany Tort de Peguera. A CEC refuge with 24 places, this may sometimes be closed. It is worth checking first at the Hotel Saurat in Espot, where the key may be obtained.

For the southern approaches to the Pica d'Estats, the Federació Catalana de Muntanya (FCM) controls the *Refugi de la Vall Ferrera,* now reached by a driveable track which runs along the left bank of the stream. The hut stands on the opposite bank among pleasant woodlands. It has places for 16 and is often busy in the high season. Some way above, in the Sotllo valley at about 2,100

The romantic little refuge la Guimbarde makes a simple base for Carlitte climbers.

metres, there is a good bivouac cave at the southern end of the first 'plain'.

Andorra has no refuges as such, but there are various *cabanes* utilised by the shepherds which one could use for an emergency bivouac. The Carlitte, on the other hand, has a number of small huts without guardians and the larger *Refuge Combaleran,* the Touring Club de France establishment on the southern end of the lake of Bouillouses. This may be easily reached by road from Mont-Louis, and makes an ideal base for explorations of the southern reaches of the Carlitte massif. For the ascent of Pic Carlitte the most convenient hut is the tiny *Refuge La Guimbarde* which is mounted on a bluff above the south-eastern bank of the Lac de Lanoux. Although very small and with the bare minimum of facilities, its position is superb.

Finally, the Canigou offers accommodation with the little *cabane, Arago,* to the south-west of the summit, a hut large enough for only five or six inhabitants; and the larger CAF owned *Chalet-Hotel des Cortalets,* a very popular centre open from June until September, and with a reputation for good food.

Additional sources of information:

Alpine Journal, 1978 - in which an article describes a lengthy ridge-walking circuit of Andorra.

Climber and Rambler, Feb. 1974 - includes first part of a series describing a walk through the Eastern Pyrenees. Mainly Carlitte and Andorra.

Climber and Rambler. March 1974 - the second part of the above series; Andorra to Viella.

Climber and Rambler, August 1977 - contains a 'fact sheet' on the Eastern Pyrenees.

Climber and Rambler, May 1979 - the last section of the High Route as far as Andorra is treated to a brief outline.

Climber and Rambler, Nov. 1980 - another article here descibes the circuit of Andorra.

The Great Outdoors, April 1979 - gives an impression of cross-country ski-ing opportunities in the eastern portion of the range.

SMC Journal, 1966 - Hamish Brown's notes on climbing in the Pyrenees includes the Encantados.

Les Pyrénées - Les 100 Plus Belles Courses by Patrice de Bellefon (1976) - continued route descriptions of some of the finest climbs.

Montagnes Pyrénées by J.L. Pérés and J. Ubiergo (1973) - covers the main peaks in words and photographs. French text.

Pyrénées 1876 - 1976 by Robert Ollivier - some brief mentions of interest in respect of the peaks east of Aneto.

The Enchanted Mountains by Robin Fedden (1962) - one of the most literary of all climbing books, deals with the Encantados and others.

Through the High Pyrenees by Harold Spender (1898) - two Englishmen 'exploring' the Pyrenees. Deals with Carlitte, Andorra and westwards.

See also: Belloc's 'The Pyrenees' (1909), Morton's 'Pyrenean' (1938), Showell Styles's 'Backpacking in Alps and Pyrenees' (1976).

Guide Books: **Pallars-Aran,** published by the CEC is the standard work dealing with climbs on the Encantados peaks, and Vall d'Aran area.

Urgellet-Pica d'Estats, and **Cerdanya,** by the same publishers, also deal with the Eastern Pyrenees. They are well-illustrated, but with Catalan text.

Pyrenees East by Arthur Battagel - Gastons/West Col, 1975 - has a number of routes between Besiberri and Sierra de los Encantados.

Pyrenees Andorra Cerdagne by Arthur Battagel - Gastons/West Col 1980 - continues the range covering the major areas.

Walks and Climbs in the Pyrenees by Kev Reynolds - Cicerone Press, 1978 - includes routes among the Encantados, Estats, Andorra and Carlitte regions.

Maps: Editorial Alpina's coverage for the section is as follows; La Ribagorca (1:25,000), Montardo (1:25,000), La Vall d'Aran (1:40,000), Sant Maurici - Els Encantats (1:25,000), Pica d'Estats - Mont Roig (1:40,000), Andorra (1:40,000). The IGN sheets covering the French slopes, and with a scale of 1:50,000 are as follows; Pic de Mauberme, Aulus-Les-Bains, Vicdessos, Ax-les-Thermes, Mont-Louis, Prades. Another sheet giving a good picture of the Carlitte and Cerdagne regions is *carte touristique,* Cerdagne - Capcir, also at 1:50,000 and published by the IGN.
There is also a new series of maps covering Andorra at a scale of 1:10,000. There are sixteen of them!

*

Further reading:

A fairly comprehensive bibliography appears as Appendix D, but this is a specifically English language list. The climber wishing to keep informed of the major developments of *Pyrénéisme* is directed to the publication of the GPHM, *Altitude,* and from time to time new routes find publicity in the GHM *Annales,* the journal of the Groupe de Haute Montagne.

The walker planning to attempt the High Route will need the paperback guide, *Pyrenees High Level Route*, by Georges Véron, the English translation of which is published by Gastons/West Col.

More than seventy years after it first appeared, Belloc's *The Pyrenees* remains the best general guide to the range. Clearly some of its contents have become dated, but much of the information with regard to mountain travel on foot is as relevant today as at the turn of the century. Several of the articles relating to the Pyrenees that have appeared in the *Bulletins* of the Alpine Garden Society contain information that will be of interest to the walker as well as to the botanist. Those of Col. G.E.M. Meadows are particularly recommended.

For the climber, again, general essays giving coverage of the range's possibilities are included in *World Atlas of Mountaineering* by Wilfred Noyce and Ian McMorrin (1969), and the more recent *Collins Guide to Mountains & Mountaineering* by John Cleare (1979). The most entertaining book dealing with mountain activity in the Pyrenees, and one which manages to convey better than most the feel of the country, is Robin Fedden's, *The Enchanted Mountains.*

*

Frontier crossing:

Throughout the range both climber and walker will frequently find themselves straying from one side of the international border to the other. As a rule the ridge which forms the frontier will be obvious, but in many instances there are no indications to show that this frontier has been traversed. Now and again a stone will be found marking a pass with a letter F on one side, and E painted on the other; and some of the Spanish valleys bear a small notice or two with the legend *'Reserva Nacional de Caza',* which indicates a game reserve. Otherwise there are no formal border signs.

The usual formalities for crossing from one country to another are naturally observed wherever a road meets the frontier post. However, there are few border patrols in the mountains, and often when one is met the bona fide climber is regonised as such, and happily ignored, There are occasional instances when in Spain the climber or the walker will be stopped and passports demanded. It should therefore be stressed that passports ought to be carried whenever there is the likelihood of the frontier being crossed. Such a precaution can saved a lot of delay and embarrassment.

*

Climate:

The weather here tends to be rather more predictable than in the Alps, and summers generally more settled. The range does, of course, have its own peculiarities so far as the climate is concerned, as do all mountain regions. The Pyrenees are subject to conflicting influences; those of the Atlantic contrasting with those of the more benevolent Mediterranean. The moist air flowing from the west brings cloud cover and precipitation to the northern slopes, while the Ebro basin collects an atmosphere of southern warmth and breathes its dryness up into the high mountains. From the east there is an overlap of heat, and when the cooler air of the French valleys meets the gusts of hot breath from the southern slopes, storms inevitably occur.

By virtue of its southerly latitude the range tends more towards bright, dry summers. The skies have a dreamy brilliance, especially above Spanish slopes. In high summer at times the days are almost too hot for energetic walking, but on the loftier summits one can usually find a breeze. The moral is to start out earlier than either altitude or snow cover might suggest, for mornings are quite often ideal when later the day might respond with too much warmth, or the sudden eruption of storm.

The main climbing season runs from mid-June until the middle of September. Earlier the mountains are shedding their snows and in the higher regions avalanches are a frequent danger. Later than September the weather threatens snow and harsh, cold winds. During the winter period, December to April, there is ample snow cover for both climbing and ski-mountaineering, as well as ski-touring in the valleys.

APPENDIX B
Flowers of Mountain and Valley

For centuries the Pyrenees have been recognised for their exceptional botanical interest. It comes as no surprise, then, to find that many of the early pioneers, both those who came to climb and those whose travels were confined to the valleys, wrote with undiluted enthusiasm for the enormous variety and profusion of flowers they found. They wrote of meadows '... starred with the white narcissus'; of gentians and asphodels and edelweiss '... fine and abundant ... and more easily found than in Switzerland.' They discovered the '... light plumy bunches of the superb long-leaved saxifrage' extending from remote limestone cliffs; cliffs too that were adorned with '... the purple flowers of the *Ramonda pyrenaica'*, one of several plants found only in these mountains. On screes and ridges and on summits themselves climbers reported colour, fragrance, life. In apparently barren gullies, on discarded boulders, and among the seductive, open faces of countless peaks, this distinctive flora survives, and thrives. The mountains and valleys of the Pyrenees offer themselves as one vast botanical garden.

The range, of course, forms a physical and climatic barrier. On the north there is a moist, rich fertility, while the south is dominated by sun-bleached aridity. In addition influences of opposing natures are inflicted, on the one hand, by the low-lying regions adjacent to the sea, and on the other by the swollen heights at the centre of the range. Consequently a common assembly of four quite distinct types of flora is formed; truly alpine, Mediterranean, and those of the Iberian Peninsular and of North-West Europe. The result is a remarkable variety of plants, incomparably richer than in any other mountain area of Europe. It is a variety composed of something like 180 species endemic to the Pyrenees; other rare plants shared only with the Picos de Europa and, in some instances, the Balkans; principally lowland species, in the eastern sector, found straying into upper regions where the warm, dry airstreams create an un-alpine atmosphere; a broad representation of alpine species from other central European mountains, and a wide distribution of plants that stretches from the Sierra Nevada to the Carpathians and beyond. Thus, a combination of circumstances specific to the Pyrenees has resulted in the establishment of a unique flora, a flora both highly satisfying to the practising botanist and to the layman who visits the mountains for other reasons.

*

Left: Elder Orchid (Dactylorhiza sambucina)
Below: Alpine Aster (Aster alpinus)

Warmed by an insistent sun the lower valleys of the Spanish Pyrenees are rich with a heady fragrance as lavender, rosemary, thyme, and other aromatic plants prosper among the stunted pines and box. Wild fruits; strawberries, raspberries, whortleberries and red currants grow in the woodlands on both sides of the watershed, the bounty of the mountains, welcoming and refreshing to the climber en route to a remote hut. In open meadows in springtime there are veritable swamps of narcissii, appearing from a distance like enormous drifts of snow, but on closer examination their perfume thickens the air and individual sub-species announce themselves with colouring from white to pale gold, natural hybrids forming colonies amongst their more abundant parents. Later, on sweeping pastures and on vegetated slopes leading to the gaunt crags, countless iris stand erect, their large flowering heads of a deep violet-blue; and the tall, feathery plumes of the Pyrenean asphodel, rank upon rank, miniature forests of white, flushed with pink. Juniper and alpenroses form calf-high cover on other slopes, and now and then spreading clumps of the pink blossomed *Daphne-mezereum* create islands of sweet scent about them.

Upper meadowlands, corresponding with the 'alps' of Switzerland, offer an immense variety of flowering plants and shrubs. Orchids are there in many forms, particularly the closely related *Dactylorhiza* with the sometimes red, sometimes yellow spike of the elder orchid (*D. sambucina*). Gentians abound, with the fairly rare Pyrenean gentian restricted to boggy areas in the eastern portion of the range, while *G. verna is* widely distributed. The martagon lily, the strikingly delicate dogs-tooth violet, and velvet-smooth Pyrenean fritillary all demand attention from the high valleys, while damp woodland areas provide a rich habitat for many diverse plants.

Specifically alpine communities in the main confine themselves to the favoured habitats of screes, moraines, precipitous cliffs and rock crevices that would appear to be insufficient to support any but the most primaeval of life forms. However, through the slow passage of innumerable decades, and despite the efforts of successive ages of glaciation, there have been a few specialized species capable of adaptation to these otherwise inhospitable regions, and they successfully exploit conditions of frost and drought and the bare minimum of stable soil that is imposed upon them. In order to survive the harsh extremes of temperature these alpines protect themselves by restricting their growth and limiting their period of flowering. They grow slowly. The majority keep low to the ground. They form dense cushions, or they creep stealthily over rocks, or form in tight rosettes. Sometimes they protect themselves with a mass of hairs, as the edelweiss and spring anemone; nearly always are they perennial, conserving energy from one year to the next.

These alpines include the stalkless white flowers of the cushion plant, *Androsace vandellii,* which favours granite shaded crevices; the pink matted moss campion, often found among limestone screes; and several different houseleeks *(Sempervivum)* that spread insistently by throwing out tiny rosettes which need very little anchorage on various types of terrain. Primulas, soldanellas, campanulas, and several members of the saxifrage family grow to advanced altitudes. They colour the climber's day, and add considerable interest to the journey from valley-stream to summit crest. They offer tempting diversions and create a dimension of harmony and fragrance to the sometimes harsh mountain landscape.

*

The limestone country west of the Aspe valley has plenty to offer the botanist, with *Campanula cochleariifolia* bringing life to several high crags reached only by the climber, and the surprise of alpine asters found on the very summits of one or two Ansabère peaks. On the Spanish slopes the huge, stemless carlene thistle appears on poor ground, while the tall, blueish thistle, Pyrenean eryngo, is found on both sides of the frontier between 1,000 and 2,000 metres. Two Pyrenean endemics; the campion *Petrocoptis pyrenaica,* and the rare woodruff, *Asperula hirta,* appear in colonies on the French side of the Col du Somport, and as spring's sun disposes of the snow cover on the pass itself, a fine display of flowers may be seen; gentians, elder orchids and Pyrenean fritillaries among them.

The Pic du Midi is noted for the *Iris xiphioides* that grows in great quantities, especially on the

Fairy's Thimble
(Campanula cochleariifolia)

slopes of the Col de Suzon; but down in the valley of Bious June encourages a lavish show of colour among the pastures, and in the woods are found the Pyrenean squill and a great many cowslips. Up beside one or two of the tarns grow clusters of the chamois ragwort, *Senecio doronicum,* a golden splash of colour to contrast the dark but shining levels of water.

Below the Pic du Midi the Ossau Valley offers many delights for the seeker of flowers. On the approach to the Col du Portalet both spring and summer give variety. Early, the slender snow gentian, *G. nivalis,* is found, while in August it has been replaced by the fringed gentian, *Gentianella ciliata.*

The Balaitous region is noted more for its austerity than its vegetation, but the approach routes through the lower valleys give plenty of opportunities for botanical diversions, while the West Ridge route, when taken from the Arrémoulit, leads past a very flowery patch beside the haunted tarn, Gourg Glacé. On the northern flanks of the region edelweiss abound, and there are a great many of the lovely Pyrenean columbine *(Aquilegia pyrenaica).*

The Ossoue Valley, that which is used for the approach to the Vignemale from Gavarnie, has long been recognised for its wealth of plants. In the lower woods many of the honey-scented Spurge laurel *(Daphne laureola)* are to be seen, while above, on the steep limestone cliffs, *Saxifraga longifolia* waves its long plumes in the early summer breeze. On the same cliffs are *Ramonda myconi,* as indeed many of Gavarnie's walls are similarly decorated in June and July. Higher in the valley grow great quantities of iris and asphodels, with alpine asters and *Reseda glauca* seen along the stream banks. Higher still the glacier crowfoot shows great resilience in surviving among the inhospitable and barren rocks, and almost on the summit of the Vignemale are one or two specimens of a stonecrop.

South of Gavarnie, the upper pastures of the Ordesa Canyon have a reputation among botanists, and Packe was one of the first to realise its potential. Writing of the Soaso meadows he said:

'I have no room to expatiate upon the wealth of flowers ... but the splendid white lilies *(Paradisia liliastrum)* were especially conspicuous, and lower down in the wood every rock was mauve-tinted with the delicate flowers of the *Ramondia pyrenaica,* which nowhere on the French side have I seen so fine.'

The splendid pink ashy cranesbill *(Geranium cinereum)* speckles the turf here, too, and the endemic Pyrenean hyacinth dominates a stretch of fine country.

The next valley to the east of Ordesa, and on the far side of Monte Perdido, is the delightful Valle de Pineta of which Ramond wrote in ecstatic prose:

'Truly this valley was ravishing, lying in the midst of the rocks, which serve as battlements to it, and of the snows which fertilise it. Rich in the luxury of nature, and lovely in its wild beauty, it is just the earth in the first days of its birth, and before man had subjected it to cultivation.'

Two centuries later the Pineta remains free from cultivation, though a road cuts along the left bank of the Cinca. There will be found the endemic bellflower, *Campanula speciosa,* as well as *C. cochleariifolia,* the Pyrenean lily, edelweiss, ramondas by the score, and countless other plants among the rich turf banks of the river, and the bright limestone walls that contain the valley and dazzle with feathery cascades.

Both the valleys of Estaubé and that which leads into the Cirque de Troumouse repay the attentions of flower lovers, as would the Nature Reserve of the Néouvielle massif, but one of the finest regions on the northern side of the watershed in the centre of the range, is that which surrounds the Lac d'Oo.

'The gorges and mountains around the Lac d'Oo', said Packe, 'especially deserve the attention of the botanist. In rising from the village of Oo to the frontier chain, the plants present almost a complete epitome of the flora of the central Pyrenees ... (and) the two lateral valleys of Medassoles and Esquierry ... are justly celebrated as the *Jardin des Pyrénées.'*

Among those plants of especial interest here are the water saxifrage *(S. aquatica), S. clusii,* and *Cardamine raphanifolia,* each of which is a Pyrenean endemic, and the rare sandwort, *Arenaria biflora,* here found a little west of its usual Pyrenean habitat. The glacier crowfoot is also reputed to be found up in the stark regions of the higher mountains, as is the alpine toadflax.

Back in Spain, the Esera and Valhiverna valleys that drain the Maladetta both offer delights when winter withdraws to its glacial levels. The pasturelands in June come alive with elder orchids, spring gentians, Pyrenean fritillaries and *Daphne cneorum.* Among the damp woods the squill, *Scilla liliohyacinthus,* brightens little glades with its bluebell-like appearance. Dwarf rhododendrons and woody sprays of *Daphne mezereum* may be seen, and clothing the wild slopes that lead up to the Col de Toro are numerous tiny daffodils. Lower, asphodels, yellow Pyrenean snapdragons and alpine forget-me-nots are abundant, and in marshy places *Eriophorum alpinum,* the alpine cotton-grass, is awash with its fluffy white tassels.

In the little Pomero valley, which leads down from the Port de la Picada to the Vall de la Artiga de Lin, is another remarkable botanical paradise. On the upper crags the spring anenome *(Pulsatilla vernalis)* finds refuge even on one or two ridges, and in the high confines of the valley, a little below the Col de l'Infern, a scattering of dogstooth violets, *(Erythronium denscanis)* emerge almost before the snow has had time to fully depart. Lower still, *Daphne mezereum* sends out its sweet perfume, and in a great carpet of colour *D. cneorum,* various members of the narcissus family, fritillaries and spring gentians jostle for attention. Among the more remote slopes there will also be found *Primula hirsuta,* and several cowslips and oxlips below.

The Vall d'Aran, green and fertile in spring bears a profusion of narcissii. In its side valleys, too, the narcissus specialist would have a field day naming the numerous members of the species which drowns the valley with bloom. The alpine anemone *(Pulsatilla alpina)* also grows here in abundant stretches alongside the white-headed Pyrenean buttercup. In another side valley, that of the Rio Unyola, another flowery region is encountered where the Pyrenean cranesbill, alongside several others, will be found. In September, the Vall d'Aran is restored again to colour, this time with a covering of *Crocus nudiflorus, Viola cornuta,* and others.

Among the Encantados the flora of the Pyrenees is well represented, and as well as many of the regular flowers, the endemic *Pedicularis pyrenaica* finds a corner in which to survive. The bird's nest orchid *(Neottia nidus-avis)* is seen in large numbers under the protection of the pine woods, and in damp areas a magnificent selection of *Saxifraga stellaris, S. umbrosa* and the lovely violet large-flowered butterwort.

Eastwards, in the Vall de Cardos, are several very fine meadows washed by the fleeting clouds of an early summer and spattered with colour. Higher, beyond Tabescán, a damp alpine stretch is white with thousands of *Paradisia liliastrum,* the beautiful St. Bruno's lily. Higher still, in the wild contortions of the mountains, the trumpet gentian *(Gentiana kochiana)* is found with sulphur anemones and crowds of narcissii. And here again may be located the glacier crowfoot.

As has already been stated, Andorra affords country more suited to the mountain walker than to the climber. To that rough generalisation should be added that it also offers one of the finest centres from which to study the flora of the range. For here will be found a good many of the plants that are among the rarest in the Pyrenees, together with several of the endemic species, and from the fact that over a thousand species of seed plants have been listed for the country it will be appreciated that the variety is quite considerable. Unhappily the dramatic changes that have taken place here over recent years have effectively reduced much of its former remote charm, but the main habitats remain virtually unscathed.

Three types of gentian; *verna, alpina* and *pyrenaica* are to be found together near the Etang de Fontnegra up by the Envalira; but from the village of Soldeu a great assortment of flowers await discovery, both in the Vall d'Incles, and to the south on the hills where now mark all the signs of winter skiing. Up here are to be found spreading mattresses of the pink *Silene acaulis,* and a number of the yellow alpine anemone; gentians again *(G. alpina),* and quantities of the Pyrenean buttercup.

In the Vall d'Incles there is an immensely rich array of plants, even allowing for the exuberance of the native cattle. Among the gentians are the Great yellow *(G. lutea)* and the little snow gentian *(G. nivalis);* there is the delicate white *Androsace vandellii* imposing itself upon one or two boulders; there are asphodels and daphnes and lilies galore; a valley of many delights. Each of the remaining valleys, with their pastures and cultivated plots, their woodlands and bare gullies and down-like rolling hills, provide ample agreeable habitats for the very many plants that survive with such evident success.

The outer slopes of the Carlitte region blaze golden with broom, as do so many parts of the Eastern Pyrenees. While Packe seemed well satisfied with his botanical discoveries, disappointment has been expressed by those who have picked at the area after spending time among one of the more rewarding regions nearby. For the walker or climber who goes primarily for exercise or sport, but who enjoys the company of flowers along the way, there is plenty to satisfy.

The path which leads from the Lanous valley up to the Lac de Lanoux goes through some lovely colourful stretches. Primulas in various forms cluster on the rocks in the spray of minor cascades, and cowslips, spring gentians and the Pyrenean gentian will be found shortly before the lake is reached. The granite of the area encourages androsace to spread in soft cushions here and there in different forms, and the upright red alpine catchfly *(Lychnis alpina)* also makes the most of the rough terrain. Up here Packe found the Pyrenean poppy growing amid the rocks not far from the summit of Pic Carlitte, and it was on the summit itself that he discovered *Erysimum pumilum,* the little yellow-flowered dwarf treacle mustard which he called the dwarf wallflower.

Approaching from the south, on the road from Mont-Louis to the Lac des Bouillouses, the woods, broken now and then with boggy glades and streams, contain *Lilium pyrenaicum* and St. Bruno's lily again, but not in the great quantities of the Val de Cardos. At the edge of the large lake countless gentians turn patches of grass blue, and as the heartland is slowly approached, the rather rare *Crocus vernus* appears in the damp turf, and surrounding several of the remote pools are white splashes of *Ranunculus pyrenaeus;* while other open slopes are clothed with alpine clover, with various gentians, and the dogstooth violet.

*Dogstooth Violet
(Erythronium dens-canis).*

June in the broad sloping Cerdagne is a time of fragrance when the meadows are awash with narcissii, but the botanist is drawn quite naturally to the Vallée d'Eyne, a valley celebrated perhaps above all others in the Pyrenees for its extraordinarily rich and diverse flora. 'To give a list of all the plants ... met on the upper rocks and in the lower valley,' said Packe, 'would be almost to give a list of the Pyrenean flora.' The yellow *Adonis pyrenaica* is one of the specialities of the valley, for it is not met in many regions; but it is pointless to choose any one flower as outstanding in a valley with such an abundance of plants. On the hillsides vast quantities of blue flax give the impression of woodsmoke drifting low against the mountains, and the alpenrose in bloom makes a blaze of brilliant red. There are small orange poppies and the rose coloured candytuft, the white of the rock cinquefoil and the violet stained *Primula latifolia* clinging to the upper crags. Colour everywhere. Colour and fragrance; a valley which well justifies its reputation.

*

Finally, a word on the preservation of these plants. It ought not be necessary to stress that the flowers which grow in such profusion in the Pyrenees are an integral part of the range's attraction. Some are protected by law, and to pick them is not only an act of vandalism, but also a breach of trust which is likely to bring resentment from local inhabitants and those who similarly use the mountains. In National Parks there are legal restraints which should be complied with. In other areas, particularly near villages or huts, the collecting of flowers would be deemed, at least, discourteous.

The man (or woman) who goes to the mountains for climbing or strenuous walking holidays is not likely to consider carrying home anything more than memories or photographs, and no other form of plant collecting is likely to bring greater pleasure. It should be remembered too, that the pressures created by modern progress are speedily encroaching upon the habitats of all of nature's living forms, and many of the plants which Ramond and Packe would have known have become rare today. Those who readily enjoy the colour and fragrance of Pyrenean flowers in the spring, summer or early autumn, must ensure that they will still be there next year, and a century hence.

*

Further reading:

The *Bulletins* of the Alpine Garden Society (Lye End Link, St.John's, Woking, Surrey) often contain articles dealing with the Pyrenean flora, and these are highly recommended. Those of specific interest are included in the bibliography.

In addition the AGS has recently (1979) published an admirable volume, *Mountain Flower Holidays in Europe* by Lionel Bacon, in which a section is devoted to the Pyrenees explaining what to find, and where. See also *Flowers of South-West Europe* - a field guide by Oleg Polunin and B.E. Smythies (1973), and *Wild Flowers of the Pyrenees* by A.W. Taylor (1971).

An article appeared in *The Geographical Magazine* for April 1958 with much of interest and some fine illustrations, but for the purpose of identification, Anthony Huxley's *Mountain Flowers* (1967), and Christopher Grey-Wilson's *Alpine Flowers of Britain and Europe* (1979), include most of the flowers likely to be found.

*

APPENDIX C
Glossary of Pyrenean Terms:

Abri:	rough shelter, suitable for bivouac i.e. Abri Michaud (Balaitous)
Ague, aigue, aygue:	water, a stream
Artiga, artigue:	pasture, or forest clearing i.e. Artiga de Lin (Vall d'Aran).
Arribet, arrieu:	small stream.
Barranc, barranco:	a gorge, or ravine.
Bat:	valley.
Borde:	stable, or barn.
Boum:	a tarn.
Cabane:	shepherd's hut.
Caillaouas:	scree slope.
Cap:	a summit.
Caperan:	individual rock tower, or aiguille i.e. Caperan de Sesques (Ossau).
Clot:	a deep pool, or a mountain basin i.e. Clot de la Hount (Vignemale).
Collade:	a broad or easy pass
Cortal:	rough pasture hut.
Coume:	narrow valley.
Estang, etang:	a tarn, or lake.
Estibe:	summer pasture.
Font, fount:	a spring, or fountain.
Forat, fourat:	a gulph, or deep hole.
Forc, fourc, fourcat:	a fork, or separation.
Gave:	mountain river, or torrent i.e. Gave de Pau (Gavarnie).
Gourg, gourc:	a deep lake.
Guell:	a resurgence i.e. Guells del Joeu (Vall d'Aran).
Hont, hount:	see font .
Hourquette:	steep pass i.e. Hourquette d'Ossoue (Vignemale).
Ibon:	see boum.
Jasse:	an alp-type pasture.
Laquette:	a small lake, or tarn.
Lis, Lit:	avalanche.
Mal, Mail:	ancient term for rocks i.e. Mail Pintrat.
Marcadau, marcat:	market
Neste:	mountain river i.e. Neste d'Aure.
Orri:	cabane, or hut built of stone.
Oule, oulette:	mountain basin i.e. Oulettes de Gaube (Vignemale)
Parador:	Spanish hotel under State control.
Pas, passet, passe:	a narrow, or difficult section.
Peña, peñe:	steep cliff, or mountain crest i.e. Pené Blanca (Maladetta).
Pla, plan:	plain, or region of pasture i.e. Plan de Estang (Maladetta).
Port, porteille, portillon:	col, or high mountain pass.
Prat:	meadowland.
Pujo, pujol:	a hill, or prominence.
Qúebe, queva:	shelter beneath a boulder, or overhanging wall.
Raillère:	chute of scree i.e. Grande Raillère (Pic du Midi d'Ossau).

Rio, riu:	stream, or river
Seil, seilh:	glacier
Serre, sierra:	mountain massif
Soum:	a secondary summit
Trou:	a deep hole, or gulph i.e. Trou de Toro (Maladetta)
Tuc, Tuqua, Tozal:	steep cliff, usually separated from the main mountain mass i.e. Tozal del Mallo (Ordesa)
Turon:	a secondary summit i.e. Turon de Néouvielle

Wild country below the Maladetta. Maladetta/Alba crest above, (Part of the ascent route used by Ramond in 1787 - then much of this was glaciated).

APPENDIX D
Bibliography

As has already been stated elsewhere this bibliography is limited to works published in the English language. It cannot claim to be fully comprehensive, but a fairly wide coverage has been attempted. It is not solely of value to the climber, but those works of mountaineering interest should be fairly obvious. Many of the earlier volumes, of course, have long been out of print and exceedingly difficult to obtain. The Alpine Club Library has a good selection of the earlier works, and most Civic Libraries can obtain old stock on request from the student of Pyrenean history.

Items marked with an * denote that the book, or article, is not devoted specifically to the Pyrenees, but contains sections of interest.

*

1813	L.F.Ramond de Carbonnieres 'Travels in the Pyrenees'	Longmans
1825	J. Hardy 'A Picturesque and Descriptive Tour in the Mountains of the High Pyrenees'	Ackermann
1837	J.E. Murray, the Hon. 'A Summer in the Pyrenees' (2 Vols)	Macrone
1838	F.H. Vaux 'Rambles in the Pyrenees'	Longmans
1843	T.C. Paris 'Letters from the Pyrenees'	Murray
1859	C.R. Weld 'The Pyrenees - West and East'	
1862	C. Packe 'A Guide to the Pyrenees'	Longmans
	C. Packe 'Port d'Oo and Posets'	Peaks, Passes & Glaciers Vol III
	C. Packe 'Table of heights of the Peaks and Passes of the Pyrenees'	Peaks, Passes & Glaciers Vol III
1864	C. Packe 'The Vignemale'	A.J. Vol I
	C. Packe 'Electricity in the Pyrenees'	A.J. Vol I
1866	C. Packe 'Flora of the Pyrenees'	A.J. Vol III
1867	C. Packe 'A Guide to the Pyrenees' (2nd edition, revised and with additions)	Longmans
	H. Blackburn 'The Pyrenees'	Sampson, Low Marston
1869	- 'Mountain Adventures' *	Seeley, Jackson, Halliday
1870	J. Ormsby 'Mont Perdu'	A.J. Vol IV
1871	H. Russell 'Pau and the Pyrenees'	
1872	H. Russell 'Mountains and Mountaineering'	A.J. Vol V
1874	J. Ormsby 'The Mountains of Spain' *	A.J. Vol VI
1876	D. Freshfield 'Spring in the Pyrenees'	A.J. Vol VII
1883	- 'Mountains and Mountain Climbing' *	Nelson
1884	F. Gardiner 'Across the Pyrenees'	A.J. Vol XI
1886	C. Packe 'Reminiscenses of the Pyrenees'	A.J. Vol XII
1889	C. Packe review of Russell's 'Souvenirs d'un Montagnard'	A.J. Vol XIV
1893	C. Packe 'Byepaths in the Pyrenees'	A.J. Vol XVI
	E.N. Buxton 'Short Stalks' * (2nd edition)	Stanfords

1897	W.P. Haskett-Smith 'In Memoriam - Charles Packe'	A.J. Vol XVIII
	H. Russell 'In Memoriam - Charles Packe'	A.J. Vol XVIII
1898	V. Hugo 'Alps and Pyrenees' *	
	H. Spender & H. Llewellyn Smith 'Through the High Pyrenees'	Innes
1899	F. Gribble 'The Early Mountaineers' *	Fisher Unwin
1901	H. Spender 'The High Pyrenees'	A.J. Vol XX
	H. Brulle 'A Pyrenean Centre'	A.J. Vol XX
1905	- 'A Tour in the Pyrenees in 1903'	A.J. Vol XXII
1907	S. Baring-Gould 'A Book of the Pyrenees'	Methuen
1909	H. Belloc 'The Pyrenees'	Methuen
	V.H. Gatty 'Early June in the Pyrenees'	A.J. Vol XXIV
	W.H. Haskett-Smith 'In Memorian - Henry Russell'	A.J. Vol XXIV
1912	C.L. Freeston 'Passes of the Pyrenees'	
1913	V.C. Scott-O'Connor 'Travels in the Pyrenees'	Long
1922	H. Brulle 'In Memoriam - Célestin Passet' (in French)	A.J. Vol XXXIV
	W.P. Haskett-Smith 'In Memoriam - Henri Passet'	A.J. Vol XXXIV
1923	W.H. Winterbotham 'Travel Memories' *	A.J. Vol XXXV
1924	J.A. Parker 'The Pyrenees'	A.J. Vol XXXVI
	D. Pilley 'Into Spain and Back Again'	Pinnacle Club Journal
1925	P. Wilstach 'Along the Pyrenees'	Bles
1928	W.M. Conway 'A Flight Over the Pyrenees'	A.J. Vol XL
	B. Williams 'The High Pyrenees'	Wishart
1929	H. Trevellyan 'In the Pyrenees'	Oxford & Cambridge Mountaineering
	E.I. Robson 'A Wayfarer in the Pyrenees'	Methuen
1931	D. Pilley 'Failure and Success in the Pyrenees'	Pinnacle Club Journal
	C. Schuster 'Men, Women and Mountains' *	Nicholson & Watson
	- 'Notes on Huts and Access'	A.J. Vol XLIII
1932	E.A. Peers 'The Pyrenees'	Harrap
1934	L.E. Bray 'Foot-Slogging in the Pyrenees'	Pinnacle Club Journal
1935	D. Pilley 'Climbing Days' *	Secker & Warburg
	R.L.G.Irving 'The Romance of Mountaineering' *	Dent
1937	E.E. Evans 'France - A Geographical Introduction' *	Chatto & Windus
	R. d'Espouy 'In Memoriam - Henri Brulle'	A.J. Vol XLIX
1938	J.B. Morton 'Pyrenean'	Longmans
1939	N.Casteret 'Ten Years under the Earth'	Dent
1946	D. Busk 'The Delectable Mountains' *	Hodder & Stoughton
1950	A. McClintock 'Gabas and Gavarnie'	A.G.S. Bulletin 18
	D.C. McKean 'Scrambling in the Pyrenees'	Oxford Mountaineering
1952	B. Newman 'Both Sides of the Pyrenees'	Jenkins
	R.P. Taylor 'Pyrenean Holiday'	Hale

1953	G.O. Jackson 'A climb in the Central Pyrenees'	Cambridge Mountaineering
1955	N. Epton 'The Valley of Pyrene'	Cassell
	R.L.G.Irving 'A History of British Mountaineering'*	Batsford
1956	S.D. Albury 'Plant Hunting in Andorra and the Pyrenees'	A.G.S. Bulletin 24
	H.V. Morton 'High Road in the Pyrenees'	National Geographical Magazine - March
1958	M. Darvell 'The Pyrenees - Easy Way'	Pinnacle Club Journal
	D. Paton 'Wild Flowers of the Pyrenees'	The Geographical Magazine - April
1960	D.H.B. Pirkis 'A High Valley in the Pyrenees'	The Geographical Magazine - August
	R. Fedden 'Russell and the Vignemale'	A.J. Vol LXV
1962	R.Fedden 'The Enchanted Mountains'	Murray
	A. Huxley 'Standard Encyclopaedia of the World's Mountains' *	Wiedenfeld & Nicholson
	A. & G. Sieveking 'The Caves of France and Northern Spain' *	Vista Books
	R. Way 'A Geography of Spain and Portugal' *	Methuen
1963	- 'Pyrenees' (Michelin guide)	Dickens Press
1964	K. Curry-Lindahl 'Europe - A Natural History' *	Hamish Hamilton
	J.M. Houston 'The Western Mediterranean World' *	Longmans
1965	S. Styles 'Blue Remembered Hills' *	Faber
	J.J. Branigan 'Europe' *	Macdonald & Evans
	A.W. Taylor 'Eastern Pyrenees'	A.G.S. Bulletin 33
1966	H.M. Brown 'Notes on the Pyrenees'	S.M.C. Journal
	A.M. Daffern 'The Pyrenees'	Mountain Craft - spring
	H.Myhill 'The Spanish Pyrenees'	Faber
	M.T. Petch 'La Cerdagne'	A.G.S. Bulletin 34
1967	A. Huxley 'Mountain Flowers' *	Blandford Press
	G.E.M. Meadows 'High Pyrenees'	A.G. S. Bulletin 35
1968	G.E.M. Meadows 'Into Catalonia'	A.G.S. Bulletin 36/2
	G.E.M. Meadows 'On Into Aragon'	A.G.S. Bulletin 36/4
	G.E. Barrett 'Carlit, Canigou and Cambras d'Aze'	A.G.S. Bulletin 36/2
	R. Laxalt 'Land of the Ancient Basques'	National Geographical Magazine - August
	V. Ingham 'Anne Lister's Ascent of Vignemale'	A.J. Vol LXXIII
1969	H. Nicol 'Pyrenean Pilgrimage'	Climbers' Club Journal
	G.E.M. Meadows 'Always a Little Further, Part I'	A.G.S. Bulletin 37/3
	J.M. Scott 'From Sea to Oceon'	Bles
	W. Noyce & I. McMorrin 'World Atlas of Mountaineering'*	Nelson
1970	J. East 'Gascony and the Pyrenees'	Johnson

	G.E.M. Meadows 'The Valley of Benasque'	A.G.S. Bulletin 38/3
1971	G.E.M. Meadows 'Plants of the Pyrenees'	A.G.S. Bulletin 39/1
	G.E.M. Meadows 'Cirques and Circuses'	A.G.S. Bulletin 39/3
	D. Scott 'Notes on High Grade Climbing in the Pyrenees'	Alpine Climbing
	A.W. Taylor 'Wild Flowers of the Pyrenees'	Chatto & Windus
1972	O. Polunin 'The Concise Flowers of Europe' *	Oxford University Press
	G.E.M. Meadows 'A Host of Daffodils'	A.G.S. Bulletin 40/2
1973	F.B. Fernandez 'The Problems of Nature Conservation and the Management of the Natural Environment in Spain' *	Nature in Focus
	O. Polunin & B.E. Smythies 'Flowers of South-West Europe' *	Oxford University Press
	H. Myhill 'North of the Pyrenees'	Faber
	C. Williams 'Women on the Rope' *	Allen & Unwin
1974	R. Laxalt 'The Enduring Pyrenees'	National Geographical Magazine - December
	S. Styles 'Pyrenean Journey Part I'	Climber & Rambler - Feb
	S. Styles 'Pyrenean Journey Part 2'	Climber & Rambler - Mar
	S. Styles 'Pyrenean Journey Part 3'	Climber & Rambler - Apr
	F.J. Monkhouse 'A Regional Geography of Western Europe' *	Longman
1975	R.P. Bille 'The Guinness Guide to Mountain Animals' *	Guinness
	J.M. Russell 'The National Park of the Western Pyrenees'	A.J. Vol 80
	A. Battagel 'Pyrenees - West'	Gastons/West Col
	A. Battagel 'Pyrenees - East'	Gastons/West Col
	S. Styles 'Backpacking in Alps and Pyrenees'	Gollancz
	N. Poulain 'Andorra, Tiny Paradise in the Pyrenees'	Readers Digest– April
1976	P. Steele 'Pierre Vergez'	A.J. Vol 81
	R.E.W. Casselton & M.J. Chapman 'Pyrenean Fact Sheet'	Climber & Rambler - April
	K. Reynolds 'The Maladetta Massif'	Climber & Rambler - July
1977	K.Reynolds 'One Man and his Mountain'	Climber & Rambler - May
	C.M. Graham 'Eastern Pyrenees'	Climber & Rambler - Aug
1978	J. Hunt 'The Age of Non-Commitment' *	Climber & Rambler - Jan
	J.C. Leedal 'Nature's Garden - The Pyrenees'	A.G.S. Bulletin 46/1
	K. Reynolds 'A Valley of Rare Perfection'	A.G.S. Bulletin 46/2
	K. Reynolds 'A Mountain called Jean-Pierre'	Climber & Rambler - July
	T.A.H. Peacocke 'The Circuit of Andorra'	A.J. Vol 83
	G.E.M. Meadows 'Always a Little Further, Part II'	A.G.S. Bulletin 37/4
	K. Reynolds 'The Last Green Valley'	The Great Outdoors - Sept
	K. Reynolds 'The Lost Mountain'	Climber & Rambler - Sept
	K. Reynolds 'Walks & Climbs in the Pyrenees'	Cicerone Press
	J.R. Carulla 'The Pyrenees - A Frontier, but no longer a Barrier'	Naturopa 30

1979	K. Reynolds 'Pyrenean High Route Part 1'	Climber & Rambler - Mar
	K. Reynolds 'Pyrenean High Route Part 2'	Climber & Rambler - April
	K. Reynolds 'Pyrenean High Route Part 3'	Climber & Rambler - May
	C. McNeish 'The Pyrenees Orientales - On Ski'	The Great Outdoors-April
	J. Cleare 'Collins Guide to Mountains & Mountaineering' *	Collins
	G. Hewitt 'Mountain Walking from the Valle de Vallibierna'	Climber & Rambler - July
	K. Reynolds 'A Progress in Pyrénéisme'	A.J. Vol 84
	C. Grey-Wilson 'The Alpine Flowers of Britain and Europe' *	Collins
	L. Bacon 'Mountain Flower Holidays in Europe' *	Alpine Garden Society
1980	J.C. Leedal 'Nature's Garden - the Pyrenees Part 2'	A.G.S. Bulletin 48/1
	G.E.M. Meadows 'Variations on an Old Theme'	A.G.S. Bulletin 48/1
	E. Pyatt 'The Guinness Book of Mountains & Mountaineering' *	Guinness
	J. Whalley 'Ring Round Andorra'	Climber & Rambler Nov
	A. Battagel 'Pyrenees Andorra Cerdagne'	Gastons/West Col
1981	D. Livingston 'The Gratuitous Helicopter'	Climber & Rambler - Feb
	H. Steen 'Ski de Raid'	Climber & Rambler - March
	G. Véron 'Pyrenees High Level Route'	Gastons/West Col
	J.G.R. Harding 'Cirques & Cañons of the Pyrenees'	A.J. Vol 86
	K. Reynolds 'The Life & Writings of Ramond'	A.J. Vol 86

*

INDEX

Note: numbers in heavy type indicate illustration pages.

147

Index

Printed by Carnmor Print & Design, 95/97 London Road, Preston.